Making Peace with Faith

Making Peace with Faith

The Challenges of Religion and Peacebuilding

Edited by Michelle Garred and
Mohammed Abu-Nimer

ROWMAN & LITTLEFIELD
Lanham • Boulder • New York • London

Published by Rowman & Littlefield
A wholly owned subsidiary of
The Rowman & Littlefield Publishing Group, Inc.
4501 Forbes Boulevard, Suite 200, Lanham, Maryland 20706
https://rowman.com

Unit A, Whitacre Mews, 26-34 Stannary Street, London SE11 4AB,
United Kingdom

British Library Cataloguing in Publication Information Available

Library of Congress Cataloging-in-Publication Data Available

ISBN 978-1-5381-0263-3 (cloth : alk. paper)
ISBN 978-1-5381-0264-0 (pbk. : alk. paper)
ISBN 978-1-5381-0265-7 (electronic)

♾ ™ The paper used in this publication meets the minimum requirements of American
National Standard for Information Sciences Permanence of Paper for Printed Library
Materials, ANSI/NISO Z39.48-1992.

Printed in the United States of America

Contents

Acknowledgments

Peacebuilders are generous people, and dozens of them have contributed behind the scenes to making this book possible. Series editor Charles Hauss of the Alliance for Peacebuilding cast a vision for featuring faith-based approaches in *Peace and Conflict in the 21st Century*, and his leadership never wavered. Matthew Scott and Mark Lorey of World Vision International shared that vision and created a space for this book to incubate while Michelle Garred was serving on their staff.

A number of colleagues were instrumental in helping to identify chapter authors, including Melanie Kawano-Chiu, Sarah McLaughlin, Charles Gibbs, Amir Akrami, Sedigheh Shakouri Rad, Kent Hill, Randy Tift, Will Elliott, Hermie Carillo, Steven Greenebaum, Amy Knorr, and Daryl Byler. The book's conceptual development was strengthened by input from Tatsushi Arai, Lucy (Moore) Salek, Mohamed Imran Mohamed Taib, Qamar-ul Huda, and Vinya Ariyaratne.

Gretchen Sandles lent her formidable communications talents to this project in quantities beyond measure. At Rowman & Littlefield, Marie-Claire Antoine gave the project an excellent start, and Dhara Snowden guided it expertly to the finish line, with the assistance of Mary Malley, Alden Perkins, and Rebecca Anastasi. Renata Nelson of the King Abdullah Bin Abdulaziz International Centre for Interreligious and Intercultural Dialogue provided exceptional support to Mohammed Abu-Nimer throughout the process, as did Mesha Arant and Teri Simon for Eboo Patel.

More people than we know have upheld this project in their prayers and meditations, including Liz Mosbo VerHage, Deborah Masten, Andrew Larsen, Krisann Jarvis Foss, Joan D. Castro, Brent Thompson, and Jana Holdrege.

Michelle Garred in particular is grateful for the formative inspiration and camaraderie of the Davao Ministerial Interfaith in the Philippines, the Harmony Centre at An-Nahdhah Mosque in Singapore, and Peter Woodrow at CDA Collaborative Learning Projects.

Introduction

Michelle Garred and Mohammed Abu-Nimer

Religion today is in everyone's newsfeed and on everybody's mind. On any given day, the headlines might include an antiminority riot backed by unexpectedly violent Buddhist monks in South Asia, a bombing event claimed by a fringe Muslim network in Europe, an attack by right-wing Jewish radicals on a Christian church in the Holy Land, or an analysis of why white evangelical Christians are voting in unprecedented droves for exceptionally polarizing political candidates in the United States. Religious conflict and violence appear to be on the increase, and they appear to be contributing to human suffering.

Social science tells us that conflict is actually shifting and changing rather than growing[1] and that religion is almost never the primary driver of such problems.[2] Instead, the drivers of conflict are multiple and interconnected, including structural, political, economic, and social factors, in addition to religious influences.[3] When the conflicting parties have different religious, denominational, or sectarian identities, religion can be pulled in as a powerful secondary element, and it sometimes comes to be perceived and experienced as central. However, social science is one thing, while public perceptions and legitimate human fears are quite another.

Fortunately, there is also an increasing recognition that rich resources for peace are found within every faith tradition. Each religion has inspired peacebuilders within it who draw on that faith's teachings and traditions to help prevent and resolve conflict.[4] Thus practitioners, policymakers, and researchers are all taking more seriously the potentially constructive role that religion can play in building social cohesion in divided societies. Various governmental aid donors and multilateral organizations, such as the European Union and the United Nations, have begun engaging religious actors in

1

their programming, resulting in fast-growing networks that link faith-based players with their secular counterparts.[5]

However, there is still a tendency among many policymakers and development and peacebuilding actors to associate religion more with conflict than with peace and to view some religious traditions with more skepticism than others. Currently, the lens of suspicion falls most frequently on Islam and becomes a paradigm that motivates or influences many of the faith-focused policies and programs that are currently unfolding. This complex reality creates a very delicate working environment for any person or organization seeking to contribute to the common good.

CHALLENGES: OUR AIMS AND APPROACHES

With the bad news about religion making regular headlines, transparent dialogue about faith-based peace alternatives is needed now more than ever. Real people of faith are doing real, self-sacrificing work every day for the cause of peace. In this book, we aim to explore the significant contributions of these faith-based peacebuilders, in a way that does not ignore the challenging aspects of religious practice but instead faces them head-on in the context of real-life practitioner experience. This project complements the important cluster of publications that unpack the "ambivalence" of religion[6] —meaning its potential to foster either violence or peace—from a conceptual point of view. It also complements publications that provide a much-needed focus on practitioner individuals and organizations,[7] yet understandably tend to emphasize their triumphs and achievements more than their challenges and difficulties.[8]

This book takes on some problematic issues because the hands-on reality is that faith-based peacebuilding is difficult. I (Michelle Garred) have joked at times that a no-nonsense title for this book might be *Wow! This Work Is Really, Really Hard.* Our hope in taking a close look at difficult things is not only to better understand the challenges involved in faith-based peace work but also to observe how practitioners cope with those challenges and to acknowledge and appreciate the sacrifice made by each of the practitioners who continue to do their peace work despite these challenges.

By "challenges" we mean the dilemmas that peacebuilders commonly face and the obstacles that they must overcome, particularly those that are inherent in the faith-based nature of their undertaking. These are challenges that practitioners, drawing on their faith, are able to address, grapple with, and often overcome.

This chapter lays a foundation for the book by analyzing what makes faith-based peacebuilding unique and challenging and previewing how those challenges manifest themselves in the experiences of the authors who have contributed to this volume. We close by identifying overarching observations and implications for the practice of faith-based peacebuilding and its improved integration with policymaking, development, and secular peacebuilding practice.

Multifaith Collaboration

This book's authorial and editorial teams are obviously multifaith in composition because no single perspective could come close to representing the fullness of faith-based experience. The diverse practitioners who have contributed chapters reflect most of the major world religions, diverse cultural backgrounds, and many different types of peacebuilding work. Some are well known, and others bring fresh new voices. However, readers will detect common themes around interfaith engagement and an emphasis on Christianity and Islam as particularly central to global conflict trends because the contexts in which we work reveal the shared, timely importance of these issues.

In our approach to multifaith collaboration, we view each faith as distinct and valuable in its own right. While we do see important common values across numerous faith traditions, such as peace, justice, and compassion, we have no aim of trying to blur the lines or meld those faiths together. Further, we support religious freedom and diversity, and we have no intention to push—or prevent—anyone's conversion from one tradition to another. However, what we do strongly advocate is people of different faiths collaborating to work together for the common good, which is a central value in all faiths and therefore a core principle in interreligious peacebuilding. Regardless of the nature and scope of the joint work, whether it is building shelters for tsunami survivors, raising chickens on a joint farm, or a student exchange program to learn about each other's faith, the important factor is the collaboration for building a sustained relationship between religiously diverse individuals and communities.

Readers who are deeply committed to one faith tradition and have not had opportunities for multifaith engagement may initially find this pluralistic approach uncomfortable. To those readers: We respectfully invite you to stay with us and to keep reading both those chapters whose content aligns with your own faith tradition and those that do not. In these chapters, as in real life, we see that faith-based peacebuilders, even those from very different religious backgrounds, often share remarkably similar challenges.

We have not asked or expected the chapter authors to formally represent their own religious traditions. In fact, with so much internal diversity in each religious tradition, it would be impossible to do so! We have simply asked each author to share how their experience as a person of faith influences their work as a peacebuilder. Moreover, we do not expect these authors to provide comprehensive solutions to the challenges posed. We simply wish to explore and recognize their diverse ways of understanding and handling those challenges, because we believe that their stories will bring new insights to the peacebuilding field. In addition, we believe that sharing these challenges and the possible ways of dealing with them by our peace practitioners contributes to the existing pool of experiences that the faith-based peacebuilding field has been accumulating in the last few decades.

Experiential Storytelling

Each chapter in this volume poses a challenge question, to which the author responds with a reflective first-person account of his or her own everyday experience. These accounts emphasize the authors' personal formation as peacebuilders, the daunting challenges they have faced, and their diverse responses to those challenges. The contributors share how they draw on their faith and on their God-given ingenuity to withstand, resolve, and sometimes even transcend the dilemmas that confront them. This is an unapologetically story-based approach, because personal stories have power.[9] Indeed, it is often said that "whoever tells the best story wins."[10] Personal experiences also contribute toward bridging the gap between theory and practice, since documented accounts of how faith-based peacebuilders wrestle with the field's biggest challenges have been in very scarce supply. We believe that these stories will encourage and maybe inspire faith-based peacebuilders, who often feel isolated when facing difficulties, by providing a way to learn from each other. We also hope to help secular partners to better understand what faith-based peacebuilding is like from an insider's perspective and to develop insights on how best to collaborate with people of faith in ways that yield positive outcomes for all.

We as editors have our own personal stories, and our experiences cannot help but influence how we have framed this book. I (Michelle) am a Christian and a U.S. American, though I have lived much of my adult life in other contexts, becoming a culturally mixed "global nomad." Most people associate me with Christianity's Protestant evangelical tradition, though I've been equally shaped by large doses of Anabaptist peace theology and Catholic social teaching. My earliest awareness of faith is that I naturally prayed to God without being taught, but I shied away from churches because my mother told me that Christians had historically oppressed women. She was not wrong—though fortunately I later discovered Christians committed to gender equality. I eventually linked up with the church as a teenager. Since that time I've been consistently compelled by the life-changing call of Jesus to love my neighbor and foster reconciliation, and I am consistently repelled by the violence and injustice that I've sometimes seen in man-made Christian practice. That ongoing tension is a key aspect of my own story and of the development of this book.

For me (Mohammed Abu-Nimer), carrying the name Mohammed (named after the Prophet PBUH[11]) as an American Palestinian Muslim does not leave me much space to avoid the effect of religious identity on my personal or professional relationships. Working in peacebuilding for the last four decades since high school and leading interfaith dialogue groups in conflict areas has shaped my beliefs and views on the importance of respecting and honoring those who practice their faith in ways different from how I was raised to believe. I was shocked to learn on a number of occasions how challenging it was for Muslims who belonged to the same faith to delve into discovering their differences and commonalities. Discovering my spiritual path through these interfaith experiences was and continues to be a life-fulfilling journey.

Structural Overview

This book is organized around four thematically linked sections. Part I, "Engaging One's Own Faith," represents an essential starting point. Effective faith-based practitioners must locate and ground themselves in relation to their own faith traditions, including both their resources for peace and their potential for exclusion, before reaching out to others. Here Eboo Patel and Rick Love both address, in varying ways, the challenges of articulating a theological case, in Islam and Christianity, respectively, for engaging believers in interfaith friendship and cooperation in the United States. Sushobha Barve examines her own religious affiliation from a different angle, as she comes to grips with violent acts done in the name of her own Indian Hindu identity group and takes steps to reconcile with the victims.

Part II, "Engaging the 'Other,'" explores the challenges of engaging with people who are not convinced of our message or who loom in our own minds as an enemy. The "other" appears in forms that readers may not expect. Azhar Hussain transcends a personally painful rift between Sunni and Shia Muslims while working to influence madrasa education in Pakistan. Yael Petretti engages strongly held views among both Israelis and Palestinians through faith-inspired Compassionate Listening, and in the process she progressively reconciles herself to both sides. Maria Ida "Deng" Giguiento, with Myla Leguro, describes how she began to work constructively with the Philippines' conflict actor she had most feared and avoided: the uniformed military.

Part III, "Engaging Policy," features practitioners navigating questions of organizational and public policy. Peter Dixon relates how a peacebuilding organization that is strongly rooted in Christian convictions can position itself to play an impartial role, even in a religiously polarized context like prepartition Sudan. Azza Karam draws on extensive experience with the United Nations to assess both obstacles and progress in involving religious actors in development and human rights initiatives. Dishani Jayaweera, with Nirosha De Silva, wrestles with the concept of "countering violent extremism," based on a Buddhism-infused analysis of international policy trends and two decades of peacebuilding leadership in Sri Lanka.

In Part IV, "Confronting Injustice and Trauma," we turn to painful legacies of violence and suppression, including some that have been perpetrated by religious institutions. Uganda's Despina Namwembe and India's Qutub Jahan Kidwai take on gender discrimination in the Orthodox Church and Islam, respectively, with a view to reducing violence and strengthening peacebuilding practice. Johonna Turner draws on the model of the "wounded healer" to narrate how Christian scripture and fellowship have helped her and the U.S. American urban youth with whom she worked to transcend past traumatic experiences.

WHAT IS FAITH-BASED PEACEBUILDING?

"Peacebuilding" in this book—and in current practitioner usage—is an overarching concept that describes the many processes and activities involved in resolving violent conflict and establishing sustainable peace. Such activities might include, for example, dialogue, reconciliation, restorative justice, trauma healing, policy reform, or peace leadership training. We use peacebuilding as an umbrella term that refers to activities intended to bring people together and address a conflict's underlying structural causes, regardless of the stage or dynamics of such conflict. This usage differs from the older, more traditional definition of peacebuilding as postconflict action.[12]

The term peacebuilding usually also implies attention to a conflict's deep causes. For example, the approach to long-term conflict in Mindanao, Philippines, that Deng Giguiento's chapter describes involves not only the negotiation of peace agreements but also the rectification of underlying grievances over control of land and resources and the transformation of polarized intergroup relationships.

A "faith-based peacebuilder," then, is someone whose faith or religious experience motivates his or her work for peace, in such a way that it influences that person's actions. This is an intentionally broad definition because we are aiming for a wide and nuanced understanding of how religion intersects with and influences peacebuilding action. Faith-based peacebuilders come not only from all the world's religious traditions but also from a wide variety of positions and roles.

The diversity of faith-based peacebuilders is reflected among the chapter authors in this book. Only a few of them carry any official religious leader's credentials; most do not. Religious leaders are indisputably important;[13] yet they represent only certain key nodes within the sprawling networks of believers who carry out the work of faith. This book casts an eye toward the full spread of those complex networks. Some of the chapter authors work in religious organizations; others, in nongovernmental, intergovernmental, or educational settings. Some work almost exclusively with religious audiences, while others work in secular contexts or in a hybrid combination of religious and secular settings. Some use words other than "peace" and "justice" to describe their work, yet make intentional contributions toward those ends.

To put forth another intentionally broad framing, "faith-based peacebuilding" is an interactive peacebuilding process in which one or more of the parties is motivated or influenced by religious identity or experience.[14] Thus a faith-based peacebuilding process may also involve individuals or organizations that are not themselves faith-based. Such wide-ranging definitions do not lend themselves to intellectually reducing the scope of analysis, and that is precisely the point. If we want to understand the influence of religion in peacebuilding, then we need to be open to considering religion in all its forms.

What Do We Mean by "Religion" and "Faith"?

This brings us to the question of what we mean by "religion" and "faith." Academics frequently debate the definition of religion,[15] while practitioners are more likely to take it at face value. When practitioners say "religion," they typically mean something apparently straightforward, such as "a set of beliefs concerning the cause, nature, and purpose of the universe, especially when considered as the creation of a superhuman agency or agencies, usually involving devotional and ritual observances, and often containing a moral code governing the conduct of human affairs."[16] When they say "faith," they typically mean "belief in God or in the doctrines or teachings of religion."[17]

Such definitions are not a bad place to start, and they do not immediately clash with our perceptions of mainstream expressions of monotheistic faiths. However, it's worth nothing that these definitions are very modern and heavily Western. Before the European Enlightenment, people probably did not think about religion as a distinct concept; rather, the spiritual permeated the holistic worldviews that shaped their day-to-day lives. They did not need a word for "religious" as a discrete phenomenon until the concept of "secular" arose to tell them that the spiritual realm might be something separate.[18] This still matters today, because it points out some ways in which westernized notions of religion may limit our understanding of religion in peacebuilding.

In the process of preparing this book, we as editors had some very revealing conversations with Buddhist and Hindu authors. One Buddhist scholar-practitioner cordially declined to write for this book because he had observed that Western-based discussions of faith-based peacebuilding often see peace-building is a way to promote one's own religion, whereas his Buddhist formation motivates him to respectfully prioritize the faith preferences of others. On the other hand, Sushobha Barve did agree to write, but only after sharing that it is sometimes uncomfortable for her as an Indian Hindu to talk about faith-based peacebuilding with Western audiences because of their rigid assumptions about faith.

Despite the above critique, or perhaps because of it, we think that there is an added value in incorporating and exploring these multiple perspectives in one edited volume. When you read Barve's chapter, as well as Dishani Jayaweera's, keep your eyes open for a faith that does not feel the need to label itself, or define its own boundaries, or declare its own existence. It simply but powerfully forms part of the complex motivational mix that makes these peacebuilders who they are. In these cases, the holistic integration of faith into life and peacebuilding makes the faith element harder to isolate and analyze but no less influential or real. It is worth noting here that indigenous faith traditions, while obviously very different from Hinduism and Buddhism, often emphasize similarly holistic worldviews. This is illustrated by the Lakota holy man Black Elk: "At the center of the universe dwells Wakan-Tanka [the Great Spirit], and that center is really everywhere."[19]

While this book uses the term "faith-based," John Paul Lederach has pointed out that "faith-inspired"[20] may a better term for capturing the diffuse aspects of the holistic influence of faith. He continues, "Sometimes people come from and are identified with a particular tradition yet may or may not consider themselves particularly religious or faithful, even while engaging in the most extraordinary acts of spiritual imagination in the midst of conflict."[21] His observation certainly applies to this book, as the authors share extraordinary stories of sacrifice, creativity, and resilience in their struggle for peacebuilding in their societies.

What Makes Faith-Based Peacebuilding Unique?

We have proposed that our view of religion should be open to the possibility of a holistic faith that permeates all of work and life, and in some cases does so quietly. In response, readers may ask, If the boundaries around faith-based peacebuilding sometimes appear fuzzy, then what makes it special? Why bother to distinguish faith-based peacebuilding from other approaches? This is an important question, and indeed there are at least three factors that distinguish faith-based approaches from secular ones.

First, all peacebuilding is shaped by the belief systems of its practitioners and participants, whether secular[22] or faith based. In the latter case, this means religious and spiritual beliefs. The specifics regarding what form the spiritual identity takes and how it affects humans vary widely by religious tradition. But faith-based peacebuilders (both practitioners and participants) believe in some sort of spiritual reality that transcends the material world, and that belief can have a profound effect on the way that they do peacebuilding. Their understanding of conflict causes may include spiritual factors, in addition to the structural and economic causes typically emphasized by secular analysts. Their impetus for action and their views of what constitutes success may be rooted in spiritual rather than professional motivations.[23] Their approaches to addressing conflict may include a strong emphasis on scriptures, symbols, rituals, and prayer or meditation.

Thus, faith-based peacebuilding practitioners intentionally bring these various aspects of spiritual belief into their work with their communities. The engagement of the spiritual component may be in the identification and recruitment of the participants, in the design of the intervention (process, structure, location, evaluation of outcomes and success), and/or in the chosen forms of follow-up over the long term.

Second, faith-based peacebuilding tends to emphasize deep personal transformative change. The emphasis on individual growth and development tends to be more consistently prominent than in secular approaches. Though evident throughout the book, that individual transformation is particularly visible in chapters like Johonna Turner's and Yael Petretti's.

When compared to political negotiation, faith-based approaches also involve a frequent insistence on pursuing "positive peace."[24] If negative peace is understood as the cessation or absence of direct violence, positive peace is understood as the presence of social justice and healthy intergroup and interpersonal relationships. Faith-based peacebuilders are rarely satisfied with negative peace because they are pursuing a much more expansive peace vision (derived from their own theological framework), known perhaps as "shanti" (in Hinduism), "salaam" (in Islam), or "shalom" (in Judaism and Christianity).

Third, the collective and institutional aspects of religion tend to shape the ways in which peacebuilding unfolds. Religious institutions are seen as potential agents of change—because they can legitimate policy choices, shape followers' opinions, and mobilize people for action—so significant effort is devoted to shaping their potential in positive ways. Further, religious identity is a powerful motivator, so coreligionists recognize themselves as belonging to networks of believers, and they may take up "insider" roles when approaching conflict that involves religious elements. These faith-based practitioners have unique access to the sacred in their own communities. Their natural capacity to enter mosques, churches, synagogues, temples, or ancestral holy grounds provides a powerful window or gate into the inner dynamics of faith communities—an entry point that secular peacebuilders will not be able to gain as easily.

Where religious leadership hierarchies are involved, they tend to shape who gets involved in peacebuilding and in what types of roles. This sometimes results in exclusion, such that people belonging to marginalized groups may find it difficult to take up prominent roles in religious institutional peacebuilding. One group that is marginalized in many contexts is women and girls, and this reality comes to the fore in Part IV. Despina Namwembe, as an Orthodox Christian peacebuilder in Uganda, opts to work for incremental change within the existing male-led religious and cultural system. On the other hand, Qutub Jahan Kidwai, as a Sunni Muslim scholar in India, is reforming shariah law to further women's protection and empowerment. Gender-based violence appears in the chapter written by Johonna Turner as part of the spectrum of violence faced by urban U.S. American youth. Interestingly, we as editors did not initially plan for this book to have such a prominent emphasis on gender. However, when we asked practitioners what they wanted to write about, gender rose to the surface, indicating the importance of gender-related challenges in faith-based peacebuilding.

Each of these faith-based uniquenesses contributes to create a peacebuilding experience that is sometimes very different from that of secular peacebuilders. During the past fifteen years, the secular peacebuilding world has seen rapid growth and professionalization, while some religious peacebuilding networks have carried on using the same time-tested modus operandi for decades. Therefore, some assumptions are simply not shared. For example, the professionalized idea of a "project," as a time-bound set of specific objectives that is funded by an external source, may seem foreign to faith-based peacebuilders who keep working tirelessly toward the same general goals, using small infusions of their own money, or sometimes no money at all, as they follow their own religious calling.

At the same time, these distinctions are not absolute, and the interconnections between religious and secular peacebuilding networks are growing rapidly. In fact, there is a significant increase in the faith-based peacebuilding organizations that began requesting and adopting professional methods of program development and integrating theories of change and other guiding frameworks into their operations. Thus, their challenge is how to keep the uniqueness of their faith identity in their operation. For example, Catholic Relief Services (CRS) has become a leader in the field of professionalized peacebuilding and at the same time has continued to pioneer faith-based processes, such as its Justice Lens analysis. This is an analytical framework inspired by Catholic social teaching that CRS suggests to mainstream in all of its initiatives and programs. It guides the group's practitioners in designing their projects by asking, How does this particular project promote justice?[25]

WHAT MAKES FAITH-BASED
PEACEBUILDING SO CHALLENGING?

The challenges that faith-based practitioners encounter come from multiple interrelated sources, which might be described as the relational work, the religious contradictions, and the global context.

Relational Work: In- and Out-Group Boundaries

The relational work of faith-based peacebuilding can be consuming, particularly for a practitioner who is working in his or her own context of protracted conflict. Lederach has recently identified several of the "dilemmas or tensions" that make it so. Peacebuilders are called upon to reach out to the "other," meaning the enemy, in ways that counter cultural peer-group pressures and personal fears. They are further called upon to recognize the humanity and transcendent value of the other and to develop compassion for the other's suffering. [26]

This work involves a deeply personal reassessment of in-groups and out-groups, of who is "us" and who is "them." Social identity theory views group categorization as a mental process that is necessary for human beings' need to position themselves in a complex world, yet potentially conflictual when it results in biased or competitive attitudes toward out-groups. [27] This is a familiar challenge to all peacebuilders, secular and faith based alike. However, in a conflict that involves religious aspects, group identity issues may be experienced as more existential, and there may be a tendency to be less flexible in accepting critical examination of identity boundaries.

The nature of religious identity touches not only sacred beliefs about life and being, but in many traditions it forces the peacebuilder to address the deep-seated fears of punishments, rewards, days of judgment, and all other beliefs that touch the core psyche of the person's existence. This possibility of an effect on the person's meaning of life and being constitutes a major uniqueness in faith-based peacebuilding processes. For a Muslim or Christian person who has been raised to avoid interacting with anyone outside his or her faith group, meeting the other can be a terrifying experience that will shake his or her core being.

Relating to this set of fears and dynamics requires the peacebuilder to reflectively process such issues in his or her own mind, as well as to connect and comprehend the reactions of other participants in a process that he or she may be leading. For example, while working in Mindanao, Philippines, I (Mohammed) observed on several occasions how the fear of losing one's own religious identity moved a participant in a Muslim-Christian dialogue to avoid coming to a workshop on Sunday (fearing the possibility of Christian prayer). A similar fear among Christian participants motivated them to insist on including pork in the dinner menu of an interfaith training session.[28]

The in- and out-group challenges can be pronounced not only between religious groups but also within faith traditions, in the complexity of the denominations, sects, or schools of thought that comprise them. There are strong views and intrafaith disagreements within many faith traditions about how their believers should relate to people of other faiths. Separation may be advocated because the "other" is seen as inferior, irrelevant, physically or politically dangerous, or a risk to one's spiritual purity and well-being, based on particular interpretations of theology.

This is why Despina Namwembe was initially "castigated" by her own religious community when she began interfaith work. This is why Shia Muslim Azhar Hussain's return to predominantly Sunni Pakistan required such personal courage, in order to overcome both his own biases and his own very practical fears. Further, this is why Eboo Patel has devoted such effort to developing alternate scriptural interpretations that reveal interfaith engagement as a "sacred value."

Interwoven into most cases of in- and out-group relations are fundamental questions of power. The power differential between majority and minority religious groups has a particularly far-reaching impact in shaping the perceptions and responses of each group toward the other. This is true to some extent even in cultural contexts that value egalitarianism, and even more so in contexts that have varying degrees of suppression. In this volume, the India-focused chapters by Sushobha Barve and Qutub Jahan Kidwai provide a unique double-faceted reflection on events unfolding in India, from the vantage points of both the Hindu majority (Barve) and the Muslim minority (Kidwai). In Kidwai's analysis of the past two decades, increasing pressure on the Muslim minority has transformed not only the circumstances in which they live but also the mind-sets and responses of the Muslim community itself. Similar power dynamics are also at play in the remaining stories and examples narrated by the other authors.

Additionally, the fear of conversion often comes up in interfaith engagement, and it is not unfounded, because numerous traditions do contain a mandate to spread the faith. In fact, in interfaith dialogue projects between evangelical and Muslim scholars and communities, fear of conversion and the competition to convert others has been identified as one of the core issues that divide certain followers of these two traditions when they interact or meet in contexts as disparate as Sri Lanka, Iraq, Egypt, Singapore, and Mindanao, Philippines.[29]

Thus, responding to perceptions and fears about conversion is one of the unique features of faith-based peacebuilding. Facilitators of interfaith dialogue must handle this suspicion at the outset of each encounter, even in the premeeting preparation. Rick Love, in his chapter, talks about the high importance among evangelical Christians of balancing the scriptural Great Commission—Jesus's command to "make disciples of all nations"—with the scriptural Great Commandment to love one's neighbor.[30]

Religious Contradictions

The relational challenges of peacebuilding are further complicated by the religious contradictions that faith-based peacebuilders experience. We refer here to the tension between the power of religious identity to foster peace and its power to fuel conflict. This paradox is increasingly widely recognized, and a number of lenses can be used to understand it. Within the research of religion-focused social scientists, the most influential concept is R. Scott Appleby's "ambivalence." According to Appleby, the experience of the sacred itself embodies "the authority to kill and to heal, to unleash savagery, or to bless humankind with healing and wholeness."[31] In a similar vein, Mark Juergensmeyer sees within religion itself a cosmic warfare between order and chaos.[32]

Though broader in scope, Robert Putnam's use of the "bridging" and "bonding social capital" concepts—in which the intragroup bonding variety can manifest a divisive "dark side"[33] —has been usefully applied to interreligious relations in the United States.[34] Mary B. Anderson's applied research on the interaction between international assistance and conflict has yielded the influential concepts of "dividers" and "connectors," which practitioners readily apply to describe their observations on the double-edged effects of religion in intergroup relationships.[35]

Those outsider explanations are often appreciated by faith-based peacebuilders and even appropriated and adapted to explain their own experience. At the same time, there are other complementary explanations for religion's dual potential that come from within religions themselves. Some faith-based practitioners experience the contradictions as a spiritual struggle between good and evil forces at work in the world.[36] For example, according to Islamic teaching, the fight between the desire to feed the self with earthly satisfiers versus the calling to nurture it with spiritual virtues is an ongoing inner struggle that accompanies humans from birth.

Others discern that violent expressions of faith are a result of linking faith too closely with ethnonational identity, politics, or the pursuit of economic gain. In other words, religions "malfunction" when they become "instruments of secular causes."[37] In this interpretation, the true spiritual essence of each religious tradition is just and peaceful, but human error or wrongdoing can cause it to manifest in destructive and violent ways.

My (Michelle's) most poignant experience with religion's ambivalence took place on September 14, 2001, just three days after the September 11 attacks in the United States. I attended the official memorial service at the

National Cathedral in Washington, DC. I was young and not nearly important enough to get myself invited to such an event—but my out-of-town boss
was on the guest list, so I attended in his place. The gathering was presided
over by one current and four former U.S. presidents and diverse religious
leaders, including the Reverend Billy Graham. From my perspective, the first
part of the service seemed mournful and respectful, an appropriate way of
processing the shocking events that had taken place and the lives that had
been lost. However, partway through the proceedings, the atmosphere
changed dramatically when a particular Christian hymn was sung. The song
was the U.S. Civil War–era "Battle Hymn of the Republic,"[38] known in part
for the lyrics

> Mine eyes have seen the glory of the coming of the Lord;
> He is trampling out the vintage where grapes of wrath are stored;
> He hath loosed the fateful lightning of His terrible swift sword,
> His truth is marching on.
> Glory, glory, hallelujah! Glory, glory, hallelujah!
> Glory, glory, hallelujah! His truth is marching on.

I chose not to sing that particular song because I had long felt uncomfortable
with the way it combined and conflated Christianity with nationalism and
military violence. So, while others stood to sing that hymn, I sat and quietly
observed. What I sensed and felt during those moments was a visceral shift in
the collective atmosphere in the room, from an attitude of mourning to an
attitude of active vengeance. I had no hard evidence to offer; yet I felt
heartsick because I was certain that I had observed my own culture taking a
very violent turn. I later discovered that other observers had also sensed the
pivotal significance of that musical moment as a launch of the U.S. "war on
terror."[39] In my view, this war involves spiritual and political distortions
from which we have not yet recovered, catalyzed in part by the militant,
nationalist theology embedded in an old Christian hymn.

Global Context

Every local context is unique, and peacebuilders invest at least as much in the
local as they do in the transnational, as the chapters in this book vividly
illustrate. Nonetheless there are constant global changes in motion that affect
us all, to greater or lesser degrees. World religions are in fact a globalizing
force, due not only to their propensity for expansion, but also to their conceptual teachings about the oneness of humanity[40] that give rise to ideas such as
human rights and humanitarian assistance. Globalization, in turn, is changing
the nature of religious experience as our connection to faraway coreligionists
and our proximity to people of different faiths both increase at a rapid pace.[41]

In today's context, the religiously related dynamics that used to be half-
way around the world now appear on our own doorsteps. The assumption of

secularization is greatly diminished but still influential. The acceptance of religion's importance is increasing, but this recognition brings with it some risk of distorted perceptions. Both of those trends have implications for the role of the faith-based peacebuilder in his or her everyday work.

The core idea of secularization theory is that as modernization increases, religion's influence will decline in public life. The religiously infused sociopolitical movements of recent decades have shown this theory to be resoundingly inadequate.[42] However, while there is a growing consensus that secularization as a prediction does not describe the *current* state of affairs, many still feel that secularism as an ideology[43] is the *preferred* state of affairs.[44] The influence of secularism varies depending on the cultural context, and it remains a relevant concept in many Western-influenced cultural spaces, if less so elsewhere. Where secularism is the predominant mind-set, religious actors must choose whether to respond by accepting it, rejecting it, or trying for a middling compromise.[45] Any choice they make may bring them into conflict with another actor, as seen in Azhar Hussain's analysis of the pressures facing conservative madrasa educators in Pakistan. Further, in secularized settings, the roles of religious peacebuilders may be viewed with skepticism. For instance, one secularist assumption is that religiously motivated peacebuilders cannot be objective or impartial when facing a conflict that involves coreligionists. However, this is an assumption that Peter Dixon and Concordis International have actively rejected in pursuing Christian-motivated yet impartial inclusive dialogue work in prepartition Sudan.

The corollary of decreasing secularism is increasing acceptance of religion's significance in public life. Azza Karam's chapter provides a fascinating assessment of how the marginalization of religious actors is slowly giving way to engagement within the United Nations system. The UN, like numerous other secular governance and development actors, appears to be rediscovering the power of religion and engaging local religious actors to improve the "reach" of its work. This is a very welcome change.[46] At the same time, it raises a flurry of new questions about how secular and religious partners can not only work together but work together well. For example, what are the differences between token engagement and genuine collaboration? Or between secular institutions that respect religion and those that instrumentalize it? How can such engagement broaden beyond official religious leaders and westernized faith-based nongovernmental organizations to achieve a more representative balance? This learning process is just beginning, and open exploration will be needed between secular and religious partners to arrive at mutually satisfactory answers.

It is also problematic that significant strands of today's apparent embrace of religion have emerged because of, and in response to, religiously related[47] violence. Many secular actors are motivated to engage religion by an underlying belief that religion is dangerous and needs to be contained. Currently, the greatest attention by far is focused on Islam. In some cases, this suspicion is made quite explicit in discussions about the supposed tendencies of Islam toward "authoritarianism," "fundamentalism," "extremism," or "terrorism." More often, the suspicion is not stated directly, but it is clearly detectable when repeated illustrations are given that focus predominantly on violent acts committed by Muslims (rather than people of other faiths). It is rare that we find a program on preventing extremism that addresses violence among Christians, Jews, Buddhists, or Hindus. This is particularly true in the Northern Hemisphere, even though there are many extremist groups actively expressing hate speech and incitement against people of other identities. This imbalance calls out for a deeper understanding of the paradox that all religions possess an unmeasurable capacity for both nurturing peace and fostering violence.[48]

It may well be true that instances of "terrorism"—if by "terrorism" one means the use of violence against noncombatants with the goal of inspiring public fear for political purposes—are more often perpetrated by Islamists at this particular point in history.[49] However, "terrorism" is simply one tactic among many—a tactic particularly well suited to structurally asymmetrical conflicts. Terrorism does not represent anywhere near the full spectrum of violence that is taking place in a given context or in the world.[50] In fact the narrow definition of the term "terrorism" has often allowed many forms of violence committed by secular institutions, including states, to be legitimized in the public eye (for example, attacks on civilian targets carried out during the wars in Vietnam in the 1960s, Lebanon in the 1980s, Afghanistan in the 1980s, and more recently in Aleppo, Syria, and as a result of post-9/11 war policies). If we expand our gaze to take in all forms of direct violence, as well as structural and cultural expressions of violence, we will find that all religions share equally in the depravity.[51] Further, if we critically examine the media reports that non-Muslims read about Islam, we will find that those reports tend to be highly selective and oversimplified, lacking the nuance that is required for cross-cultural understanding.[52]

This violence-focused mind-set, with all its partial truths and distortions, is the predominant paradigm that many faith-based peacebuilders currently encounter in their day-to-day work. It sometimes goes by the name of countering or preventing violent extremism (C/PVE), which many see as the softer side of the "war on terror."[53] In this atmosphere, Muslim peacebuilders may experience an uncomfortable tension between addressing the reality of religiously related violence among a tiny minority of their fellow Muslims and resisting the bias and discrimination with which they are being treated. Peacebuilders of other faiths are confronted with the choice of whether to play along with this mind-set, pointing a finger at Islam while overlooking the violence in their own faith traditions, or, alternatively, to constructively contest the C/PVE mind-set by bringing greater balance to the conversation and standing in solidarity with Muslim peacebuilders.

Dominant Northern and secularized processes and systems have in many ways dictated the agenda of peace and governance around the globe. Thus, operating with a faith-based peacebuilding lens in such a context requires a practitioner to continuously confront basic assumptions and misperceptions held even by those international and national agencies that promote peace and stability, particularly if one is largely dependent on their funds. To do this on a daily basis is an exhausting exercise.

In preparing this book, we have faced similar choices, and we have opted to grapple openly with the pain of religiously related violence in all faith traditions, without privileging one over the other. These themes run throughout the book but are particularly noteworthy in the chapters by Dishani Jayaweera and Yael Petretti. Jayaweera draws on her Buddhist heritage to suggest an alternate way of viewing what violent extremism is and on her extensive Sri Lankan experience for alternate ways to address it. Petretti interprets her experience in Israel and Palestine in ways that subvert common assumptions about who is who, finding partners for peace among individuals whom others might label as "extremists" and finding extremism—and transformation—equally present among her own people.

OBSERVATIONS AND IMPLICATIONS

In our effort to contribute to the development of the field of faith-based peacebuilding, we offer here a few lessons learned, gaps, and future trends that emerge from these chapters and are reinforced by our own practitioner experience. These observations will help to inform faith-based peacebuilding itself, while also supporting a call for improved engagement of faith-based practitioners with policymakers, as well as secular development and peacebuilding practitioners.

Courageous Spiritual Growth

First and foremost, the experiences in this book reveal that a key to addressing the challenges of faith-based peacebuilding and to growing as a person of faith and a peacebuilder is a willingness to reexamine and refine one's own beliefs. Many of these authors have made changes that some coreligionists might interpret as signs of compromise. Rick Love and Eboo Patel revised their theologies to better reflect a divine embrace of the "other"; Sushobha Barve held her own faith identity group responsible for violent actions; Despina Namwembe shifted from church-based to interfaith action. Yet each author appears to indicate that such renewals have enhanced, not diminished, their commitment to their own faith identity. In Namwembe's words, these changes "actually had made me a stronger believer in my faith than before."

These chapters also make it clear that many of the challenges of faith-based peacebuilding have more than one solution and that the answers may vary depending on not only the faith tradition but also the surrounding context and the unique vocation of each individual. For example, Deng Giguiento and Peter Dixon, both Christians, have faced squarely the question of whether direct violence is ever permissible. Giguiento has landed on the Christian pacifist side of that debate, while Dixon supports a rigorous application of just-war criteria. Despina Namwembe and Qutub Jahan Kidwai take different approaches to gender inequality in peacebuilding contexts—with Namwembe working powerfully with the system and Kidwai reforming it—not because one is Muslim and the other Christian but because there are multiple legitimate ways that people of faith can and do address this issue.

The authors' experiences highlight the painful reality that religious institutions, being composed of fallible human beings, do not always fulfill their highest potential—yet the core practices of faith itself are seen as consistently reliable. Johonna Turner discloses that Christian church communities sometimes fail to provide atmospheres conducive to the restoration of trauma victims—particularly victims of gender-based violence. However, the biblical scriptures themselves and the sharing of experiences with other like-minded believers together bring deep healing. Azhar Hussain explains how, in his experience, madrasas (Islamic religious schools) operating under cultural pressure may infuse education with intolerance. The answer is to go deeper into Islam, into Qur'anic theology that stresses Islam's heritage of religious tolerance, practical education, and peace. This experience points to an oft-stated paradox: "The cure for bad religion is good religion, not no religion."[54]

The Case for Engagement

As we pursue a deeper integration of faith-based peacebuilding with other fields of practice, the experiences in this book help to make the case for improved engagement by secular counterparts, including policymakers, as well as secular development and peacebuilding practitioners. Specifically, these chapters provide powerful illustrations of the transformative power of faith-based approaches within individual lives and particular case studies. More to the point, these chapters demonstrate how the challenges of faith-based work—which many still see as a reason for keeping religion limited or marginalized—can in fact be faced, overcome, and transcended in everyday practice.

What these chapters do not provide, because it lies beyond the scope and purpose of this book, is rigorous evidence for the macro-level effectiveness of faith-based approaches. This is a significant need in the field, which is being addressed through complementary efforts. For example, the Alliance for Peacebuilding, with the support of the GHR Foundation, has an initiative focusing on evaluation tools for interreligious peacebuilding. Through this process, more than forty different representatives from various faith-based organizations have worked together toward developing more rigorous methods in evaluating their work, new and appropriate evaluation tools for capturing the uniqueness of interreligious peacebuilding, and an active network for interfaith peacebuilding evaluation.[55]

Both types of evidence—project-specific case studies and macro-level proof—will be needed for the foreseeable future to help inform policy and development partners who are not yet aware of the full extent of faith-based networks, particularly at local levels, or who do not yet embrace the full power of their influence. Some secular partners still see the primary function of religious institutions as providing theological and spiritual services to communities and feel that any engagement beyond these parameters constitutes a violation of the principle of separation of church and state. Yet, as these chapters reveal, faith-based practice can in fact hold the potential for much broader forms of social and political transformation.

Religious Literacy

Secular partners who do choose to increase their engagement with faith-based practitioners reflect a broad trend toward taking seriously the potentially constructive role that religion can play in building stronger social cohesion in divided societies. It is not unusual for secular colleagues to state, "I am now convinced that I need to engage with religious leaders in the community to be effective. But how do I do that?" There is a pervasive need for capacity building to support the development of religious literacy. The experiences documented in this book suggest some basic principles that are helpful in this regard.

First, there may be a core reliance on and integration of spirituality in the program design and in the framing of the intervention. For example, when we invite religious leaders to work on a specific project related to health or girls' and women's education, we should not shy away from integrating an intentional space for prayer.

Second, there is a need for intentional provision of space for religious actors to utilize their religious rituals and sacred texts to enhance the comprehension, motivation, or application of the program in their communities. Secular partners need not understand fully how to use this space themselves or feel comfortable operating within it; they simply need to be intentional about making such space available.

Third, in much interreligious peacebuilding, the management of the uniqueness and complexity of religious stakeholders constitutes a challenge for the practitioner and the community. Lack of understanding and proper management of the intrareligious dynamics can often obstruct the implementation of many of the programs in any given community. There is a need to ensure that peacebuilders are continuously engaged in reflective processes to uncover and become aware of their own religious biases. Thus the practice of the "reflective practitioner" becomes even more relevant to faith-based peacebuilding practitioners and participants.

Hence the major emphasis in our edited volume is on this self-exploration and journey into the life of each of the practitioners. All were expected to delve into their own personal journeys and reflect on areas in which such biases were limiting to their practice. For example, Azhar Hussain reflects on his own biases as a young Shia person growing up in a Sunni-dominant community, Dishani Jayaweera identifies her journey with her own individual spiritual growth, and Yael Petretti shares the evolution of her own religious and political views as she sought out expressions of faith that consistently manifested social justice.

As mentioned earlier, interreligious peacebuilding is unique in the depth of its sensitivity for the participant due to the fact that religious identity relates to the core being of the person and his or her calling and meaning in life. Thus, any mistake or mischaracterization of the person's identity can have a damaging reaction among the participants. The existence of the sacred and profane or forbidden in many religious practices adds to the above sensitivity and reduces the space or margin of error for each of the participants and practitioners, especially if they belong to different faith groups.

Fourth, the hierarchal and authoritative nature of many religious institutions can be a unique feature that often inhibits the capacity of the participants and partners to fully engage with policymakers and development agencies without the full endorsement of their highest authorities. It is essential to respond directly and intentionally to this challenge. There are many possible alternatives available to programmers and policymakers to include women in their designs when engaging religious actors. For example, program leads can insist on the inclusion of faith-based civil society group representatives and not only theological leaders. Or they can designate parallel processes for engagement of women in interreligious peacebuilding if formal religious institutions insist on male representation.

The same practices can be applied to youth in interreligious peacebuilding programs. As observed in the chapters of many of the contributors, including Despina Namwembe, Johonna Turner, and Azza Karam, the engagement of youth and women is essential for faith-based peacebuilding.

The burden and challenges of engaging religious leaders in social or political peacebuilding not only rest on the shoulders of policymakers or secular civil society but also are often reflected among religious leaders themselves. Too often we observe certain traditional and conservative religious agencies who continue to see their role as confined to providing religious and spiritual guidance to their followers and avoid engaging in their communities' social, political, or "earthly affairs."

The above features require practitioners of interreligious peacebuilding to be equipped with specific tools that allow them to access religious communities and facilitate their engagement with other partners to build peace and harmony within and among their diverse constituencies.

Serious Engagement versus Manipulation

A final challenge remains in policymaking circles (United Nations, European Union, Organization for Security and Co-operation in Europe, African Union, various governments agencies, etc.) as to whether the recent intense increase in policymakers' interest in engaging religious agencies to support their fight against violent extremism will become an institutional commitment to work with the religious agencies on other issues. Thus, a major critical question has been raised by various actors on the ground: Can this recent engagement by policymakers with interreligious peacebuilding agencies to respond jointly to violent conflicts go beyond the diplomatic and political rhetoric?

The skeptics among interreligious peacebuilding practitioners warn against the instrumentalization of interreligious peacebuilding by policymakers. They caution against a situation in which the engagement of religious leaders is utilized mainly to serve policymakers' narrow political interests, while isolating religious leaders from other policy issues, instead of building a long-term partnership that can contribute to the transformation of the troubling and complicated relationships between secular and religious stakeholders and their respective institutions.

Despite the debates and gaps, it is essential to recognize the importance of the recent mutual collaboration and outreach to interreligious and intrareligious agencies of peace and dialogue by policymakers (reflected in hundreds of conferences, training workshops, and research projects being held or launched every month around the globe in concerted efforts to counter violent extremism and prevent violence in the name of religion). This indeed can develop into a historic shift in national and global strategies for responding to social, economic, and political problems, especially if interreligious peacebuilding agencies can sustain their efforts and engage wider audiences among their followers.

LOOKING AHEAD

Each reader will take something unique from these stories, but in them there is a cumulative impact of vision and hope. The chapter authors have the earned credibility of people who have borne the high costs of pursuing peace due to the violence and exclusion in the contexts around them and due to the challenging nature of faith-based peacebuilding itself. Despite their diverse faith traditions and cultures, they consistently illustrate transparency, humility, compassion, and spiritual depth and resourcefulness when facing adversity.

We, as editors, hope that the experiences shared in this volume will lead you to engage more deeply with faith-based peacebuilding from wherever you find yourself starting. If you are a partner to faith-based peacebuilders, may this book provide new insight to strengthen your collaboration. If you are a friendly skeptic, may this book pleasantly surprise you with more transparency, rigor, and transformation than you previously thought possible. If you are a faith-inspired peacebuilder, we hope you will find inspiration in these chapters; then, in the words of the Sufi scholar Rumi, "Don't be satisfied with stories, how things have gone with others. Unfold your own myth."[56]

NOTES

1. Mary Kaldor, *New and Old Wars: Organized Violence in a Global Era* (Cambridge: Polity, 1999); Hew Strachan and Sibylle Scheipers, eds., *The Changing Character of War* (Oxford: Oxford University Press, 2011).

2. See Institute for Economics and Peace, "Five Key Questions Answered on the Link between Peace and Religion: A Global Statistical Analysis on the Empirical Link between Peace and Religion," 2014, http://visionofhumanity.org/app/uploads/2017/04/Peace-and-Religion-Report.pdf, accessed May 12, 2017.

3. See Daphna Canetti et al., "Much Ado about Religion: Religiosity, Resource Loss and Support for Political Violence," *Journal of Peace Research* 47 (2010): 575–87; Jonathan Fox, *An Introduction to Religion and Politics: Theory and Practice* (London: Routledge, 2013), 54; Monica Duffy Toft, "Getting Religion? The Puzzling Case of Islam and Civil War," *International Security* 31 (2007): 97–131.

4. See, for example, on Islam, Qamar-ul Huda, ed., *Crescent and Dove: Peace and Conflict Resolution in Islam* (Washington, DC: U.S. Institute of Peace, 2010); on Buddhism, Thich Nhat Hanh, *Creating True Peace: Ending Violence in Yourself, Your Family, Your Community and the World* (New York: Free Press, 2003); on Christianity, Emmanuel Katongole and Chris Rice, *Reconciling All Things: A Christian Vision for Justice, Peace and Healing* (Downers Grove, IL: InterVarsity Press, 2009).

5. See, for example, the International Partnership on Religion and Sustainable Development (http://www.partner-religion-development.org).

6. See, for example, R. Scott Appleby, *The Ambivalence of the Sacred: Religion, Violence and Reconciliation* (Lanham, MD: Rowman & Littlefield, 2000); Marc Gopin, *Between Eden and Armageddon: The Future of World Religions, Violence and Peacemaking* (New York: Oxford University Press, 2000); Katrien Hertog, *The Complex Reality of Religious Peacebuilding: Conceptual Contributions and Critical Analysis* (Lanham, MD: Lexington, 2010); Monica

Duffy Toft, Daniel Philpott, and Timothy Samuel Shah, *God's Century: Resurgent Religion and Global Politics* (London: Norton, 2011).

7. See, for example, Cynthia Sampson and John Paul Lederach, eds., *From the Ground Up: Mennonite Contributions to International Peacebuilding* (New York: Oxford University Press, 2000); David Little and Tanenbaum Center for Interreligious Understanding, *Peacemakers in Action: Profiles of Religion in Conflict Resolution* (New York: Cambridge University Press, 2007); Joyce S. Dubensky and Tannenbaum Center for Interreligious Understanding, *Peacemakers in Action: Profiles of Religion in Conflict Resolution*. Vol. 2 (New York: Cambridge University Press, 2016).

8. A noteworthy exception to this focus on the positive is apparent in Marc Gopin's highly transparent exploration of the experiences of peacebuilders in the Holy Land. See Marc Gopin, *Bridges across an Impossible Divide: The Inner Lives of Arab and Jewish Peacemakers* (Oxford: Oxford University Press, 2012).

9. See Michelle Le Baron and Venashri Pillay, *Conflict across Cultures: A Unique Experience* (Boston: Intercultural Press, 2006).

10. See, for example, Annette Simmons, *Whoever Tells the Best Story Wins: How to Use Your Own Stories to Communicate with Power and Impact* (New York: AMACOM American Management Association, 2007).

11. "Peace be upon him," an expression often used following the name of Muhammed and other prophets recognized in Islam.

12. Mohammed Abu-Nimer, *Nonviolence and Peacebuilding in Islam: Theory and Practice* (Gainesville: University of Florida Press, 2003).

13. See, for example, Timothy D. Sisk, *Between Terror and Tolerance: Religious Leaders, Conflict and Peacemaking* (Washington, DC: Georgetown University Press, 2011).

14. Mohammed Abu-Nimer, "Conflict Resolution, Culture, and Religion: Toward a Training Model of Interreligious Peacebuilding," *Journal of Peace Research* 38 (2001): 685–704.

15. See, for example, Thomas A. Idinopulos and Brian C. Wilson, *What Is Religion? Origins, Definitions, and Explanations* (Leiden: Brill, 1998).

16. "Religion," Dictionary.com, http://www.dictionary.com/browse/religion, accessed December 19, 2016.

17. "Faith," Dictionary.com, http://www.dictionary.com/browse/faith, accessed August 27, 2017.

18. Karen Armstrong, *Fields of Blood: Religion and the History of Violence* (Toronto: Vintage, 2015), 4–6; Timothy Samuel Shah, "Secular Militancy as an Obstacle to Peacebuilding," in *The Oxford Handbook of Religion, Conflict and Peacebuilding*, ed. Atalia Omer, R. Scott Appleby, and David Little (New York: Oxford University Press, 2015), 380–406.

19. Black Elk, quoted in John Hart, *What Are They Saying about Environmental Theology?* (New York: Paulist Press, 2004), 63.

20. John Paul Lederach, "Spirituality and Religious Peacebuilding," in *The Oxford Handbook of Religion, Conflict and Peacebuilding*, ed. Atalia Omer, R. Scott Appleby, and David Little (New York: Oxford University Press, 2015), 541–68.

21. Ibid., 542.

22. For a rich exploration of the influence of secular beliefs, see Judith Goldstein and Robert O. Keohane, eds., *Ideas and Foreign Policy: Beliefs, Institutions and Political Change* (Ithaca, NY: Cornell University Press, 1993).

23. David Steele and Ricardo Wilson-Grau, "Supernatural Belief and the Evaluation of Faith-Based Peacebuilding" (Washington, DC: Peacebuilding Evaluation Consortium, 2017), http://www.allianceforpeacebuilding.org/site/wp-content/uploads/2017/03/Peace-and-Religion-Report.pdf, accessed April 21, 2017.

24. Johan Galtung, "Violence, Peace and Peace Research," *Journal of Peace Research* 6 (1969): 167–91.

25. Mark Rogers, Aaron Chassy, and Tom Bamat, "Integrating Peacebuilding into Humanitarian and Development Programs: Practical Guidance on Designing Effective, Holistic Peacebuilding Projects" (Baltimore: Catholic Relief Services, 2010), http://www.crs.org/sites/default/files/tools-research/integrating-peacebuilding-into-humanitarian-and-development-programming.pdf, accessed April 21, 2017.

26. John Paul Lederach, "Spirituality and Religious Peacebuilding," in *The Oxford Handbook of Religion, Conflict and Peacebuilding*, ed. Atalia Omer, R. Scott Appleby, and David Little (New York: Oxford University Press, 2015), 541–68.

27. Henri Tajfel and John C. Turner, "The Social Identity Theory of Intergroup Behavior," in *Psychology of Intergroup Relations*, ed. Stephen Worchel and William G. Austin. Nelson-Hall Series in Psychology (Chicago: Nelson-Hall, 1986).

28. Based on Mohammed Abu-Nimer's facilitation and training of Christian and Muslim dialogue groups in Mindanao, Philippines, between 1999 and 2007.

29. Mohammed Abu-Nimer, "Religious Leaders in the Israeli-Palestinian Conflict: From Violent Incitement to Nonviolence Resistance," *Peace & Change* 36 (2011): 556–80; Michelle Garred, "The Power of Mindsets: Bridging, Bonding and Associational Change in Deeply Divided Mindanao," *Journal of Civil Society* 9 (2013): 21–40; Michelle Garred, "Conflict Sensitivity and Religious Associations: An Action Research Journey in Southeast Asia" (PhD diss., Lancaster University, 2011).

30. The biblical references here are to Matthew 28:18–20 and 22:37–40.

31. Appleby, *The Ambivalence of the Sacred*, 29. See also R. Scott Appleby, "Religious Violence: The Strong, the Weak and the Pathological," in *The Oxford Handbook of Religion, Conflict and Peacebuilding*, ed. Atalia Omer, R. Scott Appleby, and David Little (New York: Oxford University Press, 2015), 33–59.

32. Mark Juergensmeyer, *Terror in the Mind of God: The Global Rise of Religious Violence* (Berkeley: University of California Press, 2000).

33. Robert D. Putnam, *Bowling Alone: The Collapse and Revival of American Community* (New York: Simon & Schuster, 2000), 350–63.

34. Robert D. Putnam and David E. Campbell, *American Grace: How Religion Divides and Unites Us* (New York: Simon & Schuster, 2010).

35. Mary B. Anderson, *Do No Harm: How Aid Can Support Peace—or War* (Boulder, CO: Lynne Rienner, 1999). See also Michelle Garred, ed., with Mohammed Abu-Nimer, *A Shared Future: Local Capacities for Peace in Community Development* (Monrovia, CA: World Vision International, 2006), http://www.wvi.org/sites/default/files/A_Shared_Future.pdf, accessed January 8, 2017; Michelle Garred with Joan Castro, "Conflict-Sensitive Expressions of Faith in Mindanao: A Case Study," *Journal of Religion, Conflict and Peace* 4, no. 2 (2011), http://www.religionconflictpeace.org/volume-4-issue-2-spring-2011/conflict-sensitive-expressions-faith-mindanao-case-study, accessed January 8, 2017.

36. For an example of this type of reasoning within Christianity, see Walter Wink, *When the Powers Fall: Reconciliation in the Healing of Nations* (Minneapolis, MN: Fortress, 1996).

37. Miroslav Volf, *Flourishing: Why We Need Religion in a Globalized World* (New Haven, CT: Yale University Press, 2015), 58.

38. Public domain.

39. See, for example, John Stauffer and Benjamin Soskis, *The Battle Hymn of the Republic: A Biography of the Song That Marches On* (New York: Oxford University Press, 2013), 4–7; Dominic Tierney, "'The Battle Hymn of the Republic': America's Song of Itself," *Atlantic*, November 4, 2010, http://www.theatlantic.com/entertainment/archive/2010/11/the-battle-hymn-of-the-republic-americas-song-of-itself/66070, accessed January 2, 2017.

40. Volf, *Flourishing*, 37–38.

41. Mark Juergensmeyer, Dinah Griego, and John Soboslai, *God in the Tumult of the Public Square: Religion in Global Civil Society* (Oakland: University of California Press, 2015).

42. The literature on this point is vast. See, for example, Jose Casanova, *Public Religions in the Modern World* (Chicago: University of Chicago Press, 1994); Peter L. Berger, *The Many Altars of Modernity: Toward a Paradigm for Religion in a Pluralist Age* (Boston: De Gruyter, 2014).

43. Shah, "Secular Militancy as an Obstacle to Peacebuilding," 380–406.

44. See, for example, Richard Dawkins, *The God Delusion* (London: Bantam, 2006); Sam Harris, *The End of Faith: Religion, Terror and the Future of Reason* (New York: W. W. Norton, 2004).

45. Fox, *An Introduction to Religion and Politics*, 32.

46. Note that the rediscovery of religion may arguably have started a bit earlier in foreign policy and official diplomatic circles than it did in other spheres of governance and in development practice. See Douglas Johnston and Cynthia Sampson, *Religion: The Missing Dimension of Statecraft* (Washington, DC: Center for Strategic and International Studies, 1994).

47. The term "religiously related"—borrowed from Mark Juergensmayer, Margo Kitts, and Michael Jerryson, *Violence and the World's Religious Traditions: An Introduction* (New York: Oxford University Press, 2017)—is useful because it encompasses all the diverse ways in which religion and violence can be interrelated, without imposing specific assumptions about causation.

48. For examples of violence in faiths other than Islam, see ibid.; Arie Perlinger, "Comparative Framework for Understanding Jewish and Christian Violent Fundamentalism," *Religions* 6 (2015): 1033–47.

49. Jonathan Fox, *An Introduction to Religion and Politics: Theory and Practice* (London: Routledge, 2013), 52.

50. Ibid., 52.

51. Galtung, "Violence, Peace and Peace Research." For insight on how the multifaceted analysis of direct, structural, and cultural violence can help in understanding the full spectrum of religiously related violence and in developing a "self-reflexive critical analysis," see also Jason A. Springs, "Structural and Cultural Violence in Religion and Peacebuilding," in *The Oxford Handbook of Religion, Conflict and Peacebuilding,* ed. Atalia Omer, R. Scott Appleby, and David Little (New York: Oxford University Press, 2015), 146–81.

52. Edward W. Said, *Covering Islam: How the Media and the Experts Determine How We See the Rest of the World, Revised Edition* (New York: Vintage, 1997).

53. Marc Ambinder, "The New Term for the War on Terror," *Atlantic*, May 20, 2010, https://www.theatlantic.com/politics/archive/2010/05/the-new-term-for-the-war-on-terror/56969, accessed April 21, 2017.

54. Jonathan Sacks, *The Great Partnership: God, Science, and the Search for Meaning* (London: Hodder & Stoughton, 2011), 11.

55. Jennie Vader, "Meta-review of Inter-religious Peacebuilding Program Evaluations" (Washington, DC: Peacebuilding Evaluation Consortium, 2015), http://dmeforpeace.org/sites/default/files/Peacebuilding%20Evaluation%20Consortium%20Meta-Review%20of%20Inter-Religious%20Peacebuilding%20Program%20Evaluations_July2015FINAL.pdf, accessed April 21, 2017. Note that a book on the evaluation of interreligious peacebuilding and dialogue is under development by the King Abdullah Bin Abdulaziz International Centre for Interreligious and Intercultural Dialogue.

56. Jelaluddin Rumi, "Unfold Your Own Myth" (excerpt), in Roger Housden, *Ten Poems to Set You Free* (New York: Harmony Books, 2003).

Part I

Engaging One's Own Faith

Chapter One

Articulating a Personal Theology of Interfaith Cooperation

Eboo Patel

*Challenge: How do we convince faith communities that interfaith coopera-
tion is a central value of their tradition rather than something ancillary or
even against their faith?*

Interfaith leaders and peace practitioners who work in the religion space
know that faith communities are quick to affirm the civic value of diversity,
but they also ask themselves an additional question: Are positive relationships with people who orient around religion differently a *sacred* value also?
In other words, when invited to participate in interfaith peace and cooperation projects, faith communities are apt to ask, "Can we as [Muslims/Chris-
tians/Hindus/Jews/Buddhists/etc.] work in partnership with people who we
think are *wrong* on significant cosmic matters?" Emphasizing the civic value
of interfaith cooperation, however important, might not get faith communities over the religious hurdle. To effectively connect with such communities, interfaith leaders will need to articulate *a theology of interfaith cooperation*.

In my experience, developing and articulating such a theology not only
helps interfaith leaders more effectively engage certain faith communities in
interfaith work but also helps them connect more deeply with their own
highest values. The renowned philosopher Alastair MacIntyre expresses this
sentiment well when he writes, "I can only answer the question 'What am I to
do?' if I can answer the prior question 'Of what story or stories do I find
myself a part?'"[1] Those of us who view ourselves as part of religious traditions want our work in the world to be aligned with the "story" of our
tradition. Articulating a theology of interfaith cooperation offers us the

29

chance to develop an interpretation of that story and live out its values in our work.

This chapter will elaborate on the need for and design of a theology of interfaith cooperation, using my experience as an Ismaili Muslim who founded Interfaith Youth Core (IFYC) as a case study.

FOUNDATIONS—HOW I BECAME AN INTERFAITH LEADER

As an adolescent, I viewed religion as irrelevant, something my mom made me do every so often. That changed during my college years. As an undergraduate, I was heavily involved in both service and social justice work, a set of commitments that led me to Dorothy Day and the radical social movement that she founded, the Catholic Worker. The St. Jude's Catholic Worker House of Hospitality was one of the local homeless shelters in my college town. When I volunteered there, it felt qualitatively different from the Salvation Army or the Men's Emergency Shelter or any of the other agencies where I spent time. There was no staff-client distinction at St. Jude's, and there was a lot more joy. It was a community, not an agency. When I inquired about how that came to be, the Catholic Workers told me to read the work of Dorothy Day. I found her writing luminous, particularly because it cut through the noise of theory and analysis with a simple and beautiful philosophy: poverty and war were not only unjust but against the will of God. It is our purpose to end both. Living in community with those on the margins was what God wanted of us, Jesus showed us how to do it best, and following that path was the most fulfilling life possible. Day had walked it herself for fifty years.

I wanted Day's sense of purpose and strength of conviction. In both her writing and her life, she seemed to say, "If you want this, go to the source: God."

My admiration for Dorothy Day and the Catholic Worker movement helped me see religion through new eyes. It occurred to me that many of my heroes—Martin Luther King Jr., Mahatma Gandhi, Malcolm X, Mother Teresa, Archbishop Desmond Tutu, His Holiness the Dalai Lama—were people of deep faith, leaders whose religions played a central role in the work they did for the world. What's more, they were from different religious communities. Dorothy Day was a Catholic, King a Baptist, Tutu an Episcopalian, Gandhi a Hindu, Malcolm a Muslim, and the Dalai Lama a Buddhist. Something about how these people connected with their respective traditions had given them great courage and power. How could I ever have thought religion was irrelevant?

At the same time, I was getting a clearer picture of the dark side of religion in the world. As an undergraduate, I was deeply involved in the campus diversity movement and enjoyed nothing more than lecturing my father about what I liked to call "people-of-color consciousness." Generally speaking, he received these lectures with good humor, figuring, I suppose, that it was part of the cost of sending his son to college. But at some point, I must have crossed a line as he got frustrated and said, "Listen, the next time you want to lecture me about diversity, why don't you first tell me how you are going to solve the most important identity challenge in the world: conflicts over religion."

The following week, my girlfriend at the time called me and, choking back tears, said, "Yitzhak Rabin has just been assassinated." My girlfriend was Jewish and regarded Rabin as one of the great faith heroes of the twentieth century, the man who would lead Israel and the Jews to peace with the Palestinians. She was utterly heartbroken over the assassination, and what was left of her heart after the murder was shattered by the fact that the killer was Jewish and claimed that his accomplice in the assassination was God. For me, it was a wake-up call to the ugly role that religion was playing in world affairs. Protestant-Catholic conflict in Northern Ireland, Hindu-Muslim conflict in India, Christian-Muslim conflict in the Balkans, Buddhist-Hindu conflict in Sri Lanka, and, of course, the granddaddy of them all, the Jewish-Muslim conflict in the Middle East. Why hadn't I noticed the religious dimension of global affairs before? And why was religion never part of the diversity discussion in college?

Add to this another insight. The foot soldiers of religious extremism always seemed to be young. Yigal Amir, the man who murdered Prime Minister Rabin, was twenty-six at the time. But my faith heroes had begun their journeys when they were young as well. Martin Luther King Jr. was the same age as Yigal Amir when he led the Montgomery Bus Boycott. The Dalai Lama and Mahatma Gandhi were even younger when they began their movements. What's more, all of my faith heroes seemed to have had an intense experience with another faith during their formative years. Gandhi read the Bible as a young man in law school, and Martin Luther King Jr. read Gandhi as a young man in seminary.

In the summer of 1998, I was lucky enough to be at the United Religions Initiative Global Summit at Stanford University and to meet a group of like-minded young people from around the world. We talked excitedly about the prospect of creating programs that would bring young people with different religious orientations together to do service projects and engage in conversations about how their various faiths inspired them to serve. It aimed to increase the amount of service being done in the world, strengthen relationships between diverse communities, enhance the leadership of young people, and raise the volume on faith as a positive rather than a destructive force. Organizations like Teach for America, City Year, and Public Allies were intentional about bringing people of different racial, ethnic, and class backgrounds together around service, but they didn't touch faith. The project we envisioned would employ the same basic approach of using service as a common table to gather diversity, but the dimension of identity we would emphasize was faith.

A small group of us launched an initiative called Interfaith Youth Corps and started running interfaith service-learning projects with young people in different parts of the world. After defining a methodology that seemed to work across a range of settings—and changing the "Corps" part of our name to "Core" to reflect our vision of being at the heart of a larger movement—we started to build the foundation of an organization that could improve and scale our program. In addition to continuing to organize interfaith service projects, we began to write and speak about interfaith service learning, hold conferences for colleagues in the growing movement, and design curriculums for the emerging field.

I was in graduate school during those first years of launching Interfaith Youth Core, writing a DPhil thesis at Oxford University on the educational programs of the Ismaili Muslim community. This is the community I was born into but had not been active in since I was a child. My academic work allowed me to connect with the tradition in an intellectual way, which is the manner in which I feel both most comfortable and most inspired. I read the writings and speeches of the past two Ismaili leaders (Aga Khan III and Aga Khan IV), built relationships with Ismaili intellectuals, and had a chance to participate in Ismaili conferences. I discovered how deeply the theme of pluralism was woven into the fabric of the tradition and how much the Ismaili leadership was seeking to nurture people with interfaith knowledge and skills. It felt like a match made in heaven (and because I am now a much more devout person, I believe perhaps it was!). The value of pluralism that I had discovered through my social justice work and seen vividly displayed through the lives of other faith leaders was an integral part of the religious community into which I was born; I had just not paid attention until I became a young adult. As I was doing intellectual work in the Ismaili community, I was also reconnecting with my grandmother in India, who I discovered regularly took destitute women into her home and nurtured them back to health and wholeness. When I asked her why she put herself at risk by doing this kind of work, her response was, "Because I'm a Muslim. This is what Muslims do."

It was at that point that I recognized a deep personal desire to delve into the Muslim tradition, especially the Ismaili interpretation of it. To reference the MacIntyre quote from earlier, I realized that I was part of the "story of Islam" and that learning that story, especially the parts that spoke to pluralism, would guide and inspire my life and work long into the future. I wanted my life to be a small thread in the larger fabric of Islamic pluralism. As I became more widely involved in Muslim circles and interfaith efforts, I realized that my felt personal desire to learn and articulate a Muslim theology of interfaith cooperation overlapped with a need within both the Muslim community and the broader society.

ELEMENTS OF A MUSLIM THEOLOGY
OF INTERFAITH COOPERATION

A theology of interfaith cooperation means interpreting the key sources of a tradition in a way that puts forth a coherent narrative and deep logic that calls for positive relationships with people of diverse religious orientations. When I say key sources, I mean both the central texts of a religious tradition and also important historical moments, examples of archetypal figures, writings of significant scholars (philosophers, theologians, and jurists), and art that seeks to tap into the ineffable dimensions of the tradition. A coherent narrative is a theme that is clearly traceable throughout the different dimensions of a cumulative historical tradition (texts, history, archetypal figures, scholarship, etc.).

My own Muslim theology of interfaith cooperation begins with important stories from the life of the Prophet Muhammad that speak to interfaith cooperation. In fact, the first people to recognize Muhammad as a prophet were actually Christian: Bahira, a Christian monk, noticed that Muhammad, when he was a boy, had the mark of prophethood on his back. Waraqa, after Muhammad's earth-shattering experience on Mount Hira in the year 610, explained to Muhammad and his wife, Khadija, that what Muhammad had experienced was God's revelation. The person most responsible for protecting Muhammad during the early years of Islam, when he and his fellow Muslims were hounded and harassed in Mecca, was a pagan, Abu Talib. One of Muhammad's first acts when he emigrated from Mecca to Medina was to create what became known as the Constitution of Medina, which allied the various religious groups and tribes in that area in an alliance of goodwill and common defense.

There are powerful moments from the classical period in Muslim history that affirm the value of interfaith cooperation, from the Prophet Muhammad inviting a group of Christians to pray in his mosque to the Caliph Ali writing to his governor in Egypt, "All those there are your brothers in faith or your equals in creation."[2] Many Muslim groups have since followed in this tradition of respecting and protecting non-Muslims. The only country in Europe with a higher Jewish population *after* the Holocaust was Albania. The reason is that the people of that majority-Muslim country made it a part of their public honor to protect Jews during that dark time. Similarly, the Muslims of Rwanda appeared to be the only organized group who protected Tutsis from the machete-wielding Interahamwe militia during the genocide of the 1990s.

Like stories from the lives of exemplary figures and key moments in history, religious art is an important contributor to a theology of interfaith cooperation. Muslim poets have long been known for their respectful attitudes toward other religions. Take Ibn Arabi, who wrote,

> My heart has become capable of every form:
> it is a pasture for gazelles and a convent for Christian monks,
> and a temple for idols and the pilgrim's Kaa'ba,
> and the tables of the Torah and the book of the Quran.
> I follow the religion of Love: whatever way Love's camels take,
> that is my religion and my faith. [3]

There are also key ideas in the Islamic tradition that can be interpreted as embracing diversity. Take for example the term *ayat*, commonly understood as a "verse of the Quran" but more literally translated as "sign." God gives us his signs in many places—in his revealed scripture, in our relationships with others, in the natural world, and in the culture of the societies in which we live. In this way, the growing diversity of our societies may be viewed as an *ayat* of God and therefore something sacred.

Finally, any theology of interfaith cooperation has to take seriously the central text or texts of a tradition, interpreting them in ways that support positive relationships with those who believe differently. This requires not only highlighting the parts of the text that support cooperation but also developing a hermeneutic that explains the dimensions of the same scripture that seem to highlight the opposite.

In a brilliant essay titled "The Place of Tolerance in Islam," Islamic scholar Khaled Abou El Fadl lists various verses from the Quran that are clearly intolerant toward other religions alongside verses that command positive interfaith relationships and essentially asks, Why should we follow one set of verses rather than the other? The verses in question could not be more different. Here is an example on the intolerant side: "Fight those among the People of the Book (Jews and Christians) who do not believe in God or the Hereafter, who do not forbid what God and his Prophet have forbidden, and who do not acknowledge the religion of truth—fight them until they pay the poll tax with willing submission and feel themselves subdued."[4] And an example that calls for interfaith cooperation: "O humankind, God has created you from male and female and made you into diverse nations and tribes so that you may come to know each other. Verily, the most honored of you in the sight of God is he who is the most righteous."[5]

Which view is the "correct" one? When it comes to relating with Christians and Jews, what should a conscientious Muslim do? To answer this question, Abou El Fadl puts forth a four-part hermeneutic for approaching the Quran that is the key to interpreting sacred texts (including the difficult parts) in a manner that advances a theology of interfaith cooperation.

The first part of the hermeneutic addresses the historical context of the text. Muslims believe that the Quran was revealed over the course of twenty-three years, years during which the Prophet Muhammad was not only spreading the message of Islam but building an ideal Muslim society. As in any real-world movement, there were moments of tension and conflict both within the fledgling Muslim community and between Muslims and other groups—Jews, Christians, Sabians, pagans—in the area. According to Muslim belief, God would reveal Quranic verses that helped the Prophet Muhammad deal with particular situations. Many Muslim scholars, Abou El Fadl among them, say that the verses from the Quran that are intolerant toward other groups are meant to be specific advice for particular times and places and not meant to be applied broadly. The verses that speak of interfaith cooperation, on the other hand, contain an ethic that is meant to be understood in a universal and eternal way.

The second part of the hermeneutic deals with the overall moral thrust of the Quran. Abou El Fadl points out that at the center of the Quran is a set of "general moral imperatives such as mercy, justice, kindness, or goodness" and that the entire text must be read "in light of the overall moral thrust of the Qur'anic message."[6]

The third part deals with the conscience of the reader. In addition to the historical context of the text and the general principles of the Quran, Abou El Fadl emphasizes that morality is not only contained in the text but also in the heart or conscience of the reader. After all, according to Muslim belief, God gave all people his breath (*ruh*). People are required to bring this inner morality to their reading of the Quran and their lives in general. As Abou El Fadl writes, "The meaning of the religious text is not fixed simply by the literal meaning of its words, but depends, too, on the moral construction given to it by the reader. . . . [T]he text will morally enrich the reader, but only if the reader will morally enrich the text."[7]

Finally, Abou El Fadl emphasizes that the context of the reader matters. Like all texts, the Quran emerged in a particular time and place. And like all people, we read it in particular times and places. In interpreting the Quran, both the context of the text and the context of the reader have to be taken into account. To support this view, Abou El Fadl gives the following example: "The Qur'an persistently commands Muslims to enjoin the good. The word used for 'the good' is ma'ruf, which means that which is commonly known to be good. Goodness, in the Qur'anic discourse, is part of what one may call a lived reality—it is the product of human experiences and constructed normative understandings."[8] In other words, the Quran expects readers to approach the text not only with their God-given *taqwa* but also with ideas of what is "good" from their own context. For Abou El Fadl, this means that evolving notions in culture and civilization, from progress in science to ideals like universal human rights and the benefits of diversity, ought to be brought to bear when interpreting the Quran.

At the end of his essay, Khaled Abou El Fadl emphasizes that any tradition, including Islam, "provides possibilities for meaning, not inevitabilities. And those possibilities are exploited, developed and ultimately determined by the reader's efforts."[9] No doubt one can understand the Quran and the Islamic tradition as one that compels building bunkers of isolation or barriers of division. However, this is not the only possibility. One of the fascinating things about religious traditions is that they contain a multiplicity of potential interpretations and expressions. Some of these seem, at least from the outside, contradictory, even opposing. Islam can be read as a religion that seeks both converts and emphasizes cooperation. The real question is therefore not, What does Islam say? It is, Which of the many possibilities and logics within Islam do I most want to emphasize? That has as much to do with the reader's understanding of the tradition and the times as it does with anything else. What is crystal clear is that the tradition of Islam, like other major world traditions, has ample resources through which a faithful Muslim can construct a theology of interfaith cooperation.

It is important to highlight that Khaled Abou El Fadl is not alone in his approach to the Quran and the Muslim tradition. Other important Muslim scholars have developed similar themes in their writings. For example, in his essay "Islam and Cultural Imperative," Dr. Umar Abd-Allah emphasizes that the genius of Islamic civilization is its ability to integrate its sacred law within various cultural contexts. In fact, he writes, one of the five maxims of Islamic law is to respect sound custom across time and place. Islam is meant to be a tradition that harmonizes with a range of cultures, not one that sets out to destroy them. To support his point, he quotes from a renowned thirteenth-century Islamic legal scholar, Al-Qarafi: "Persons handing down legal judgments while adhering blindly to the texts in their books without regard for the cultural realities of their people are in gross error. They act in contradiction to established legal consensus and are guilty of iniquity and disobedience before God."[10]

CHALLENGES AND RESPONSES

While there is a range of possible challenges involved in advancing a theology of interfaith cooperation, in this section I want to highlight an issue that is very particular to my situation. As noted earlier, I am an Ismaili Muslim, part of a small Shia Muslim community viewed as somewhere between heterodox and heretical by many Sunni Muslims. Ismaili doctrine states that God will provide a rightful interpreter of the Quran (known within the community as "Hazir Imam" for "Present and Living Imam" and to the broader world as

His Highness Aga Khan IV) from within the Prophet Muhammad's lineage to guide the community of believers through different times and places. Ismailis, in keeping with the guidance of past imams, have established their own houses of worship and have prayer practices that are distinct from those of most other Muslims.

Being an Ismaili actually makes developing a personal theology of interfaith cooperation easier. Aga Khan IV has made pluralism a central value of his imamate, one that he makes clear emanates directly from the broader tradition of Islam. As he stated in his Jodi lecture at Harvard in November 2015, "At the very heart of the Islamic faith is a conviction that we are all born of a single soul. We are 'spread abroad' to be sure in all of our diversity, but we share, in a most profound sense, a common humanity."[11]

But being an Ismaili has created interesting challenges for me when it comes to engaging the broader Muslim community. For example, I remember being given a tour of a Muslim education center, when the spiritual leader of the institution made some offhand negative comments about Muslim minorities in general and heaped special scorn upon Ismailis in particular. While most Muslim leaders at this point know that I'm an Ismaili and would not say such things to my face, I have heard from several sources that not a few have made disparaging references about my Ismaili identity behind my back.

So why is it that my interfaith efforts have had at least modest success, both within and beyond the Muslim community? I think the explanation lies in how social conditions have shifted in a manner that created an opening for American Muslim civic leaders to emerge, leaders whose particular Muslim identity is secondary to their work in the world.

The shift began with the attacks of 9/11, which were a triple shock to American Muslims. The first shock was the one that everyone in America experienced—the massive devastation of an attack on one's homeland that affected family, friends, neighbors, and fellow citizens. The second shock was that it was other Muslims who had carried out the attack, leading to significant soul-searching among American Muslims regarding the hateful theology that motivated those Muslim extremists. The third shock was the sudden requirement to defend Muslim identity to a questioning American public.

At the time of 9/11, I was finishing my doctorate at Oxford University and launching Interfaith Youth Core. As I stated earlier, I had recommitted to Islam during my graduate school years and was especially moved by the theology of interfaith cooperation that I found in the Ismaili interpretation. My newfound religious zeal found expression in building IFYC and in writing and speaking. After 9/11, America provided me with ample opportunities for such expression. There were liberal audiences associated with college campuses, civic institutions, and media outlets like National Public Radio that were eager to hear an interpretation of Islam that was consonant with America's best traditions of inclusion and cooperation. I had come about such an interpretation honestly, and I offered it proudly and freely. Because most Americans were at a point where they were learning the basics of Islam, it seemed like overkill to spend time explaining the differences between various communities within the house of Islam (Sunnis versus Shias, etc.). To most audiences, I was simply an American Muslim, albeit a liberal one, who was able to articulate the tradition of Islam in a manner that they understood. I did dozens of public speaking appearances every year and wrote a book, *Acts of Faith: The Story of an American Muslim, the Struggle for the Soul of a Generation*, that became required reading on campuses across the country. Everywhere I went, I explained that I was neither a religious leader nor a scholar, simply a devoted member of the Muslim tradition inspired by my faith to build a nonprofit organization dedicated to interfaith cooperation.

In the American landscape, there has long been a category for civic leaders who are religiously inspired. Think of Millard Fuller of Habitat for Humanity, or even Jimmy Carter. They are not viewed first and foremost as religious leaders, but their faith is directly connected to the way they are perceived by the public. I was one of several Muslims (others include Reza Aslan, Daisy Khan, and Wajahat Ali) who came to occupy this space in the American public square.

In the post-9/11 era, changes were afoot within the Muslim community that made the category of "civic Muslim leader" more salient as well. For many years, the immigrant Muslim community (I admittedly know much less about the African-American experience) was content to build up its internal institutions—mosques, Islamic schools, places to get married and buried, and so forth. Little thought was given to presenting Islam or the Muslim experience to the broader American public. In fact, as with Catholics, Jews, Mormons, and evangelicals in earlier eras, the institutions of the Muslim community were meant to be protective bunkers from what was viewed as a secularizing culture that had little respect for traditional religious identity. As such, the leaders of the community were largely local imams adept at erecting and maintaining bunkers. Needless to say, such figures did not translate well to the task of explaining Islam to the broader society in the post-9/11 context. Nor would they have ever accepted me as a public exponent of the tradition.

But in the post-9/11 era, power within the Muslim community had shifted away from local imams to a national-level intellectual Muslim leadership characterized by figures such as Hamza Yusuf, Zaid Shakir, Ingrid Mattson, Umar Abd-Allah, and Sherman Jackson. Almost all of these figures were black and white converts to Islam who had studied in both Western universities and traditional Muslim settings. Their understanding of Islam was broad, deep, and highly intellectual. They recognized, for example, the historical and cultural contributions of the Ismaili community to Islamic civilization, even while they disagreed with dimensions of the doctrine. And while fiercely critical of some American policies and practices, these Muslim intellectuals proudly called America home and believed that Islamic wisdom could be beneficial to the nation. They found the insular interpretation of Islam prevalent in many mosques highly frustrating.

At the same time, the second and third generations of American Muslims were coming of age and seeking their place in the national landscape. Unlike their parents and grandparents, they had no memories of mid-twentieth-century village life in Egypt or Pakistan and found Muslim leaders whose interpretations seemed stuck in those places to be out of touch, especially in a society increasingly looking upon Muslim identity with suspicion.

The shock of 9/11 accelerated a meeting that was likely to happen anyway, between a cadre of towering American Muslim scholars and a new generation of young Muslims who wanted a more intellectual understanding of their tradition, especially its place in the national landscape.

Both groups recognized the importance of American Muslim civic leaders—writers, artists, nonprofit professionals, policymakers, athletes—who could represent and articulate ways in which Islam was part of the American mosaic, an approach that required at least an implicit understanding of a Muslim theology of interfaith cooperation. I was lucky to be among the earliest such leaders on the scene in post-9/11 America. Muslim scholars took me under their wing and vouched for me in Muslim circles; the emerging generation invited me to speak on their campuses and asked for my help with their fledgling American Muslim projects (books, plays, nonprofit organizations, etc.).

I never hid that I was an Ismaili from anybody; nor did I use my platform to defend or advance my community. I have always believed that my work and my manner should do the talking. To the broader society, I hoped that it would cast a favorable light on Islam and Muslims. To the Muslim community, I hoped that it would cast a favorable light on the Ismaili interpretation of Islam.

There are myriad examples of public leaders—black or Latino or Jewish politicians, for example—who at one point in time or another were considered by significant segments of their respective communities to be "not black" or "not Latino" or "not Jewish" enough. That was certainly the primary danger that my Ismaili identity presented. So why didn't such a threat come to pass for me?

In a word, circumstance. A particular moment in American and Muslim history needed my particular way of presenting what it meant to be Muslim in America, an approach that emphasized the ethic of pluralism in both traditions. The same articulation of a Muslim theology of interfaith cooperation might have found itself without an audience—both within the Muslim community and amid the broader American public—just a few years earlier.

In fact, it could easily have been dismissed as marginal chatter from a marginal Muslim.

This is not something that makes me sad. It's simply how human societies work. Consider that Barack Obama was viewed as "too white" by South Side blacks when he ran against Bobby Rush for a congressional seat in 2000. Eight years later, he was widely embraced as "one of ours" by that same community when he ran for president.

I was and am proud to be of service.

CONCLUSION

In this conclusion, I'd like to tell another story about timing and make the case that theologies of interfaith cooperation are necessary beyond the confines of the academic and priestly class.

I'd like to do this by highlighting the example of one of the cofounders of Interfaith Youth Core, April Kunze Mendez. April grew up as a devout evangelical Christian, attending church several times a week, leading Bible studies, and going on mission trips. The turning point in April's faith life came when she was president of the Christian student group at her undergraduate institution. A mosque suffered an arson attack in nearby Minneapolis, and April received an email requesting that the religious leaders in the area support the Muslim community in its time of need by attending a candlelight vigil. April instinctively sent back a yes. When she brought the idea to the next meeting of the Christian student group, she discovered that some members had different instincts. A few suggested that this was a good time to proselytize to the Muslims whose prayer space had been destroyed.

When April said she had already sent back an email saying she would help and thought that turning service into evangelism was disingenuous, one person spoke up with indignance: "Those people aren't Christian. They do not believe in Jesus Christ. They pray to a false God. If you help them, you are supporting devil worship." The problem is, those people had not just their instincts; they also had a very clear interpretation of scripture. April found herself subject to a session of bigotry against Muslims, decorated with biblical proof-texts.

Some members of the Christian student group told April that if she went to the candlelight vigil, she would be crossing a line into a territory they viewed as "unchristian," and they felt she would no longer be fit to lead their group. April was at a loss. Every fiber in her being told her that supporting a different community in its time of loss and need was a Christian thing to do, but she did not have a Christian vocabulary with which to express that conviction. She lacked a theology of interfaith cooperation.

The chapter has a sad ending, but the larger story of April's life points to something more hopeful. April went to the candlelight vigil, and she was voted out as president of the Christian student group. The situation caused a temporary crisis in faith for her. She told me that she left the church for a while, stating that she could not be part of a tradition that would rejoice at the devastation of another community's house of worship.

It was only when April started to work in interfaith organizations and share the story above that she came across Christian theologians who told her that going to the candlelight vigil in support of a Muslim community was actually a *very* Christian thing to do and offered biblical support for this view. April renewed her faith commitments largely through a new understanding of cornerstone Christian scripture.

Like most people, April had long loved the story of the Good Samaritan. She loved how an "unlikely other" was the hero of the tale, helping the man stranded by the side of the road while the priest and the Levite passed him by. She hadn't paid much mind to the particular identity of the Samaritan.

But as she studied Christian theologians engaged in interfaith work, she learned that a primary characteristic of the Samaritan tribe was that they worshipped differently from the Jews whom Jesus was leading. In fact, Jesus had actually pointed out to the Samaritan woman at the well that she was praying to a God that she did not know. The fact that Jesus, in the Good Samaritan story, would use a member of this same community as an exemplar of righteousness and tell his followers "to go and do likewise" is a powerful illustration of how someone with different beliefs can be viewed positively, even heroically. That the Good Samaritan story begins with the deeply theological question "How do I attain eternal life?" shows that it is not only a story about earthly ethics but one with cosmic, even eschatological significance.

How many of us, in the diverse communities in which we live, have been asked to pray for a sick friend from a different religion, or attended a colleague's wedding at an unfamiliar house of worship, or found ourselves at a volunteer project that benefits a family who prays to God differently than we do. Many of us take part in such events because we are nice and polite, but we feel a little uncomfortable. Am I involved in something against my faith if the couple that is getting married in front of me are saying prayers that are not fully consistent with my belief system? We wind up leaving a little part of our "faith" and try not to think about it too much.

This splitting of ourselves is problem enough, but as April's story illustrates, the truly difficult moment comes when someone from our own faith community says that our engagement across religious lines is actually treasonous to our own tradition. Then we face a crossroads. Go one way, into the faith "bunker," and try to have as little to do with people outside our own doctrinal community as possible—an increasingly difficult task in our pluralistic world—or go the other way and say that faith doesn't matter that much, that we are just going to be "nice" to everyone. That leaves many of us cold, as it did April. Faith commitments are, after all, at the heart of who we are. We believe, deep in our bones, that the reason we are nice—that we are involved in this volunteer effort, that we feel deep sympathy for our sick friend—is *because* of our faith commitment.

In *Why Did Jesus, Moses, the Buddha, and Mohammed Cross the Road?* Christian writer Brian McLaren notes that people generally believe that strong faith is connected with hostile views toward other communities. People with appreciative knowledge of other traditions and positive relationships with other communities consequently are viewed as having weak faith. This means that anytime an interfaith leader proposes an interfaith activity to a group that thinks strong faith is a virtue, group members are likely to think that such a path is meant to water down their faith. McLaren writes, "Many faithful Christians see our plea for them to become less hostile as a temptation to love God, their religion, their community, their ancestors, their history and their future less. Before they'll listen to our case for a new kind of strong-benevolent Christian identity, they must be convinced it is the path to more love and fidelity, more strength and meaning, not less."[12]

The power of theologies of interfaith cooperation is that they give us language that strengthens our connection with our faith, language deeply rooted in authentic interpretations of our holiest traditions, language that allows us to be both fully Christian or Jewish or Hindu and also fully in relationship with others.

NOTES

1. Alasdair MacIntyre, *After Virtue: A Study in Moral Theory* (Notre Dame, IN: University of Notre Dame Press, 2007), 250.
2. Sermon 53 in Imam Ali ibn Abu-Talib, *Nahjul Balagha: Peak of Eloquence*, comp. Sayyid al-Sharif ar-Radi (Elmhurst, NY: Tahrike Tarsile Qur'an, 1996), 184.
3. Mahmood Jamal, *Islamic Mystical Poetry: Sufi Verse from the Early Mystics to Rumi* (New York: Penguin Classics, 2009).
4. Seyyed Hossein Nasr, ed., *The Study Quran: A New Translation and Commentary* (New York: HarperOne, 2015), 9:29.
5. Khaled Abou El Fadl, *The Place of Tolerance in Islam* (Boston: Beacon Press, 2002).
6. Ibid.
7. Ibid.
8. Ibid.
9. Ibid.
10. Umar Abd-Allah, "Mercy: The Stamp of Creation," Nawawi Foundation, 2004, http://www.nawawi.org/wp-content/uploads/2013/01/Article1.pdf, accessed July 20, 2016.
11. Aga Khan, "The Cosmopolitan Ethic in a Fragmented World" (lecture, Samuel L. and Elizabeth Jodidi Lecture Series, Cambridge, Massachusetts, November 12, 2015), http://wcfia.harvard.edu/lectureships/jodidi, accessed July 20, 2016.
12. Brian McLaren, *Why Did Jesus, Moses, the Buddha, and Mohammed Cross the Road?* (New York: Jericho Books, 2013), 44.

Chapter Two

How Being a Jesus-Centered Peacemaker Guides, Inspires, and Sustains My Peacemaking Efforts with Muslims

Rick Love

Challenge: What is it about your faith that inspires and sustains your work for peace?

As an evangelical Christian, I affirm a distinctively Jesus-centered approach to peacemaking. I learn much from academics and practitioners of diverse perspectives, but my ultimate focus is on Jesus Christ—his person, teaching, example, death on the cross, and second coming. In this chapter I will describe the difficulties of peacemaking between Christians and Muslims and then explain how these five theological truths about Christ guide, inspire, and sustain my peacemaking efforts with Muslims.

FOUNDATIONS

First a word about my personal journey. I am on my fourth career. I began as a pastor; then I became a missionary. Next I led an international missionary organization. And finally, I sensed God's call to peacemaking. In other words, the path to becoming a Jesus-centered peacemaker had many twists and turns and lessons learned.

I began the journey as a youth pastor. There was a conflict between two leading families in the church, and their kids were in my youth group. Each family accused the other of gossiping about them. I did not even know what the word "mediation" meant back then, but I felt intuitively I needed to get both families together to talk through their issues. After tense moments and many tears, hearts softened, and reconciliation began. It felt good.

But things didn't go so well when I become pastor of missionary outreach. Since I was planning to move to Indonesia to be a missionary, I had been mentoring a gifted man to take over my role at the church. We had a strong difference of opinion about how we should fulfill Jesus's Great Commission to make disciples of all nations (Matthew 28:18–20)—such a strong difference of opinion, in fact, that it led to a church split. Instead of a peacemaker I was a peace breaker!

In my zeal to fulfill the Great Commission, I had failed to obey Jesus's Great Commandments: "'You shall love the Lord your God with all your heart, and with all your soul, and with all your mind.' This is the greatest and first commandment. And a second is like it: 'You shall love your neighbor as yourself.' On these two commandments hang all the law and the prophets" (Matthew 22:37–40). [1]

God was trying to teach me that these Great Commandments govern the Great Commission. In other words, central to my task of making a disciple is being a disciple! If I had been as committed to the Great Commandments then as I was to the Great Commission, things might have turned out differently.

I continued to face conflict when I arrived in Indonesia. Two conflicts in particular stand out. I welcomed a couple to our team who were close friends with one of our veteran couples (they had attended the same church in the United States). I thought this would enhance team dynamics. But only a short time later I ended up doing shuttle diplomacy between them, driving back and forth between their houses, relaying their messages to one another. They had intense differences of opinion over their approaches to ministry and lifestyle issues that hadn't been evident during their friendship in the United States. I learned that culture shock not only throws off people's equilibrium but also heightens conflict. [2] And again I was in the middle of it. So I continued learning how to mediate conflict.

On another occasion my Western team and some Indonesian church members gathered at my house for a mini-retreat. I was called into one room to mediate conflict between members on my Western team. They had been arguing about the best way to relate to Indonesians and adapt to the culture. When I walked out of that meeting, I was immediately ushered into another room, where the Indonesian church members were in conflict. They had offended each other and were nursing grudges. What a day! Two conflicts, two cultures, and a budding mediator thrown into the fray.

Personal experiences of conflict like this weren't the only things shaping me into a Jesus-centered peacemaker. Over a decade later, the evil of terrorism crashed into my life. The events surrounding 9/11 pushed me further into peacemaking. I realized that this attack and subsequent attacks would be perceived as a "clash of civilizations,"[3] that many people would view Muslims—all Muslims—as terrorists. My focus until 9/11 had been on interpersonal peacemaking, but now God was leading me to intergroup peacemaking.

So I went on a sabbatical at the Yale University Center for Faith and Culture's Reconciliation Program as a postdoctoral fellow. I looked forward to a time of writing and reflection as I transitioned into the role of peacemaker. But my time at Yale was anything but reflective.

On October 13, 2007, 138 influential Muslim clerics, representing every school and sect of Islam from around the world, wrote an open letter to Christians everywhere, calling for dialogue based on the common ground of "love of God and neighbor." This open letter was called "A Common Word."[4] One of the most famous responses to this call for dialogue was issued by the Yale Center for Faith and Culture's Reconciliation Program, which in turn resulted in a global conference at Yale University on July 24–31, 2008.[5]

Seventy-five high-level Muslim leaders joined seventy-five high-level Christian leaders for a week of dialogue about the Great Commandments (love of God and neighbor). This unprecedented global conference was truly a turning point in my life. I have never met so many Muslim scholars, sheikhs, grand muftis, and princes! More importantly, learning about Islam directly from these Muslim leaders and getting to know them personally over meals impacted me profoundly. Because of this, I've devoted myself to becoming a full-time peacemaker—specifically between Christians and Muslims.

CHALLENGES

A conversation with one of my partners in peacemaking illustrates a core challenge of this work. Professor Salaam[6] had asked me to lecture on war and peace at his university, so he treated me to lunch before class. While enjoying the meal at Ali Baba's Grill he asked, "Why do you talk about peace and peacemaking so much? Why not talk about seeking 'mutual understanding'?" (Professor Salaam had attended a few Peace Catalyst International events.) I said, "Because Jesus taught about peacemaking in the Bible, and we seek to be a Jesus-centered peacemaking organization."

He seemed a bit frustrated and then asked, "What does it mean to be a Jesus-centered peacemaking organization?" I answered, "To be Jesus centered means we recognize the centrality and priority of peace for Jesus. Jesus's person, teaching, example, death on the cross, and second coming all focus on peace."

Then he spoke candidly. "Rick, do you know that many Muslims are suspicious of you?" I responded, "That's okay, Salaam. So are many Christians!"

Many Christians think that, as an evangelical peacemaker, I am compromising my faith, and many Muslims are afraid we are trying to evangelize them. So Christian-Muslim peacemaking faces significant barriers and misunderstanding on both sides.

First of all, from the Christian side of things, my organization, Peace Catalyst International, works with evangelicals. According to Ed Stetzer, 59 percent of evangelical pastors say Islam is dangerous and promotes violence. They agree with Franklin Graham's characterization of Islam as "a very evil and a very wicked religion."[7]

Bradley R. E. Wright notes in *Christians Are Hate-Filled Hypocrites . . . and Other Lies You've Been Told* that Christians act very ethically compared to the rest of society. However, Wright also observes that Christians in general and evangelicals in particular do not like people of different races, religions, and sexual orientations.[8] To add my own observations to Wright's work, evangelicals seem to struggle most with three communities: Muslims, undocumented immigrants (usually Latinos or Hispanics), and the LGBTQ community.

Second, many conservative evangelicals assume peace is for liberals, whether theological or political. Other evangelicals, who appreciate the Bible's emphasis on peace, tend to have a narrow view of God's peace purposes, focusing primarily on interpersonal peacemaking among believers. Peace for them is unrelated to the gospel, the kingdom of God, or the pressing social issues of the day. In other words, peacemaking is generally not on the agenda of most evangelicals.

Here's what my friend Steve Norman learned when he did a survey about peacemaking for his doctoral studies: "I recently conducted a research project that collected data from 15 pastors in personal interviews and 297 pastors through an online survey. Their feedback on this issue was almost unanimous: 'Yes, I affirm the theory of peacemaking as a biblical value. No, it's not something our church is currently doing. Honestly, we'd have no idea where to start if we wanted to.'"[9]

The term "evangelical" comes from the Greek word *euaggelion* in the New Testament, which means "good news."[10] But mobilizing evangelicals to be good news people who work for peace with Muslims has its challenges. I often tell people, "Peacemakers are like bridges between the two faith communities. And they get walked on by both sides!" Frankly, it gets discouraging. That's why having a robust theology of peacemaking centered on Jesus is so important for us. It pushes us beyond our comfort zone and calls us to embrace everyone. It keeps us walking into the winds of opposition because it is the right thing to do.

The fact that Jesus was a peace disturber (explained below) as well as a peacemaker sustains me in my work of mobilizing evangelicals. I realize I need to disturb the status quo when it comes to Christian-Muslim peacemaking. I do this in two ways. First, I spend much of my time countering the negative and inaccurate views of Muslims in the media. My book *Grace and Truth: Toward Christlike Relationships with Muslims* is an example of this kind of work.[11]

Second, I often end my talks to evangelicals with words like this: "Yes, there is a minuscule number of violent extremists who want to do us harm. But the Muslim world is diverse, and the vast majority of Muslims are just like you and me. *They want to be faithful to God, love their families, and be productive members of society.*"

But even if I were wrong about Muslims and Islam (and I am not!), Jesus's teaching about love of neighbor and enemy is straightforward, indisputable, and pervasive. We need to reach out in love to our Muslim neighbors regardless of how we view them!

So how do I handle questions and suspicions from Muslims? One of the things I do when I meet a new imam is say, "I know that you want me to embrace Islam, and I want you to follow Jesus. So let's just admit it and then figure out the practical ways we can work for peace and the common good." That usually works.

Another way I address Muslim suspicions is to be consistent and persistent. I usually take them out for a meal and discuss ways we might get our congregations together. Then we actually put on an event together. So effective peacemaking involves eating lots of hummus and drinking lots of tea!

RESPONSES

As the stories above demonstrate, mediating conflict demands wisdom, courage, and perseverance. Those of us who work in the field of Christian-Muslim peacemaking need guidance and inspiration to sustain our peacemaking efforts. For my organization, Peace Catalyst International, that guidance and inspiration comes from Jesus.

It was during my sabbatical at Yale that I began digging deeper into what the Bible teaches about peacemaking. I pride myself on knowing the Bible. But as I studied the topic of peace from Genesis to Revelation, the beginning of the Bible to the end, I realized that the idea of peace and peacemaking is much bigger than I thought. And over time it was clear that peacemaking did not just consist of a few commands about conflict resolution. It centered on Jesus.

The following five truths lay the biblical foundations for peacemaking in the way of Jesus. These are the truths that fortify our souls, guide our steps, and sustain our efforts.

The Person of Christ

In two of the best-known prophecies of the future Messiah in the Bible, Jesus is called the Prince of Peace (Isaiah 9:6–7) and described as the one who is our peace (Micah 5:2–5). Paul's letter to the Ephesians also makes this affirmation: "But now in Christ Jesus you who once were far off have been brought near by the blood of Christ. For he is our peace" (Ephesians 2:13–14).[12]

Thus, peace "is not merely a concept nor even a new state of affairs, it is bound up with a person."[13] The phrase "he is our peace" is emphatic in the original Greek language and should be translated "he himself is our peace." Jesus embodies peace, according to Paul. He is the source of peace and the one who brings peace.[14]

The Teaching of Christ[15]

Jesus's teaching about peacemaking begins with the famous beatitude "Blessed are the peacemakers, for they will be called children of God" (Matthew 5:9).[16] In the original language, the term "peacemaker" combines two Greek words: "peace" (*eirene*) and "to make, do, or produce" (*poieo*), implying that peacemakers not only resolve their personal conflicts but also take the initiative in helping others resolve conflict. Thus, the very term "peacemaker" implies some form of mediation.[17]

This blessed work of peacemaking is an urgent priority, according to Jesus: "Therefore, if you are offering your gift at the altar and there remember that your brother or sister has something against you, leave your gift there in front of the altar. *First* go and be reconciled to them; *then* come and offer your gift" (Matthew 5:23–24).[18] Jesus commands us to stop worship and seek reconciliation. In other words, reconciling with our brother or sister even trumps worship! "First go and be reconciled" teaches that we must take responsibility for broken relationships. Even if I don't have anything against my brother or sister, if he or she has something against me, I must take the initiative. This passage also indicates that the Great Commandments—love of God and love of neighbor—are inseparable. One cannot truly love God without loving one's neighbor—which is demonstrated by our commitment to pursue reconciliation.[19]

Jesus's brand of peacemaking also begins with humility. "Why do you see the speck in your neighbor's eye, but do not notice the log in your own eye? Or how can you say to your neighbor, 'Let me take the speck out of your eye,' while the log is in your own eye? You hypocrite, *first* take the log out of your own eye, and *then* you will see clearly to take the speck out of your neighbor's eye" (Matthew 7:3–5). With a sense of humor, Jesus the carpenter exhorts us *first* to get the metaphorical log out of our own eye; *then* we can take the speck out of our neighbor's eye. Again, Jesus gives us clear steps in the peacemaking process: "first . . . then."

Sadly, it is human nature to be part of speck-finders.org. We specialize in speck finding in others and tend to be blind to our own issues. But instead of being speck finders, Jesus calls us to be log removers! He calls those in conflict to begin with humble introspection.

This is especially important in Christian-Muslim relations. Christians tend to compare the best interpretation and practice of their faith with the worst interpretation and practice of Islamic faith. This natural tendency fosters a sense of superiority, blinds Christians to the darkness in their own community, and hinders them from seeing any light or beauty in Islam. Moreover, it is the opposite of what Jesus taught.[20]

During a Vineyard Great Lakes Regional Conference in Columbus, Ohio,[21] Yale theologian and peacemaker Miroslav Volf shared with the pastors in attendance a story about the Common Word Dialogue between Christians and Muslims at Yale:[22] "Prior to the dialogue, we inserted a brief apology in the Yale response to the Common Word, asking for forgiveness. People got so upset! They said you should not ask for forgiveness until Muslims ask for forgiveness first!" Volf paused and with a big smile on his face asked, "Since when is my moral behavior predicated on the moral behavior of another?"

Jesus's teaching on love of neighbor and love of enemy also pushes us toward peace. If we truly love others, we will want to be at peace with them. Making peace or working toward reconciliation is an act of love.

Immediately after teaching about the Great Commandments (love of God and neighbor), Jesus told the famous parable of the Good Samaritan in response to a religious expert's question, "Who is my neighbor?" This religious leader wanted to limit the definition of neighbor so that the demand of neighbor love remained within his comfort zone (Luke 10:29–37). Like most people of his day, he believed that "neighbor" referred to someone of his race or faith. It meant someone "like me" or a person "I like."

But Jesus's revolutionary parable shattered the religious leader's relational categories. Jesus showed that love for one's neighbor reaches beyond race or religion, color or creed. The hero of the story was a Samaritan! At the time, Jews despised Samaritans as heretics who were syncretistic in faith, ethnically inferior, and excluded from the true worship of God (John 4:9). In other words, "good Samaritan" would have been an oxymoron for a Jew. Yet this Samaritan showed compassion toward his enemy the Jew, demonstrating that love of neighbor includes the people whom we find it hardest to love. An accurate understanding of love of neighbor means we love even our enemy.

But in case this isn't clear, Jesus makes it explicit: "You have heard that it was said, 'You shall love your neighbor and hate your enemy.' But I say to you, Love your enemies and pray for those who persecute you, so that you may be children of your Father in heaven" (Matthew 5:43–45).[23]

The Example of Christ

Jesus's hospitality reverberates with peacemaking implications.[24] Jesus freely and habitually ate with people regarded as "sinners" to the extent that he had a reputation as "a glutton and a drunkard, a friend of tax collectors and sinners" (Luke 7:34).[25] The stories of Jesus with the tax collectors Levi (Luke 5:27–32) and Zacchaeus (Luke 19:1–10), the "sinful" women at Simon the Pharisee's house (Luke 7:36–50), the adulterous woman (John 8:1–11), and the Samaritan woman at Jacob's well (John 4:1–43) are perhaps the best illustrations of Jesus's practice.

What I find amazing is that Jesus also ate with his greatest critics—the Pharisees. He accepted their hospitality while at the same time boldly confronting them about their hypocritical traditions of ritualistic washing (Luke 11:37–42) and Sabbath observance (Luke 14:1–6).

Jesus's hospitality reflected inclusive love. Unlike the Pharisees and many evangelicals, Jesus engaged the "other" without fear of compromise or contamination. Jesus taught and modeled both exclusive truth claims and inclusive love aims.[26] Jesus made exclusive truth claims: "I am the way, and the truth, and the life. No one comes to the Father except through me" (John 14:6).[27] At the same time, he made inclusive love aims. He commanded his followers to "love their neighbors as themselves" and even "love their enemies" (Matthew 22:39; Matthew 5:44).

Jesus was also a nonviolent activist.[28]

> Jesus answered, "My kingdom is not of this world. If my kingdom were of this world, then My servants would be fighting so that I would not be handed over to the Jews; but as it is, My kingdom is not of this realm." (John 18:36)[29]
> Jesus said to him, "Put your sword back into its place; for all those who take up the sword shall perish by the sword." (Matthew 26:52)[30]

However, being nonviolent did not mean that Jesus was passive. He was also a peace disturber! Perhaps the most striking example is when he cleansed the temple.

> Then they came to Jerusalem. And he entered the temple and began to drive out those who were selling and those who were buying in the temple, and he overturned the tables of the money changers and the seats of those who sold

doves; and he would not allow anyone to carry anything through the temple. He was teaching and saying, "Is it not written, 'My house shall be called a house of prayer for all the nations'? But you have made it a den of robbers." And when the chief priests and the scribes heard it, they kept looking for a way to kill him; for they were afraid of him, because the whole crowd was spellbound by his teaching. (Mark 11:15–18)[31]

This is the one place in the gospels where Jesus appears to be violent. It is true that Jesus was forceful and angry, but he did not physically attack people. Despite a reference to his making a whip of cords, there is no mention of him whipping people. As Ben Witherington notes, "Jesus did not burn anything, nor did he lead any troops or bandits into the temple; he simply interrupted the economic activities there temporarily."[32]

Religious leaders allowed merchants to sell animals in the outer courts of the temple. Instead of being the "house of prayer for all the nations" (Mark 11:17)[33] that God had intended, the temple had become an ingrown religious club. So Jesus confronted this religious corruption.[34] The cleansing of the temple was a passionate prophetic act against the discrimination of Jewish religious leaders toward Gentiles. It was an act of radical reform, intended to shake up the status quo.

Perhaps the best modern example of a peace disturber is Martin Luther King Jr. He confronted white hypocrisy, racism, and injustice. But his goal was not to defeat white people in America; rather he sought to reconcile with white America.

The Cross of Christ

The death of Christ on the cross is a central tenet of the Christian faith and the ultimate peacemaking event in history. Through his death, Jesus ushers in peace to a broken, alienated world (Colossians 1:19–20; Ephesians 2:13–17). In fact, the gospel (the story of the life, teaching, death, and resurrection of Jesus) is referred to as the gospel of peace five times in the New Testament (Acts 10:36; Romans 5:1; Ephesians 2:13–17; Ephesians 6:15; Colossians 1:20).

At the cross Jesus cried out, "Father, forgive them for they do not know what they are doing" (Luke 23:34).[35] Jesus loved and forgave those who crucified him. In other words, Jesus's death on the cross not only procures peace but also demonstrates love for enemies—a key to making peace and an important part of the gospel (Romans 5:10; Colossians 1:21–22).

My brother-in-law once asked me, "Rick, your peacemaking work with Muslims seems to ignore the stumbling block of the cross,[36] and this is the heart of our faith. How do you respond to that?" I said, "In our peacemaking efforts we demonstrate the cross. We seek peace and model love. And if we model it well they will be much more receptive to hearing the message of the cross." He liked my answer!

The Second Coming of Christ

According to the Hebrew scriptures (called the Old Testament by Christians), the end times will be both a day of judgment and the ushering in of a universal reign of peace (Micah 4:1–4; Isaiah 2:2–4, 11:1–9; Ezekiel 37:24–27).

The New Testament teaches that Jesus is the promised Messiah who ushers in this age of peace in two stages—at his first coming and ultimately at his second coming (Matthew 1:1, 16:16; Ephesians 1:10; Revelation 21–22).

Jesus-centered peacemakers follow the person of Christ. They obey the teaching of Christ. They imitate the example of Christ. They believe and share the message of the cross of Christ, and they long for the return of Christ.

Jesus-Centered Peacemaking in Action

I attended the Marrakesh Declaration in Morocco on January 25–27, 2016. There, three hundred Muslim scholars, government officials, and non-Muslim observers like myself gathered from over one hundred countries to address the rights of religious minorities in Muslim-majority countries. [37]

When I arrived at the event, Halima (who works for the Moroccan embassy) waved me over and invited me to sit down next to her. We had met previously at a Christian-Muslim dialogue at Eastern Mennonite University in Virginia. She shared a few things about the conference, and then we both turned our attention to the speakers.

Later, during a break, I told her I appreciated how much she went out of her way to make me feel at home at the conference. With a big smile on her face, she said, "I will never forget your message at the dialogue at Eastern Mennonite University. You began your talk by asking for forgiveness for the way Christians have failed to love Muslims. I could never forget your message."

I began that dialogue as I do at similar events. I obeyed Jesus's command to first get the log out of my own eye (Matthew 7:3–5). I started with my heart, and I touched her heart. Jesus-motivated humility breaks down lots of barriers.

Peacemaking between Christians and Muslims is what I call intergroup or social peacemaking. Interpersonal peacemaking focuses on specific conflicts between individuals, whereas intergroup peacemaking focuses on barriers between groups. In other words, in Christian-Muslim peacemaking we seek to break down prejudices and stereotypes between the two faiths.

A Christian woman attended one of Peace Catalyst's "Love Your Neighbor" dinners, where Christians and Muslims gathered to discuss love of neighbor and enjoy a meal together. That simple experience of meeting Muslims in a safe space helped her see that they are people just like her. She said, "I no longer fear Muslims. In the past when I saw a woman wearing a head covering [hijab] at a store I was fearful and avoided her. Now I go up to her and greet her warmly!"

During one of my visits to Indonesia, I had lunch with an Islamic teacher named Ahmed. As we ate our rice meals together, Ahmed confessed that he was prejudiced against Christians.

When I asked him why he was prejudiced, he said that his teachers taught him that the focus of true devotion to God in Islam is prayer, while true devotion in Christianity is evangelism. Thus, he said, he believed that Christians only wanted to attack his faith and convert him. I told him this is true of some Christians, but the vast majority are not like that.

Then Ahmed asked me what prejudices Christians have toward Muslims in America. "Most Christians fear that Muslims are terrorists, Islam is violent, and thus Muslims want to kill them," I explained. Ahmed said, "Wow! Both of our faiths fear each other because we think the other wants to attack us!"

After lunch we visited Adi Sutanto, director of a Christian denomination called Jemaat Kristen Indonesia (JKI). Without knowing anything about what Ahmed and I had talked about during lunch, Adi shared a fascinating vision of JKI: "We have bought property and want to make a prayer garden. In fact, during a time of prayer recently we had a vision that this prayer garden will be used for Christians, Muslims, and Buddhists."

I turned to Ahmed and said, "See, Christians *are* committed to prayer, not just evangelism!" We both laughed, as he shook his head in agreement. Prejudices were starting to melt away.

This is how intergroup peacemaking works!

Peace Catalyst International sponsors a number of programs that bring Christians and Muslims together. Almost all of them focus on a meal.

Peace feasts
"Love Your Neighbor" dinners
"Quick to Listen" dinners
Jesus dialogues
Communities of reconciliation
Visual peacemaking
Service events[38]

Here is the "behind-the-scenes" work necessary to make these events happen. First, the peace catalyst takes the initiative to visit mosques and meet Muslims. Before we get groups from the church and the mosque together, we build bridges with the imams and other Muslim leaders.

The peace catalyst also spends time with the pastors or Christian leaders to discuss the kind of program that meets their need. The pastor and the imam sometimes meet before the formal program, but often they trust the peace catalyst enough to wait for the program before they actually meet.

Thus, the peace catalyst functions as a "go-between" or a mediator between the two groups. She or he prepares the leaders, prepares the program, and creates a safe space for the two groups to meet.

Here's how peace catalyst Tim McDonell described one of his events.

> We recently had the pleasure of putting on a "Quick to Listen" luncheon with friends from three local churches in Ventura County and friends from the Islamic Center in Oxnard. We met at an Indian restaurant in Ventura that is owned by a member of the center, a setting that provided an opportunity for us to meet and to ask questions about each other's faith.
>
> By taking the time to meet our neighbors, new friendships can be formed. There may be many things we don't agree on, but there is one thing that we do agree upon: God is great and he is our creator. He desires that his children love and care for one another. Our aim is to learn to love our neighbors as God loves us and to develop lasting friendships. [39]

CONCLUSION

Peacemaking between Christians and Muslims is not rocket science. But it is demanding. We take initiative and build relationships. We overcome prejudice on both sides. We often get discouraged, and the work is slow.

But we find strength as we remind ourselves continually of what it means to be Jesus-centered peacemakers:

1. Jesus is the embodiment of peace and peacemaking.
2. If we follow Jesus's teaching, we will see reconciliation as an urgent priority. We will practice humility and become proactive peacemakers. We will go beyond our comfort zones to love our neighbors and even our enemies.
3. If we follow Jesus's example, we will pursue peace nonviolently, we will demonstrate inclusive hospitality, and when necessary we will disturb the status quo to work toward true peace.
4. Jesus's death on the cross procures peace and demonstrates the priority of love of the enemy.
5. We joyfully anticipate universal, comprehensive peace at Christ's return.

The peacemaking implications of these five truths are staggering. They guide us, inspire us, and sustain us as we wage peace in the way of Jesus!

NOTES

1. Holy Bible, New Revised Standard Version (National Council of Churches of Christ, 1989), BibleGateway.com, accessed May 29, 2017.

2. When people enter a new culture, they become disoriented because of linguistic barriers and cultural differences. This usually results in significant stress.

3. See Samuel P. Huntington, *The Clash of Civilizations and the Remaking of World Order* (New York: Simon & Schuster, 2011).

4. A Common Word (http://www.acommonword.com, accessed August 24, 2016).

5. "'A Common Word' Christian Response," Yale Center for Faith and Culture, http://faith.yale.edu/common-word/common-word-christian-response, accessed August 24, 2016.

6. This is a pseudonym, out of respect for the individual's privacy.

7. Lisa Cannon Green, "Pastors Grow More Polarized on Islam," Lifeway Research, October 22, 2015, http://lifewayresearch.com/2015/10/22/pastors-grow-more-polarized-on-islam, accessed August 24, 2016.

8. Bradley R. E. Wright, *Christians Are Hate-Filled Hypocrites . . . and Other Lies You've Been Told* (Minneapolis, MN: Bethany House, 2010), 155–79.

9. Rick Love, "Do You Have a Bible Sized View of Peace? The Peace Gap in Evangelical Churches," Rick Love, http://ricklove.net/?p=2848, accessed August 24, 2017.

10. This good news refers to the coming of the kingdom of God through Jesus's life, healing, teaching, death, and resurrection.

11. See Rick Love, *Grace and Truth: Toward Christlike Relationships with Muslims* (Arvada, CO: Peace Catalyst International Publications, 2013).

12. New Revised Standard Version.

13. A. T. Lincoln, *Ephesians* (Dallas, TX: Word, 1990), 42:140.

14. "It does not say that he gives peace but rather that he is our peace, probably echoing Micah. 5:5 (cf. Isaiah. 9:6)." B. Witherington III, *The Letters to Philemon, the Colossians, and the Ephesians: A Socio-rhetorical Commentary on the Captivity Epistles* (Grand Rapids, MI: Wm. B. Eerdmans, 2007), 259.

15. It is beyond the scope of this chapter to give a detailed summary of all that Jesus taught about peacemaking. So I will focus on Jesus's teaching that is most relevant to peacemaking with Muslims.

16. The context of Jesus's ministry provides an important insight into the meaning of peacemaking. Jesus lived under Roman rule, ministering in an occupied territory. In the original context of the beatitudes, this emphasis on peacemaking was most likely directed against the Zealots, Jewish revolutionaries who hoped to throw off the yoke of Roman oppression and to establish the kingdom of God through violence. In contrast to the Zealots, Jesus speaks of a peaceable kingdom and a nonviolent extension of that kingdom.

17. Mediation refers to third-party peacemaking. The ideal of scripture is that the two parties in conflict work it out between themselves—in cooperative resolution. But often people in conflict need help. So they turn to a trusted third party to aid them in resolving their dispute. See Matthew 18:16; 1 Corinthians 6:1–8; Philippians 4:2–3; and Philemon.

18. Holy Bible, New International Version (Colorado Springs, CO: Biblica, 2011), BibleGateway.com, accessed May 29, 2017.

19. It is noteworthy that the first mention of the command to love one's neighbor in the Bible is linked to peacemaking. "You shall not take vengeance or bear a grudge against any of your people, but you shall love your neighbor as yourself: I am the LORD" (Leviticus 19:18). Love is contrasted with vengeance and bearing a grudge. In other words, when we overcome vengeance and grudges (i.e., peacemaking), we are truly loving our neighbor.

20. Point 3 of "Seven Resolutions against Prejudice, Hatred and Discrimination" says it well: "We seek to be accurate when we speak about one another's faith. Overstatement, exag-

geration and words taken out of context should not be the case among people of faith. The Torah teaches us 'not to bear false witness against our neighbor' (Ex 20:16). The Gospel teaches us to 'do unto others as you would have them do unto you' (Matt 7:12). The Qur'an teaches us to 'stand out firmly for justice as witnesses to God, even though it be against ourselves or our parents' (Qur'an 4:135). Thus we strive to speak truthfully about one another's faith, to respect each faith community's own interpretation of themselves, and not to compare the best interpretation and practice of our faith with the worst interpretation and practice of others. We encourage every person be discerning re: how media and literature portray the 'other.'" See Peace Catalyst International, http://peace-catalyst.net/initiatives/7-resolutions, accessed August 24, 2016.

21. The conference was held in Columbus, Ohio, at the Columbus Vineyard, May 15–17, 2012.

22. "'A Common Word' Christian Response," Yale Center for Faith and Culture, http://faith.yale.edu/common-word/common-word-christian-response, accessed August 24, 2016.

23. New Revised Standard Version.

24. "Hospitality is at the heart of the gospel and practice of the early church; its themes and language pervade the NT." C. D. Pohl, "Hospitality," in *New Dictionary of Biblical Theology*, ed. T. D. Alexander and B. S. Rosner (Downers Grove, IL: InterVarsity Press, 2000), 561 (electronic ed.).

25. New Revised Standard Version.

26. In a personal email to me, my friend Andres Duncan exclaimed, "Jesus shatters our theological and political categories. Exclusive truth challenges the liberal, while inclusive love challenges the conservative. Jesus is so exclusive in His truth claims as to shame the most exclusive conservative. And he is so inclusive in His love aims as to shame the most inclusive liberal."

27. New Revised Standard Version.

28. When I speak about the blessing of being a peacemaker, people often counter with this question. "Yes, but Jesus also said he did not come to bring peace but a sword (Matthew 10:34). So how do you reconcile these two verses?" Matthew 10 described Jesus's commission of his disciples to extend the kingdom. Before any mention of a sword, he told them to go in peace: "If the house is worthy, give it your blessing of peace. But if it is not worthy, take back your blessing of peace" (Matthew 10:13, New American Standard Bible). When Jesus sent out the seventy disciples, he described this process in a slightly different way: "Whatever house you enter, first say, 'Peace *be* to this house.' If a man of peace is there, your peace will rest on him; but if not, it will return to you" (Luke 10:5–6). This passage implies that in some sense, those on mission are bearers of peace (see John 14:27), whose fruitfulness depends on the discernment of peace when sharing their faith. Jesus's followers are peacemaker-witnesses who speak the blessing of peace on families where they stay. Nevertheless, response to the message of the kingdom will be mixed: some will accept the message; others will reject it. Because of this, families will be divided, and conflict will ensue. But please note: Jesus used the metaphor of the sword to describe the divisive fallout that sometimes accompanies the extension of the kingdom. This is confirmed by the parallel passage in Luke: "Do you think I came to bring peace on earth? No, I tell you, but division" (Luke 12:51). Jesus did not use the metaphor of the sword to depict any form of violence or belligerence on the part of his followers. Among evangelicals, Matthew 10:34–38 ("I came to bring a sword") rather than Matthew 5:9 ("Blessed are the peacemakers") seems to provide the dominant perspective regarding peace and witness in the New Testament. In other words, there is the assumption that conflict will prevail. With this mind-set, could it be that conflict sometimes ensues because of the nonirenic manner in which we communicate the message? Could this be something of a self-fulfilling prophecy? How do we reconcile Matthew 10:34–38 with Matthew 5:9? At the very least we need to affirm both truths, since the Bible does. Walter Kaiser gives wise guidance: "When Jesus said that he had come to bring 'not peace but a sword,' he meant that this would be the *effect* of his coming, not that it was the *purpose* of his coming." W. C. Kaiser, Peter H. Davids, and F. F. Bruce, *Hard Sayings of the Bible* (Downers Grove, IL: InterVarsity Press, 1996), 378. As children of God, our purpose is to represent the Prince of Peace, regardless of the effect.

29. Holy Bible, New American Standard Bible (Lockman Foundation, 1995), BibleGateway.com, accessed May 29, 2017.

30. New American Standard Bible.

31. The parallel passage in John says he made a whip of cords and "drove all of them out of the temple, both the sheep and the cattle. He also poured out the coins of the money changers and overturned their tables" (John 2:15, New Revised Standard Version).

32. B. Witherington III, *The Gospel of Mark: A Socio-rhetorical Commentary* (Grand Rapids, MI: Wm. B. Eerdmans, 2001), 315.

33. New Revised Standard Version.

34. "The point of Jesus' complaint, however, seems to be that it all took place in the Court of the Gentiles. Hence (17) quoting Isaiah 56:7, the bone of contention is that the place intended for Gentiles ('*all nations*') to pray was being misused by the Jews for trade (and profit). '*Den of robbers*' (17) is very strong language, and may have its origin in Jeremiah 7:11. The anger of Jesus is clear." D. English, *The Message of Mark: The Mystery of Faith* (Downers Grove, IL: InterVarsity Press, 1992), 190.

35. New Revised Standard Version.

36. In 1 Corinthians 1:23, Paul the apostle says, "We proclaim Christ crucified, a stumbling block to Jews and foolishness to Gentiles" (New Revised Standard Version). Paul called Jesus's death on the cross a stumbling block to Jews because it was inconceivable to a Jew that the promised messiah would die on the cross. Paul did not want Christians to shrink back from sharing the message of the cross, even if it seemed inconceivable to others.

37. For more on the Marrakesh Declaration, see "The Marrakesh Declaration: A Game Changer for Christian-Muslim Relations?," Peace Catalyst International, February 1, 2016, https://www.peacecatalyst.org/blog/2016/2/1/the-marrakesh-declaration-a-game-changer-for-christian-muslim-relations, accessed August 24, 2016; "Religious Freedom and the Marrakesh Declaration: A Behind-the-Scenes Account," Peace Catalyst International, February 6, 2016, https://www.peacecatalyst.org/blog/2016/2/6/religious-freedom-the-marrakesh-declaration-a-behind-the-scenes-account, accessed August 24, 2016.

38. "Programs," Peace Catalyst International, http://www.peace-catalyst.net/programs, accessed August 24, 2016.

39. "A Special Luncheon," Peace Catalyst International, http://peace-catalyst.net/blog/post/a-special-luncheon, accessed August 24, 2016.

Chapter Three

Journey of Redemption

The Role of an Apology in Reconciliation

Sushobha Barve

Challenge: How do you acknowledge and work to transform any wrongs committed by people of your own faith tradition?

Our world today is witnessing violence linked to religion and religious identities. As a multireligious country, India too has been grappling with religious polarization that is provoking extreme verbal, written, and physical violence, mainly targeted at minorities. Each form of violence against minorities strikes at the roots of social coexistence and at the foundations of the Indian constitution that gives each individual the right of freedom to practice his or her religious beliefs. When the atmosphere is thus polarized, the moderate majority feels intimidated and silenced by the more aggressive elements. In present-day India, peace practitioners face the challenge of acknowledging and working to transform wrongs committed by people of their own community. What role can individuals play at such times so that the social compact is not destroyed? Any effort at changing the public narrative of exclusion to one that recognizes the benefits of social coexistence seems an uphill task. This means going against the tide of the times and acting according to the promptings of one's heart, or what some would call conscience or the inner voice.

This chapter gives an account of my journey of the past thirty years and how it has led me from a very personal experience of dealing with prejudice against a Muslim friend to growing out of cowardice to face violence, stepping out of my comfort zone to reach out to people whom I did not know, and being part of larger public peace processes with others for larger impact and change. This journey has been far from smooth and a constant process of

59

learning and unlearning, evaluating and reevaluating in the context of changing India and the world. On this journey my own commitment to dialogue and reconciliation has only grown and deepened by the year. But before I launch into my personal experiences, I need to give some historical and political context.

Indian Context

The current political environment within India and the surrounding region is very complex. India is the largest country in South Asia and one of the most diverse. It is a land of unparalleled diversity in language, culture, caste, and creed held together simply by an idea, the idea of India. India has a population of over 1 billion people. Hindus form approximately 80 percent of the population. Muslims form about 14 percent, Christians 2 percent, Sikhs 2 percent, and other faith groups 2 percent. Jammu-Kashmir is the only Muslim-majority state in India, and a few states in the northeast of India are majority Christian.

Indian civilization goes back almost five thousand years, and Hinduism has very strong roots across the length and breadth of India, although the Hindu faith is practiced differently in different parts of the country. For nearly one thousand years, Muslim invaders from Northwest and Central Asia came to India. Large areas of the Indian subcontinent (present-day India, Pakistan, and Bangladesh) were ruled by Muslims for several centuries. But not all Muslim foreigners came to conquer. Many came as traders through sea routes, settling in coastal towns, while others came as Sufi preachers. India has shown remarkable capacity to absorb different faith traditions, intermingle and allow synthesis of varied cultural traditions, embrace languages coming from outside, and evolve a new syncretic tradition, known also as Sufi or Bhakti tradition. This tradition has allowed various faith traditions to live in harmony for centuries despite occasional tensions.

Besides the multireligious nature of Indian society, another historic feature has been the caste system, which originally divided Hindu society according to occupational groups and over a period became hereditary, dividing the society into tight compartments within a hierarchy. This system has survived till today. The caste system is unjust, as those on the lower rung of the ladder have remained outside social and economic privileges for centuries without any hope of ever being lifted out of their wretched condition. For centuries they were treated as untouchables. Many compare the caste system to apartheid. The Indian constitution has given equal rights to all citizens of India irrespective of caste or religion. But translating this into social and civic attitudes in daily lives remains a challenge. The Indian constitution has also provided reservations (or affirmative action) to the underprivileged castes, which has caused social friction between caste groups as more have become aware of and demanded their constitutional rights.

India's diverse communities have lived in harmony and peace for centuries with shared culture and deep bonds of brotherhood. The Indian subcontinent saw the first major rupture between Hindu, Muslim, and Sikh communities in the 1940s, when some Muslim leaders demanded that the British should grant a separate homeland for Indian Muslims consisting of Muslim-majority provinces of British India. This also led the Sikh community in the Punjab to demand a separate homeland for the Sikhs. There were many people in those provinces against division on the basis of religion. While political leaders sparred over their respective political views without thinking of the consequences of their positions, ordinary people from all communities were unaware of what lay ahead for them. Polarization increased, and minorities began to come under violent attacks, being driven out of small towns even before the partition of India and Pakistan was officially announced. That was a bloody period of history when almost every religious community committed unspeakable atrocities against one another, with 1 million people killed and 20 million displaced from their ancestral lands.

Unfortunately, that has left a legacy of hatred and distrust between the peoples of India and Pakistan that has deepened due to three major wars and several unresolved disputes. Since independence the sentiments of bitterness have extended across the India-Pakistan border and have yet to be healed and transformed into a normalization of relations. Despite attempts to normalize relations, mistrust has so far continued to derail the official dialogue process. One of the unfortunate impacts of this mistrust between India and Pakistan is that the minority Muslim community in India is a frequent target of attacks. The chain of Hindu-Muslim riots that started during partition has continued from time to time since independence, usually tracing to the instigation of political groups or parties. During situations of strife, people have witnessed how old bonds of brotherhood between communities become the first casualty, and personal friendships are snapped and consigned to flames of hatred.

It is only in recent decades that Indian and Pakistani historians have begun to write about the social upheavals of partition, recording the personal testimonies of survivors of violence on both sides of the border. Among recent books, Pakistani historian Dr. Ishtiaq Ahmed's *Punjab Bloodied, Partitioned and Cleansed*, Rajmohan Gandhi's *Punjab*, and Urveshi Butalia's *The Other Side of Silence* have added to new understanding.[1] These testimonies reveal that all religious communities committed cruelty and violence against the innocent and unarmed. But many testimonies also tell us about the humanity shown by countless numbers from each religious community who protected, gave shelter to, and helped with safe passage those who were under attack from their own community during that madness. These books provide glimpses of both good and bad sides of human nature, and they have contributed to some extent to restoring our faith in "humanity." These public testimonies perhaps are among the first steps in the healing process.

FOUNDATIONS

I am a Hindu and belong to a Brahmin upper caste considered a privileged group. In India, people can recognize our religious identities from our names. Thus, there is no need for us to declare our religion for identification. As peace practitioners, our most valuable asset is our belief in and respect for the pluralism of faith traditions and our capacity for trust building.

I grew up in a home where my parents and grandparents were religious and observed all religious rituals. Despite this, there was never any talk or ill speaking or discrimination against any other caste or religious community in our family. No seeds of prejudice toward other religions were planted in our minds at home. There was also no discussion of the undesirability of mixing with the lower castes or Muslims.

One day my youngest uncle brought home his college friend, who was seriously ill and needed to be looked after, as he lived in the college hostel at the time. He belonged to a lower caste. But I don't remember any elder rebuking my uncle for bringing his friend over to our home. My orthodox grandmother looked after this young man for several weeks in our home. Another uncle had two Muslim college friends who came home during Hindu festivals, and my uncle went to their homes during Muslim festivals to take part in the festivities. From early childhood, though our family identity of higher-caste "Hindu Brahmin" was ingrained in me, the above-mentioned encounters with those from other castes and religions who came to our home were also deeply imprinted in my consciousness and demonstrated to me that one could have normal, good relations with those who did not belong to our "set."

My parents were liberal and not rigid in their attitudes. We lived in that part of Mumbai City with a predominantly Hindu population. I went to a school where we did not have any non-Hindu students except for a lone Jewish girl who traveled a long distance each day to attend school. Hence my first encounter with people of other religions came when I went to college in mid-1960.

Abida was my classmate. As we got to know each other, she told us of her relatives in Pakistan. I was surprised to hear her family saga from the partition of India and how it uprooted and separated families. This catastrophic event that shook the Indian subcontinent had not touched people of Maharashtra, my state in western India, on the same scale as it had the partitioned states of Punjab and Bengal. It was like opening a window to a world that was unknown to me. It was also my first glimpse into Mumbai City's varied communities. Although there was nothing offensive in the way Abida spoke of her faraway relatives in Karachi, my own reaction was unexpected. I decided to distance myself from Abida because she had relatives in Pakistan, a country that India considered an "enemy" and had fought against a couple of years earlier. Although we never spoke about this, clearly an invisible wall had come up between Abida and me.

One day a thought flashed through my mind: I had no right to distrust Abida because she had done nothing to deserve this attitude from me. On one occasion when our college group was together, I found myself telling Abida about the reason for my changed attitude and telling her that I was sorry. Although she had sensed this, she did not know the reason. I am glad we were able to talk. We must deal with the distrust and prejudice in our own hearts if we are to bring harmony and reconciliation between communities.

This episode made me aware of the Muslims of India and desire to learn more about them. Little did I know then that my future life would be devoted to working with the diverse communities of India, and particularly working closely with the large Muslim community in India and also in Bangladesh and Pakistan. The following years guided me toward the field of peacebuilding.

CHALLENGES AND RESPONSES

1984 Anti-Sikh Riots

In October 1984, India's prime minister Indira Gandhi was assassinated by her two Sikh bodyguards. Not knowing what had happened in Delhi, a friend and I got on a train in Mumbai for a thirty-six-hour journey to a small town in the northern Indian state of Uttar Pradesh. Our copassengers were a Muslim couple, two Sikh businessmen, and an army officer. Such a diverse mix of passengers is not uncommon in Indian train compartments. Our first stop came after five hours of the journey, and someone got down and brought a newspaper. It carried news of Prime Minister Gandhi's assassination at the hands of her bodyguards. There was discussion among the fellow passengers as we continued the journey. By nighttime we got reports that Sikh passengers were being pulled out of trains and beaten up to avenge the prime minister's death. Our fellow Sikh passengers became silent with troubled expressions on their faces. By morning our train too was stopped at unscheduled places by mobs, and the Sikhs sensed trouble and changed their seats. They went to the upper berths and covered themselves with blankets. They gave their belongings to us for safekeeping, along with a piece of paper with a family address scribbled on it. In case anything happened to them they wanted us to take their belongings to their families.

Before long mobs walking up and down the train compartments discovered the Sikhs and dragged them away. I tried in vain to tell them the two Sikh passengers were innocent. I was pushed aside. The Sikhs were taken out of the compartment, beaten up with bamboo sticks, and stoned. After some time the injured men were put back in the compartment, and the train moved. At another stop the bodies of injured Sikhs were thrown out, and the mob this time decided to burn them. As the train moved, we saw our two injured copassengers being set on fire. We were numbed by witnessing these events.

Following the train incident, I was deeply troubled for weeks and months. At night the images of the attack returned and, with them, guilt at not being able to save innocent lives, anger toward Hindu mobs for what they had done, and a sense of deep shame and hurt that I could not resolve. I wanted to distance myself from those who had blood on their hands as I felt I was different from them. But could I really detach myself in this manner? Was it self-denial? Should there be collective guilt? Would I have felt the same emotions had I not witnessed the violence and brutality on that train?

I wrestled with these questions in the aftermath of the anti-Sikh riots. The act of assassinating the prime minister was dastardly. But the actions of the Hindu mobs who avenged this act by targeting hundreds of innocent members of the Sikh community and lynching them could not be justified. It is wrong to hold an entire community responsible for the action of two individuals. What is the role of an individual and that of the society when such violence breaks out? Does such violence erupt spontaneously, or does such an eruption come out of a long-simmering pot? Are we not all responsible for such violence through our attitude of indifference, sitting on the fence when we are required to act in some small way to prevent a brewing crisis from exploding?

The train incident had shattered the myth about Hindus as peaceful, tolerant, and incapable of cruelty and violence. I was suddenly face-to-face with the ugly side of human nature and the truth that my community was capable of vengeance and cruelty just like other communities. This truth was very difficult to digest. For several weeks I lay awake during the nights. I was afraid for India. One always has an idealistic view of oneself, one's family, one's community, and one's country. When they don't live up to this ideal, it is indeed very painful to face the truth and accept it.

I kept thinking, What is my role in preserving India's social fabric and preventing its disintegration? What should I do?

One night several thoughts flooded into my mind. When there are upheavals in any society, no one factor or individual is responsible for them. Each one of us in some way has contributed to the turbulence through our attitudes—through taking sides, prejudice against one group or the other, or just indifference. Do such attitudes make people blind to what's happening around them and to the wider interest of their societies? History too has played an important part in shaping attitudes of various communities, particularly those with bitter experiences from the partition of India. Are people aware of these blind spots?

I certainly was not. If all of us are responsible for what has gone wrong, then we must share collective responsibility for it. In that sense, each individual can also play a small role as a citizen in repairing and restoring personal and social relations that have broken down. How can I as an ordinary individual help in this process? A clear thought flashed through my mind: you must take moral responsibility for the violence unleashed against the innocents as part of a collective and apologize to the Sikh community. So strong and persistent was this thought that it brushed aside all doubts.

Around this time, news came that perhaps one of the two Sikh passengers whom we thought were dead might be still alive. I decided to visit, as the scrap of paper with the address of one of the Sikhs was preserved and could help in tracing them. A friend from Delhi agreed to travel with me to Kanpur, the North Indian town where the two men lived. Scores of people offered help in tracing the address. Finally, one morning, accompanied by my Delhi friend, I visited one of them whose address we had. His house showed signs of being targeted during the riots—blackened walls, empty holes where doors and windows should have been, and a bare house with no furniture. We were not sure what reception awaited us. Would the family be hostile to us? Would they believe my story that all their belongings given to us for safe keeping were stolen by the mobs?

The Sikh man was lying on his bed surrounded by his family. Both sides were surprised to see each other. He had not fully recovered from his broken limbs and burns. The family had great difficulty in tracing him as they too had to move to a relief camp when their home was attacked. They narrated the difficulties they had gone through and how the two Sikh passengers were taken to the hospital by the police from the railway tracks in an unconscious state. It was in this home that we learned that the second man too had survived. They gave us his address.

When I apologized for their physical and psychological ordeal at the hands of the Hindu mobs and for not being able to protect their belongings, the wife of one of them replied, "The fact that my husband is alive and you are unharmed is a gift of the almighty. Please, don't ever worry about those belongings. These material things don't matter compared to human lives." I wondered if the first family who had lost everything in their home also felt the same way. Both the men felt that we must think of how to heal the wounds between our communities now. The words spoken by the two men were without anger and bitterness. This was remarkable, particularly as they were victims of terrible physical violence. To this day their words remain a challenge for me and nudge me to continue to face the truth about myself and my people. This was also to reveal a deep truth: just as not everyone supports the violence committed by a few members of their majority community, not all the victims nurse the desire for revenge for their suffering and humiliation.

Making an apology or seeking forgiveness (*Kshama* in Sanskrit or *Maafi* in numerous Indian languages) has several references in the Bhagavad Gita[2] and other Indian religious texts and is an accepted sociocultural norm among the Hindus as well as other communities. Yudhisthara, one of the characters of the epic Mahabharata,[3] says in reply to his wife Draupadi's demand for revenge,

> How will the world run?
> If bitterness rewards bitterness,
> Injury is returned for injury, hate for hate,
> If fathers suspect sons, sons suspect fathers,
> If trust disappears between husband and wife?[4]

In Chapter 16, verses 2 and 3, in the Gita, Krishna describes Ahinsa (nonviolence), Peacefulness, Forgiveness, and Compassion as divine qualities.

The Kanpur visit helped me to complete the inner journey. I could now move on. Visiting these men in their homes was the most difficult encounter of my life till then. I don't know how I found courage for it. As we left their homes and the town that night, I said to myself, "I owe it to these two men and many others like them to commit my life to the work of healing and reconciliation."

The burden of guilt I had carried till then was gone. Though we had not been able to protect the Sikhs on the train, others—policemen and doctors in the hospitals—had given protection and medical aid, which saved their lives. If we had not made the journey to their homes, I would not have known the ordeal they and their families had gone through. The journey helped me discover new meaning and calling for my life. I saw in those victims a capacity for gracefully accepting apology and a vision of a higher purpose for the future through their trauma and suffering. Such individuals, fortunately, challenge the perpetrators to face the consequences of their actions and also challenge the silent majority who allow such violent upheavals to take place. The visit convinced me that although the task was difficult, the relations that were breached between communities could be restored. Once the burden of guilt was lifted, creative ideas started to come for the next step.

New Delhi

I spent the following two years in New Delhi, which was the scene of intense riots and massacres in several slums around the city during the anti-Sikh riots of 1984. The house I lived in was on the road where many commercial furniture shops belonging to Sikh businessmen had been looted and gutted. Many residents of a Hindu colony (or neighborhood) across the road were frequent visitors to our house. During one such visit, I told the group of my experience during the anti-Sikh riots and the visit to Kanpur to meet the Sikh passengers. This prompted a discussion about those riots and how the very neighborhood in which we sat had been affected. The Hindu visitors spoke frankly of how shameful these acts were and admitted that some from their colony had taken part in the looting and burning of furniture shops. They wondered if there was something they could do about this.

I arranged a meeting for them with Justice R. S. Narula, a respected retired Sikh judge. He agreed to receive them in his home. The group was given a gracious welcome. The judge personally served tea to each one in the group. After this, when everyone settled in, one member of the group said to the judge, "We have come to tell you that we are deeply ashamed of the acts of looting and burning of shops on our road by some men from our colony and offer our apologies. We want to help in building bridges." The judge graciously accepted their words and agreed to visit their colony. The judge and one of his grandsons went on to be part of initiatives with me for several years. Many such encounters took place in the following weeks and months in Delhi, thus bringing personal healing to individuals.

I am convinced that if, in a situation, one sees that one's own community is wrong, there should be no hesitation on the part of an individual to take responsibility and apologize on behalf of his or her community. This is the only way to rebuild the social compact.

However, there are many Sikhs who have a grievance that those guilty of the mass crimes have not yet been punished and that many victims have not received appropriate compensation. I cannot fault them for these sentiments and over the years have come to realize that justice and compensation issues are important for the victims. There has been no successful prosecution of perpetrators of heinous crimes committed during the 1984 riots, so even after three decades many Sikhs feel there is no closure. Some Sikhs have kept the demand for justice and waged legal battles against perpetrators and a few Hindu political leaders for over thirty years in India and in recent years also in the United States. The government of India recently announced that it would reopen fifty-nine serious cases from the 1984 riots.

After 1984, I worked for some time among the Sikhs in New Delhi who were trying to cope and restart their lives following the anti-Sikh riots. Decades ago, the Sikhs in Punjab had suffered grievously from the violence and displacement that took place when British India was partitioned to form India and Pakistan. During several encounters, some of the Sikhs would bitterly recount memories of partition and explain that they were fearful of the prospect of being uprooted again from their new dwellings in different towns and cities of India. As a witness to the 1984 riots, I began to understand the nature of such violence and its lingering impact on individuals and communities for a long time into the future. This understanding equipped me with sensitivity to the impact of violence in conflict areas and with a sense of how to initiate and conduct peacebuilding work.

Jammu-Kashmir

Since 2001, I have been working with the Centre for Dialogue and Reconciliation, focused on Jammu-Kashmir. There, an armed uprising in the early 1990s by Kashmiri Muslims for independence was just winding down, but violence had not stopped completely when we started our work. Our efforts focused on postconflict peacebuilding. But this was different from our previous work, which had been directed at healing in the aftermath of communal riots. When the riots ended, the violence stopped, making it easier to start reconciliation work. But in Jammu-Kashmir, the nature of violence was longstanding, and the availability of guns was widespread, aftereffects of the armed insurgency and counterinsurgency measures by the Indian security forces. All these had severely impacted people in a manner that I had not seen earlier. Besides, Kashmir is an almost seven-decades-old dispute between India and Pakistan, and its international dimension complicates the situation on the ground. Kashmiri anger and grievances are directed against India. It took me a while, as an Indian citizen, to win the trust and confidence of important stakeholders there and start initiatives that would make a difference to people on the ground.

On numerous occasions, I have acknowledged that India has failed in fulfilling many promises given to the Kashmiri people and that specific cases of human rights abuses by Indian security forces went beyond normal security duties and fell into the category of criminality. I have observed how a sense of victimization has hampered the capacity of Kashmiri people as a direct result of historical traumas. Through empathizing with their suffering, I have tried to go beyond "us and them." I have also evolved to a belief that Kashmiris are empowered people who can develop solutions to their own problems. This has been central to our various dialogue conferences, which include women and youth, people from different regions and communities and across the Line of Control, as well as our peace education for teachers and India-Pakistan Track 2 dialogues with a Pakistani partner called the Jinnah Institute.

One of the important dialogue series was between Kashmiri Muslims and Kashmiri Pandits (Hindus) and between Muslims of Kashmir Valley and Hindus of the Jammu region. Kashmiri Pandits are a small minority who were forced to migrate out of Kashmir in the wake of the armed uprising in the early 1990s. This has left a vacuum, resulting in the disappearance of Kashmir's famed composite culture. Both communities have their own sets of grievances and narratives of events; they do not agree on the causes of the exodus or on what should be the modus for the return home of the displaced

Kashmiri Hindus. After one of the dialogues between Kashmiri Muslims and Kashmiri Hindus, the participants went to meet Kashmiri political leaders of different ideological viewpoints to inform them of their views regarding the return of the Hindus. This became public, and the Kashmiri Hindus came under severe criticism from some in their community, who asked who had given permission to the group to speak on the community's behalf. Although the participants never claimed that they were spokespersons for their community, the dialogue initiative had run into serious trouble. There was a temporary setback. In fragmented societies, rebuilding the social compact is a hard task.

My own viewpoint is that an individual can speak as a member of his or her community and enter into a dialogue with members of the other community. After all, such a dialogue is not always for negotiating a political settlement but can be for addressing misinformation, prejudice, and other societal issues of coexistence. Intercommunity relations are led and built by individuals or groups at the community level to develop possibilities for living together again. My work since 1984 has been entirely based on individual conviction and action. I never once felt that I needed to request the permission of my community or any political party to initiate dialogue and reconciliation.

In 2015, during a raging controversy over a religious matter in Jammu-Kashmir, a Kashmiri Muslim truck driver was killed by a radical Hindu group in the Jammu region. Tension rose across the two regions. In an inspired initiative, the Hindu president of the Jammu Chamber of Commerce, Rakesh Gupta, flew to Kashmir and made a public statement with his Kashmiri Muslim counterpart by his side. Gupta said, "We condemn such acts of killing of the Kashmiri truck driver. Action must be initiated against the culprits and their handlers. Business communities of both regions want to have cordial relations with each other. We will not allow anyone to disturb socioeconomic conditions in the state. That is why we have come together."

In the context of Jammu-Kashmir, Gupta belongs to the minority Hindu community in the majority-Muslim state. His courageous statement demonstrated that any public apology for any wrong act committed by either majority or minority community can help to assuage public anger and act as a balm in volatile situations. He told me later that some of the radical Hindus were not happy with his press statement. On the other hand, a large number of Hindus appreciated Gupta's courageous statement and were glad that someone had spoken up. The statement reduced communal tension and helped to prevent a further outbreak of violence.

Despite temporary setbacks at times, Kashmiris who have been part of our initiatives realize the importance and value of such dialogues in peace-building processes. In the dialogue meetings, people of Jammu-Kashmir belonging to diverse religious communities have responded to their counterparts by acknowledging the failings of their own group. Such an "acknowledgment" is important as it registers wrongdoing on the part of one's community and becomes a first step in the reconciliation process. Those I work with are supportive of each other as our own understanding of peacebuilding dimensions grows wider.

In Jammu-Kashmir, I have also been confronted with the question of human rights, and I have come to realize the importance of justice issues when one is engaged in larger peacebuilding efforts. Close friends have occasionally challenged me, asking, Why do you want to start peacebuilding without considering how to hold perpetrators accountable for the crimes they have committed? The slow and weak criminal justice system has emboldened people to commit heinous crimes with impunity during communal conflagrations, while the Indian state has shown its incapacity to bring the criminals to justice and subject those holding public office to accountability. I have come to realize that indeed human rights and justice issues cannot be brushed under the carpet. For some victims closure may only come through the justice they seek. The pursuit of justice and reconciliation are complimentary but may be carried out by different groups. This is not always easy, but it is very clear that justice without reconciliation, or vice versa, will not work.

At times, the goal of resolving the international dispute over Kashmir seems distant and complicated. Yet, through many ups and downs, our organization has succeeded in creating a statewide peace infrastructure in Jammu-Kashmir that has widened the peace constituency and contributed from time to time with constructive ideas for the official Track 1 dialogue.

CONCLUSION: SILENCE OF THE MAJORITY

During the past thirty years since the train incident, my life has completely changed course. Since then, I have worked in different parts of India—north, west, and east—among communities deeply impacted by violence. I have become more aware of my role as a member of the majority Hindu community as well as the role of any majority group toward minorities in democracies. Both these aspects have dominated all the dialogue and reconciliation work I have done. It has encouraged me to read and learn more about the impact of India's syncretic tradition, which intermingles Hinduism, Buddhism, Jainism, Sikhism, Islam, and Christianity, as well as Persian and Central Asian languages, art, architecture, and music. I began to observe how the interdependence in social and economic relations among different religious communities has developed into deep intercommunity bonds and how numerous worshiping places dotted around the country where diverse religious communities gather for worship have provided glue for bonding them. I have grown to appreciate the grounding I have received during the growing-up years from my family that never encouraged hate, prejudice, and discrimination toward the "other."

Over the years I have wrestled with the "silence of the majority" as a difficult question that one is confronted with constantly. That is the cause of greatest injury to victims in such conflicts. Such silence allows a conflict to simmer over a period before exploding into violence because people have not raised their voices or acted at the initial signs of something going wrong, which might have prevented violence later. Unfortunately, this silence is usually interpreted by the victim community as complicity of the majority in violence committed against them, and this sense of betrayal brings further pain and estrangement.

The silence of the majority has so many aspects to it. Without doubt some among this silent majority do in fact support the perpetrators of violence in thought and conviction, but they would not join the mobs, as this does not suit their "social status." The instigators of violence are aware of such sentiments and feel emboldened by this. But the majority of people, who watch violent incidents as "bystanders," do not approve of violence and criminal acts.

Another important angle to why the silent majority remains silent is that they are struggling to keep out of trouble themselves and to survive. Even so, there are numerous examples in India's history of how silence has saved lives, as recorded by authors about people who quietly protected and rescued people during the partition violence as well as during numerous riots.

It is crucial to address the trouble when early-warning signals are first seen because it may be too late to speak or act after violence erupts. My experience during the 1984 riots showed that confronting an already-violent mob as an individual may not be enough to protect the intended targets. But the continued silence of the majority even after the violence subsides and facts about the atrocities come to light is problematic for the victims, who feel let down by this "silence," resulting in bitterness and distrust of one and all in the "other" group. This is what leads to bleeding sores in intercommunity relations. As Martin Luther King Jr. said, the ultimate tragedy is "not the glaring noisiness of the bad people, but the appalling silence of the good people."[5]

During my work, I came across many among "the silent majority" in the violence-affected areas who did not know how to respond to the aftermath of violence through small individual acts and were therefore unable to reconnect with their neighbors. But when such persons are encouraged and facilitated, they play a splendid role in the reconciliation process, as I witnessed during the Mumbai work in the 1990s.

The silence of some persons may also represent an inner conflict of loyalty to one's own community that demands "you protect the wrongdoer to save family or community honor," even if this goes against your conscience. In this case, one would not utter words that paint one's family or community in a bad light. I do know of families and communities where such discussions have gone on, preventing individuals from stepping out of line and forcing the silence of individuals who might otherwise speak out.

In some contexts, there is also a social belief that bad memories should not be revived as they cause pain and prevent people from moving on in life. As time is the best healer, the past should be buried. But this can also become an excuse to cover up one's feelings of guilt and shame over criminal acts committed by people of one's own community. Unfortunately, brushing things under the carpet most often does not work, as it brings neither healing nor closure. The past has a way of reemerging in unexpected ways and at awkward moments.

One may need to nudge and challenge those who are silent by asking, "What is more important—shielding a wrongdoer or upholding values of humanity and rule of law?"

I know from my own experience that most people who have witnessed violence can never shut their minds to what they have seen. Violence has a deep impact. An individual can work through the issues of "loyalty," the "burden of shame," and the feeling of "what can an ordinary person like me do anyway"—as I did—and take small steps that can make a difference to affected individuals. This is a painful process, as it requires courage and deep change in one's "own self." Through such individual steps, one can shake off the "shame" that immobilizes individuals and become an instrument for reconciliation. Helping and encouraging individuals to break their silence and shed their shame is important. The dynamism of any society to overcome difficult moments and challenges will depend on the capacity of its people for independent thinking and expression.

After the Mumbai riots in 1993, I talked to a Hindu woman who was alone in a ground-floor flat with her five-year-old daughter on the worst day of the riots and panicked after hearing the rumor that Muslim mobs were coming to attack their area. I informed her that these were just rumors. But she was angry and retorted, "Muslims must be taught a lesson." When I asked, "What kind of a lesson?" she was not sure, as she had not thought about it. So I narrated the gruesome killings that had taken place in different parts of the city and asked if she hoped for this kind of lesson to be taught to the Muslims. She was shocked and told me she certainly did not mean or wish for the killing of innocent people. I realized how such un-thought-through sentiments become the support base of the perpetrators of violence.

There is also another important aspect when someone speaks out, as seen in the public statement made by the Hindu business leader of Jammu. His apology preempted further violence and more importantly gave courage to those who felt disturbed by what had happened to break their silence. Hence acknowledging the horrific acts committed by one's community can act as balm for the victim community. Such expressions also help in isolating the wrongdoers rather than blaming their entire community. Going further, words of regret and apology born of remorse have the power to rally opinion and public support for victims that to some extent can assuage the harm to the victims and restore broken relations.

After the anti-Sikh riots in Delhi, and later on in Mumbai and Gujarat, when the nature and the extent of violence became known, citizens mobilized themselves to go out to help the victims and assist in rehabilitation efforts at a time when there was a prevailing general sentiment that the government had failed. These citizen initiatives that reached out to the victims made powerful statements. On the one side there was a display of cruelty and criminality, and on the other side there was strong mobilization of citizens who disapproved of violence against other human beings and cherished human values of peace, compassion, and empathy by reaching out to victims. At any given time and place, we can see the presence of both these strains of good and bad in human behavior side by side. The constant presence of good in human behavior, I believe, is the strength of Indian society and the human family. The challenge before us is to not allow evil to overwhelm us and to strengthen the "good" instead.

It is important therefore to discern the silence and engage with the silent majority in helping to think through their emotions and reactions to injustice and violence. This too is an important aspect of peace and reconciliation work. The burden of responsibility must always rest on the majority community in this task.

NOTES

1. Ishtiaq Ahmed, *The Punjab Bloodied, Partitioned and Cleansed: Unravelling the 1947 Tragedy through Secret British Reports and First-Person Accounts* (Karachi: Oxford University Press, 2012); Rajmohan Gandhi, *Punjab: A History from Aurangzeb to Mountbatten* (Delhi: Aleph, 2013); Urveshi Butalia, *The Other Side of Silence: Voices from the Partition of India* (Durham, NC: Duke University Press, 2000).

2. The Bhagavad Gita is contained within the Mahabharata. See *The Mahabharata: Complete and Unabridged*, trans. Bibek Debroy. 10 vols. (Penguin Books India).

3. Ibid.

4. Rajmohan Gandhi, *Revenge and Reconciliation: Understanding South Asian History* (London: Penguin, 1999), 12.

5. Martin Luther King Jr., "Some Things We Must Do" (address delivered at the Second Annual Institute on Nonviolence and Social Change at Holt Street Baptist Church, Montgomery, Alabama, December 5, 1957).

Part II

Engaging the "Other"

Chapter Four

Listening Our Way to Peace

Yael Petretti

Challenge: What difficulties do you face in engaging people with extreme religious views, and how do you address those difficulties?

"An enemy is someone whose story we have not heard."
—Gene Knudsen Hoffman [1]

The Israeli-Palestinian conflict has seemed intractable for decades, and by virtue of my living in Jerusalem for close to thirty years, I have been a part of it. Along with so many other residents whose religious sentiments connect them viscerally to this ancient land, I have internalized the ecstasy of its transcendent spiritual energies and the agony of seeing the hearts and bodies of its inhabitants ripped apart by hatred and violence. There is no comfort in Zion, no peace in Palestine. Perhaps the greatest single challenge I have experienced in Israel has been persuading people to lay their defenses down for just long enough to listen to those around them, those on the other side of the street or those beyond the wall. To ask themselves, "Can they really be human beings?" As a Jew who cares deeply for both peoples, it has pained me very deeply to hear my fellow Israelis say that they couldn't care less about Palestinian suffering or that they "deserve it anyway." When one challenges the casual apathy expressed in this kind of remark, angry accusations like "It's as though you've never lived here," "You are naïve and a self-hating Jew," or "Whose side are you on?" follow. The barricades are up, and you are shut out and isolated.

In this chapter, I will attempt to illustrate how the skill of deep, empathic listening can be a powerful aid to us as we work to build peace with people who hold strong, perhaps even "extremist," views about the conflict.

I have always felt that if people from both sides could just *see* each other close up and listen to each other, they would find ways to end the pain and destruction they were causing in each other's lives. It seemed impossible to simply stand by and watch it go on. Leviticus 19:16 enjoins us not to stand idly by while our brother's blood is at stake. As I understand this commandment, "brother" means "everyone," although there are some Jewish political and religious figures in Israel who would disagree with that. Witness the rabbis who gave actual written approval to assassinate Prime Minister Yitzhak Rabin for taking steps to end the conflict. Pushing back against xenophobic and exclusivist religious interpretation is another painful challenge to peacebuilders in this region.

Despite the challenges, there are Palestinians and Israelis who are determined to join hands to end the fighting and misery. They began by listening. Being a good listener is not always easy, even when we interact with members of our families and our friends. Listening deeply to someone with whom we are in conflict is even more difficult, but I believe that it is the key to understanding, reconciliation, and peace.

FOUNDATIONS

As a child, I had a favorite fairy tale. It took place in a walled medieval town. The people of the town were very afraid of a dragon who lived outside the walls in a cave, but there was a small girl who would sneak out of the gates to visit the dragon and bring him cakes to eat. He revealed to her that he was miserably lonely and could not understand why the townspeople were so afraid of him. One day, she took him by the paw and brought him into the town center square so that everyone could see that he was harmless and friendly. And, of course, they all lived happily ever after as good neighbors. Obviously, I wanted to be that girl. The aspiration of bringing "enemies" together to see that they could be friends has been the thread that has run though my entire life. I was raised a Catholic but grew disillusioned with the exclusivist tenor of the doctrine at the time. So many of my friends were not Catholic, and I could not accept that they were not going to heaven with the rest of us, as the nuns had warned. As a teenager, I got deeply involved in peace and social justice work, which led me directly to Judaism and the concept of *tikkun olam* (repairing/healing the world).

Since my teen years, I had been involved in one sort of campaign or another. I was disheartened to learn that "peace people" are often not very peaceful. I have seen deeply rooted personal anger channeled into peace work, and that anger always found ways to express itself in ways that only perpetuated the conflict. I have also been guilty of harboring too much self-righteous anger at times.

Early in 2001, I learned about a practice called "Compassionate Listening." From the first day of training, its message of "humanizing the other" resonated deeply for me. It just made sense: if you take sides in a conflict, you become part of the conflict. If, on the other hand, you don't take sides and are able to listen deeply to each person involved, it might be possible to bring down others' defenses and soften their attitudes a bit. Here was another way to approach peacebuilding that I wanted to try. I became a Compassionate Listening facilitator.

The principles of Compassionate Listening were inspired and developed by Quaker activist Gene Knudsen Hoffman (1919–2010) and distilled in the Middle East over two decades by Leah Green, founder of the Compassionate Listening Project (www.compassionatelistening.org). The practice of deep, respectful listening has proven to be a powerful peacebuilding tool there and in other places. In the Middle East, Israelis and Palestinians have actually been able to create peaceful interrelationships—the bonds on which future coexistence and reconciliation can be built—by learning to cultivate compassion for each other. Building on the foundational skill of being able to hear hard things, they are learning to acknowledge the suffering they have caused each other. But how does one go about "cultivating compassion" for a perceived enemy? How can we sit and listen to someone whose words and quite possibly even deeds are reprehensible to us, offensive to all our sensibilities? How can we seek to understand the killer of our child, spouse, or parent and see that individual as a fellow human being? Can we learn to identify some positive motivation with which we might connect on a human level beyond the hurtful words or behavior? If we are able to learn not to interrupt or correct what we think are mistakes or untruths in what we're hearing, does it mean that we are giving our tacit agreement to it? Why do we need to be "right" so urgently that we often think our lives depend on it? Are we willing to look inward at our own carefully cultivated prejudices and stereotypes and recognize them as such? And more, are we ready to entertain the possibility that we, ourselves, might be part of the problem?

Compassionate Listening gives us one path toward coexistence and the concrete steps that must be taken to build that coexistence. It teaches us to open our hearts wide and listen deeply and respectfully. This means being face-to-face with people who may frighten us or make us very angry. It means making these "enemies," even the extreme ones, feel safe enough in our presence to let down their guard and to begin to share their suffering with us. When this happens, our innate ability to empathize with another's suffering makes us aware of our shared humanity, and the melting of hearts toward one another begins. Attitudes and behavior can shift, sometimes quite dramatically.

The poet Henry Wadsworth Longfellow once mused, "If we could read the secret history of our enemies we should find in each man's life sorrow and suffering enough to disarm all hostility." This is precisely the aim of Compassionate Listening: disarming hostility and creating a heart-to-heart connection among former "enemies." Again, it does not necessarily signal agreement, but once the connection is made, the logistics of peaceful coexistence can be worked out together. By that I mean we can find the concrete solutions to each problem as it comes up. Obviously, there are going to be times when not everyone is happy with the new arrangements, but if enough trust can be established, people can allow themselves more flexibility as they journey toward everyday peace.

In 1978, as a newly converted Jew motivated by *tikkun olam*, I took the next logical step of moving to Israel. I eagerly anticipated the chance to help build this new country on the Jewish humanitarian values I had studied. And there was the attraction of being part of the traditionally underdog Jewish people. We would show the world what being "A Light Unto the Nations," the biblical command to be a shining example of moral and ethical behavior, was all about.

For the first few years, as I studied and became a licensed tour guide, I was totally infatuated with "the Land," the biblical term Israelis use for the country. I became familiar with every town, village, holy site, wadi, and path. I was thrilled to touch the stones of ancient history and to learn about all that had happened there.

But I hadn't learned about *all* that had happened. As I paid more attention to things I saw in everyday life, I realized that there were major omissions in the official story of our modern history. The oft-repeated mantra of "a people without a land coming to a land without a people" was simply not true. There had been a people there who became engulfed in conflict and displacement when the modern state of Israel was born in 1948, and they resisted, sometimes violently. Following on the heels of the Holocaust in Europe, the Jews who came to Palestine, as it was called before 1948, were too traumatized to care about these "Arabs" and often behaved as though they weren't there.

As a tour guide, I traveled constantly throughout Israel and the West Bank Palestinian towns and villages. It seemed to me that until the First Intifada of 1988, there was an air of resignation in the Palestinian areas conquered by Israel in the 1967 war.

Despite the cautious coexistence that prevailed in most places, they were always friendly and welcoming when I visited with a tourist group or alone. Even after that, especially during the time of the Oslo Accords in 1993, we celebrated the new, hopeful atmosphere of peace amid anticipation that there would be Palestinian autonomy and independence very soon. The hope died with a gunshot at a Tel Aviv peace rally on November 4, 1995, the evening that Israeli prime minister Yitzhak Rabin was assassinated. Peace has retreated further and further away since then. Violence and polarization have brought the two peoples into agonizing gridlock. I used to tell my tourists occasionally that in Israel both life and death are intensely real. There is not very much theoretical about this conflict. On both the Palestinian and Israeli sides, we are completely inundated with our cultural narratives about it, and they are diametrically opposed. This conflict saturates the heart, mind, and spirit of every person living in it. Israelis are perpetually frightened of Arab attack and see themselves as victims of Palestinian hostility as well as of worldwide anti-Semitism. Conversely, the Palestinians feel thoroughly victimized by the occupation of their lands by the Israeli state and by the discrimination they feel at the hands of Israel and Israelis. There are myths, songs, media story lines, and individuals to perpetuate and increase the mutual fear and distrust. Each side sees itself as a victim of existential danger from the other side, and here the cycle has remained and intensified.

RESPONSES

"Compassionate Listening" is the name given to this kind of deep listening by Buddhist monk and teacher Thich Nhat Hanh. The reader can find the concept in many of his books, especially *The Art of Communicating*,[2] or listen to his August 31, 2014, "Super Soul Sunday" interview with Oprah Winfrey. This practice has as its basic premise that every human being is born with an innate goodness, a natural longing for love and connection with other human beings. We know it as the heart, soul, psyche, "that of God," our pure essence, or whatever we choose to call it: that place within each of us that longs for peace and connection. Thus, every human being deserves the chance to have his or her feelings and experience acknowledged. It is the "wounds" that each person receives throughout life that close down this heartfelt longing for peaceful connection—be they physical or emotional abuse, racism, sexism, war, poverty, or any sort of marginalization from others. In Israel and Palestine, these wounds are horrifically deep. Almost every family has lost one or more relatives to war, violence, and imprisonment. The pain and anger are, for many, insurmountable, or seemingly so.

What, then, can we as peacebuilders do?

Almost every spiritual tradition over the ages has held that love is the central guiding force for our lives, that we must love one another. Our hearts, therefore, are our best resource for creating peace within ourselves and in our surroundings. The Catholic background I had as a child and the Jewish path to *tikkun olam* that I chose as an adult have both sensitized me to the suffering of others and to the importance of compassion. As Compassionate Listeners, we work hard to discover what keeps our hearts closed—the fears, stereotypes, judgments about others, and so on. As we become more clearly aware of these obstacles to our connection with others, we can put them aside as we listen to them. We strive to become fully present to the person who is speaking, not giving advice or solutions but unobtrusively accompanying him to his own wisdom deep down inside. This is a tremendously healing gift in itself. In the supercharged context of the Israeli-Palestinian conflict, just the act of stating, "I am ready to listen to you. I want to learn about your feelings and experiences," is revolutionary and monumental. Many of my fellow Israelis are on hair-trigger alert for any suggestion that Israel's actions might be less than righteous. When such a suggestion is made, even in mild terms, they become hyperdefensive. I have always joked that it is against the law to allow anyone to finish a sentence in Israel. Humor aside, getting Israelis to listen is one of the biggest challenges I have ever faced in peace work. I have lost many friendships over this, which saddens me greatly. The Palestinians, on the other hand, are far more willing to listen, in general, but quickly become frustrated with talk when they see no subsequent action to alleviate their plight. In the course of a Compassionate Listening Project delegation to Israel/Palestine, which Leah Green and I co-led in June 2010, we met Bethlehem University Professor Elias al-Hazin. As he spoke to us, he was vehement about what he viewed as the "uselessness of $20 million spent on 'dialogue' programs" that take Israelis and Palestinians abroad to discover each other's humanity. "It must happen *here*," he thundered. He decried the "too many conferences [we have] with Israel," because when they are over, Israelis return to their home communities, and there is no organizational follow-up to solve the conflict.

The frustration is understandable, particularly as conditions deteriorate further with every passing day. Our Compassionate Listening delegations and local workshop sessions do not formulate specific plans or actions to solve the problems to which we bear witness. It is painfully clear, however, that there will never be social and political justice for the Palestinians in Israel and in Israel-controlled Palestine without radical and foundational change in Israeli official policy. Here it is important to differentiate between the role of the Compassionate Listener and the role of the advocate. When we are Compassionate Listening, giving our undivided, nonjudgmental attention to a speaker, we hope to offer at least some degree of healing by letting him know that he is important enough to be heard and that we care about how he feels. Advocacy is a very different undertaking. It requires that the advocate take a stand on behalf of someone who is suffering injustice or hardship at the hands of a more dominant power. The advocate confronts the more pow-erful party that is perceived to be causing the harm and demands that it stop. Advocacy is obviously a good and necessary thing, especially if it can be done in nonviolent ways such as the ones demonstrated by Mahatma Gandhi. In terms of the Israeli-Palestinian conflict, it is often difficult for the Com-passionate Listener to keep him- or herself from straying into the realm of advocacy because the conflict is so self-evidently lopsided. Israel is by far the stronger party and maintains almost complete control of everyday life.

Yet Thich Nhat Hanh reminds us that if we take either side in a conflict, we forfeit our role as peacemaker.

During the time that I lived in Jerusalem, I struggled with the tension between remaining only a "neutral" listener and taking part in active advocacy. In searching for an answer, I decided to follow Gandhi's lead, reasoning that while he never said a bad word about the British, individually or collectively, he succeeded in completely dismantling the Raj's rule there. I would engage in advocacy as a separate activity, not as part of Compassionate Listening work. Once, while taking part in a peaceful demonstration against the establishment of another West Bank Jewish settlement, I thanked the policeman who threw his body between our small group of protesters and the hundreds of infuriated settlers who had gathered there for the cornerstone-laying ceremony. Although my thanks came as an unfamiliar shock to him, I could see by his expression that there was an instant of friendship and connection.

But even in that situation, Compassionate Listening was helpful because it trains us to maintain our inner peace, to stay "anchored in the heart," even when subjected to intense emotion or physical threat—what Arnold Mindell refers to as "sitting in the fire."[3] One of the keystone principles of Compassionate Listening, as mentioned above, is learning to find the positive motivation behind acts or words to which we object. As I looked into the angry faces of those settlers and heard their shouts, it was very helpful to remember that they believed that they were doing the right thing, perhaps because they thought they were building a safer society for their children or for some other reason that I could understand (but not necessarily agree with). It was possible to gaze back at them without anger and without adding to the hatred in the air.

There are many ways to build peace, but I believe that the healing power of empathic listening cannot be overestimated. As part of my 2012 Compassionate Listening delegation of Americans to Israel/Palestine, we spent a night in the Galilee village of Tamra with my Bedouin friends of many years, Amal and Yassin Hamdouni. Tamra's population, half Palestinian and half Bedouin (now identifying as Palestinian for the most part), are Israeli citizens. In response to my request, Yassin invited some English speakers from the village to meet with us in the evening after dinner. An English teacher at the high school came along with a history teacher and the mayor of Tamra. As I introduced the members of our group to these people and explained that we had come to listen to them, I could see that the realization that this was a different kind of meeting was dawning on them. In typical Bedouin fashion, they had thought that they were just coming to welcome visitors from abroad; it was part of their culture of hospitality. When they learned that these Americans had actually come from as far away as Hawaii just to hear how their lives were, they were flabbergasted. Shyly at first, they began to speak. We listened fully and respectfully. Soon the floodgates burst open, and for hours they told us of the painful reality of living as Arabs in Israel, even though they are Israeli citizens. They described the difficulty or near impossibility of attaining a permit from the Israeli government to build new homes for their grown children who were ready to marry but could not until a house was ready for a new couple. The mayor took us to a hilltop overlooking the village and showed us how it is hemmed in on four sides by a road, a Jewish National Fund forest, a Jewish kibbutz, and fields. Therefore they cannot expand to accommodate the natural growth of the town's population. There were many other things that they told us about, such as not being able to communicate with or visit poverty-stricken relatives in Gaza. Although I had been a regular part of the Hamdouni household for over twenty years, I was hearing many things for the first time. I realized that Yassin and Amal had never complained about any of these issues because they did not want to make me, as an Israeli Jew, feel uncomfortable. My heart broke.

At the end of the evening, our hosts and speakers expressed how much they felt respected by our coming to hear them. They said that they were so amazed and happy that people from so far away were truly interested in them and their lives. The warmth of their farewell moved everyone deeply. When our group left Tamra the next morning, we boarded our bus laden with more fresh fruit and small presents than we could carry.

Often, however, persuading someone to speak to us is more difficult than it was in Tamra, particularly if that person is on the right side of the political spectrum, which is where more conservative, more ethnocentric feelings reside. In Israel, the prevailing belief is that if you are also listening to "the other side" (i.e., the Palestinians), you are automatically "anti-Israel." The same is true if you admit to being involved with "peace work" of any kind. A good number of Israelis do not ascribe to this and work very hard to promote understanding and peaceful relations among Palestinians and Jews. But in my experience, the majority of Jewish Israelis view any openness to hearing the other side with suspicion. The wounds are deep and defenses strong. For them, it is frightening to open their ears and hearts to hear about Palestinian suffering, to "humanize" the enemy. Likewise, many Palestinians are only now beginning to understand that without understanding Jewish suffering, there will never be peace. Courageous leaders like Sami Awad, Palestinian founder of the Holy Land Trust, teach their people about the Holocaust by visiting Auschwitz and Yad Vashem. He helps his fellow Palestinians develop empathy for Jewish Israelis by showing them what the Jewish people experienced in the not-so-distant past.

A few years ago, I wanted to bring a Jewish settler leader to speak at a Compassionate Listening group I'd brought to Jerusalem. For five days, she would not return my phone calls. When I reached her at last, I persuaded her to come and promised that our group would be very respectful of her, and she would not be attacked in any way. She felt that we had probably already made up our minds that she, as a settler, was in the wrong, but much to her credit, she came anyway. She spent an hour or two detailing her history and beliefs. She had actually been one of the first to convince the government to allow Jews to live in the West Bank, which she called by the biblical names of "Judea" and "Samaria." We learned that one of the main reasons that it had been hard to reach her was due to a terrible terror attack on a settlement neighboring hers. Just a few days before our meeting, two Palestinians had entered a West Bank settlement and murdered an entire family there. She had been given the task of going to tell the parents of that couple that their children and grandchildren were dead. The story shook all of Israel. This trauma made it much harder to meet with us, a group that was meeting also with Palestinians, but, as I said before, she did it. I will forever admire her courage for this.

Our group was attentive, and as we had practiced in our Compassionate Listening training, participants asked her many questions, always couched in respectful language. As the meeting broke up, she told me that she was very surprised at the kindness and friendliness of the group. She was so thrilled, she said, that she couldn't wait to tell her sister, who had advised against her meeting with us. A year later, I asked our settler friend if she would be willing to talk to another group, and this time she invited us to her home in Neveh Tsuf, a settlement near the Palestinian village of Halamish in the West Bank, Samaria. When we arrived, she had even baked us a cake. She did indicate that she had to do something later in the morning and could only talk with us for an hour or so. Three hours later, she was still talking. As the morning wore on, she grew more comfortable with us and filtered her statements about "the Arabs" less. At one point, for example, she exclaimed, "They have no more maternal instinct than a cat!" She did not actually know any personally but told of skirmishes that her neighbors had regularly with the people of Halamish. She feared for her many children, most of them grown and studying in religious schools throughout the West Bank. Here was one of the points at which we could connect, for example: a mother's concern for her children's safety. Although it was hard for many of us to hear some of the things she said, we were able to speak to that concern. Like most Jewish settlers, our hostess was convinced that all Arabs wanted to kill the Jews and throw them out of the Land. When she was finished speaking, I asked her if she had ever heard of Sami Awad, and she had not. I told her about his trips to Auschwitz and his teaching fellow Palestinians about nonviolence and the need to understand their Jewish neighbors. She leaned back in her chair and was quiet for a moment. Then she said, "Well, maybe there *is* some hope."

Sometimes when there is a conflict, the mediating parties may draw the line at speaking with certain persons or groups involved in the conflict. These "blacklisted" people are just too far outside the parameters of dialogue, and it is felt that meeting them would undermine the credibility of the mediating parties. In our Compassionate Listening work in Israel/Palestine, we have no blacklist. We believe that every person has the right to be heard. This principle applied, for instance, to our meeting in 2010 with a member of Hamas. "Hamas" is an acronym for the Arabic name for the Islamic Resistance Movement. It is a Palestinian Sunni offshoot of the Muslim Brotherhood and is dedicated to abolishing Israel as a Jewish political state.

His name was Farhan, and he was the former mayor of Beit Ummar, a village not far from Jerusalem. He had just been released from Israeli prison the day before our meeting. Israeli authorities had jailed him the day after he had been elected mayor of Beit Ummar a year previously. They had told him that if he would resign, they would release him, but he refused since he had been elected by the people of his town. We met in the home of his mother.

For most Israelis, Hamas is the ultimate demon. The United States follows the same line. But Compassionate Listening tells us that if we don't listen to our enemies, we have no hope of understanding what they want and how to find solutions to our conflict. So our delegation entered the home of a Hamas leader.

Forty-six-year-old Farhan was perhaps the least frightening person I had ever seen. A gentle man who sat with his five-year-old son, Salahadin, in his lap throughout our meeting, Farhan said, "I teach my three daughters and two sons to love, not to hate. To love is to be brave; it is stronger than hate. We may hate behaviors but not the person." He tells his children, "There are good Jews, not like the soldiers." We asked him to tell Salahadin how sorry we are for the long separation from his father. Farhan did this. He explained the Hamas understanding of Zionism: that Jews, Christians, and Muslims had lived there together in peace under the Ottomans, but when European Jews formed the Zionist movement to come there and rule over everyone, without giving equal rights to the people already there, the people who follow Hamas could not accept it. That is the context in which "eliminating Israel" should be understood, Farhan said. It is not eliminating the Jews; it means eliminating the political entity, the Zionist state, which does not give equal rights to the Muslims and Christians who have lived here for centuries. He added, "Making peace is harder than making war. Mohammed taught that it would be better to take the Qa'abah [the sacred black stone block in Mecca] apart stone by stone than to kill one human being." Obviously, there are other voices in Hamas, ones more prone to violence. Stepping back and seeing the bigger picture, we can understand that the violence has erupted out of frustration.

As we left Farhan's home, I told him that I was an Israeli who was very glad to meet him and hear what he had to say. As a religious Muslim, Farhan could not offer me his hand (just as religious Jewish men will not have physical contact with any unrelated woman), but he said, "Then, please let us work together." As our group could readily see, keeping people from meeting one another face-to-face and talking together is the best way of maintaining the conflict. When we cannot be together, we can much more easily succumb to the "us-against-them" narrative, and the conflict grows and endures.

While the more violent elements in Hamas make terrifying declarations about destroying Israel and fire rockets at Israeli settlements near the Gaza Strip, there are also renegade groups in Gaza who fire the rockets with or without Hamas's permission. The result for Israelis is the same: ongoing trauma.

For those who follow events in this conflict, the name Sderot will be familiar since it is often cited in news reports as the target of rocket fire originating in Gaza. Sderot is a city of approximately twenty-five thousand people located in the northern Negev just outside the Strip. The campus of Sapir College, an enormous institution that provides kindergarten through college education and comprehensive social services to the local population, is located there.

Professor Julia Chaitin teaches psychology at Sapir College, specializing in the psychological effects of ongoing trauma. She, along with Dr. Tsvi Fierman, director of Sha'ar haNegev Psychological Services, and two other psychologists/educators, Shimona and Ortal, described life in their area to our group. We met in one of the bomb shelters, because over thirty rockets had already landed by the time we arrived. Every day, between twenty and seventy-five rockets are fired at the Sderot area. The red-alert system sounds with each one, and the people of Sderot have fifteen seconds to reach a shelter before it lands. Shimona described the day before when she had her five-year-old child by the hand but her toddler had wandered to the other side of the playground area when the alarm sounded. In horror, she realized that she did not have time to retrieve the toddler and get both of her children into the shelter within fifteen seconds. For a split second, she thought that she would have to choose one of her children to save. The rocket had already slammed into the ground nearby when she got her children into the shelter.

Professor Chaitin and Dr. Fierman discussed the near impossibility of coping with ongoing trauma. In traditional circles, trauma is usually one terrible event that the victim experiences, and then he or she goes on living and finds ways to deal with the trauma through therapy of some kind. Here, the traumatic events happen constantly. Dr. Fierman asked, "How can we treat a child for PTSD when another bomb falls in the middle of our conversation and we have to run to the shelter?" He estimated that at least 75 percent of the local population suffers from posttraumatic syndrome disorder, a condition first identified by the Israel Defense Forces among its soldiers in the 1980s. Many of the psychologists themselves are traumatized, he continued, and have great difficulty in restraining themselves from leaving their classrooms to find their own children on the campus during red alerts.

In Gaza, the population of 1.8 million suffers profound and relentless trauma. Since January 2009, there have been three concerted Israeli incursions into Gaza. Deafening nightly overflights and their targeted attacks continue. Besides the nearly four thousand Palestinians killed (the vast majority of whom were civilians), many thousands more have been wounded, and over a quarter of the population has been made homeless.

Here is an excerpt from the "Informed Comment," published by the International Middle East Media Center on July 25, 2015:

> The high percentage of Palestinian families in Gaza that is suffering from mental and psychological issues is not a new topic, nor a surprising one. According to Save the Children, "Homelessness and repeated exposure to violence, coupled with soaring unemployment for parents and limited mental health support, have prevented children from recovering from the mental trauma of war." Save the Children CEO Justin Forsyth said in a statement, "Many children in Gaza have now lived through three wars in the past seven years, the last one notable for its brutality. They are emotionally and, in some cases, physically shattered." According to the organization's report, "An average of 75% of children surveyed experience unusual bedwetting regularly. In one area, al-Shoka, nearly half the children interviewed wet the bed every night. Up to 89% of parents reported that their children suffer consistent feelings of fear, while more than 70% of children said they worried about another war. On average seven out of 10 children interviewed suffer regular nightmares."

One can only wonder how many future generations have been damaged by the devastation. How long will it take to recover?

Amid this chaos, there are still Israelis and Palestinians who maintain contact and strive for peace. Professor Chaitin and an Israeli friend of hers named Roni belong to an organization called Other Voices. Both live in Israeli communities abutting or near the wall surrounding the Gaza Strip. Until recently, members of this group, Israelis and Gazans, would gather in a living room around a speaker phone to talk with each other. They inquired about each member of the group on the other side and related their sorrow and distress about the ongoing misery. Each side has succeeded in humanizing the other.

One truly heartrending story is that of Dr. Izzeldin Abuelaish, a Harvard-educated Palestinian doctor born in Gaza who chaired the department of obstetrics and gynecology at the Soroka Medical Center in Beersheba, Israel. His life had been a model of what peaceful coexistence could look like. Then, on January 16, 2009, Israeli tank shells killed his three daughters and a niece. On the road outside Tel HaShomer Hospital in Israel, priests, imams, rabbis, and many of us laypeople held prayer vigils for the recovery of another member of his family. Dr. Abuelaish blessed us as he passed. Rather than succumb to hatred and despair, the "Gaza doctor" wrote a book titled *I*

Shall Not Hate,[4] in which he insists that all of the people of the region must listen to each other to bring about peace

CONCLUSION

Inspired by examples such as these, we witness the transformative power of openhearted listening. By anchoring ourselves in our hearts and by allowing ourselves to be guided by healing intention, we create the possibility of deep, human connection. We build a true and lasting peace.

As we work toward this goal of transforming conflict into connection, especially with people who hold extremist views, we indeed face challenges that can be daunting as we "sit in the fire" of intense emotions. I have found, however, that the transformative shift in attitude and behavior can be stunning in its rapidity and depth. It is as though the longing for peace has lain just below the surface, waiting only for recognition and release. Often the change of heart takes much longer, but it is knowing that it may happen at any time that keeps us going.

Compassionate Listening has transformed me as well. Coming from a family with some very strongly opinionated members, I had learned two ways of handling disagreement: either outshout them or flee the field. Learning to listen with genuine respect and care to people whose words and/or actions seemed outrageous to me has been both demanding and eye-opening. I discovered that by forgoing the temptation to prove how right I am, several things happened: (1) I did not die; (2) the one expressing these intense feelings or opinions visibly calmed down when he realized I was really listening without interruption or judgment; and (3), perhaps most meaningfully, the speaker would often muse that perhaps he had expressed himself in more extreme terms than he really felt, admitting that he could be at least partially wrong. One of the greatest challenges for each of us is to recognize our own fallibility and not feel threatened by it. As we engage in our peacebuilding work, one of the most powerfully disarming things we can do is to model this approach.

Another helpful tool is to ask open-ended questions of the speaker, inviting him to elaborate on his experience and feelings. These are questions that accompany the speaker into deeper clarity and understanding for both him and for us as listeners. Perhaps the most powerful tool that Compassionate Listening gives us, however, is to look for the positive motivation beneath what we see as objectionable behavior and to speak to that. Learning to discern in this way is not always easy, especially at first. But finding these things about which we can agree—for example, the settler mother's fear for her children—gives us the bridge we can cross to connect with a fellow human being.

It seems so clear to me that the practice of building heart-to-heart, human connections is precisely what so many spiritual paths have at their core: the belief that we are truly one.

At the end of this chapter, I offer a short list of books that have inspired me to see the world and our humanity in this way. Perhaps you, the reader, will feel buoyed by their wisdom as you work to build peace in various parts of the world. As we know, it is often difficult.

As first-century Rabbi Tar'fon put it in the Babylonian Talmud (the ancient scholarly commentary on the Hebrew scriptures), "It is not incumbent upon you to finish the task, but neither are you free to absolve yourself from it."[5]

NOTES

1. Gene Knudsen Hoffman, *Compassionate Listening and Other Writings*, ed. Anthony Manousos (Torrance, CA: Friends Bulletin, 2003).
2. Thich Nhat Hanh, *The Art of Communicating* (New York: HarperOne, 2013).
3. Arnold Mindell, *Sitting in the Fire: Large Group Transformation Using Conflict and Diversity* (Florence, OR: Lao Tse Press, 1995).
4. Izzeldin Abuelaish, *I Shall Not Hate: A Gaza Doctor's Journey on the Road to Peace and Human Dignity* (Toronto: Random House, 2010).
5. Babylonian Talmud, Pirkei Avot (Ethics of the Fathers) 2:16, compiled by Rabbi Yosef Marcus (Brooklyn: Kehot Publication Society), http://www.chabad.org/library/article_cdo/aid/2011/jewish/Chapter-Two.htm, accessed June 2, 2017.

RECOMMENDED READING

Armstrong, Karen. *Twelve Steps to a Compassionate Life*. New York: Alfred Knopf, 2011.
Barasch, Marc Ian. *Field Notes on the Compassionate Life: A Search for the Soul of Kindness*. Emmaus, PA: Rodale, 2005.
Brady, Mark, ed. *The Wisdom of Listening*. Boston: Wisdom Publications, 2003.
Cohen, Andrea, Leah Green, and Susan Partnow. *Practicing the Art of Compassionate Listening*. Indianola, WA: Compassionate Listening Project, 2011.
Fellman, Gordon. *Rambo and the Dalai Lama: The Compulsion to Win and Its Threat to Human Survival*. Albany: State University of New York Press, 1998.
Gobodo-Madikizela, Pumla. *A Human Being Died That Night: A South African Woman Confronts the Legacy of Apartheid*. Boston: Houghton Mifflin, 2003.
Hwoschinsky, Carol. *Listening with the Heart: A Guide for Compassionate Listening*. Indianola, WA: Compassionate Listening Project, 2001.
Keith, Kent M. *Anyway: The Paradoxical Commandments*. New York: Berkley Books, 2001.
Macy, Joanna, and Molly Young Brown. *Coming Back to Life: Practices to Reconnect Our Lives, Our World*. Gabriola Island, BC: New Society Publishers, 1998.

Chapter Five

Faith-Based Peacebuilding in Pakistan

Not for the Faint of Heart

Azhar Hussain

Challenge: How can a perceived adversary promote tolerance and meaning-ful change in a traditional, conservative context?

> "If they charge thee with falsehood, say: 'My work to me, and yours to you! ye are free from responsibility for what I do, and I for what ye do!'"[1]
> —Al-Quran, Chapter 10 [Yunus]: Verse 41

Our workshops aren't boring. During a workshop with rural imams, one of the participants was crying. His name was Ibrahim. He hailed from an isolated mountainous area and was initially trained in one of Pakistan's many madrasas (religious schools). We asked him why he was crying. He said, "Mr. Azhar, what I've learned here has opened my eyes. Something terrible is about to happen in my village, and I am to blame." We asked him to explain.

"Our *jirga* [village court] sentenced a sixteen-year-old girl to be executed in two days because she snuck out at night and secretly called a boy. Her mother and sister were sentenced to have their noses cut off because they allowed this to happen. Now I see this wasn't Islamic at all. It's wrong, and I am responsible." We discussed possible solutions and decided to buy Ibrahim a plane ticket to return home immediately to convince the *jirga* to reverse its harsh decision. He flew home, and the sentence was rescinded.

You are probably skeptical. How can centuries-old cultural practices be reversed by a workshop? But what if false narratives taught under the guise of safeguarding tradition, culture, and religious identity and incorporated in schools and madrasas nurtured these intolerant practices? Sectarian violence in Pakistan is fueled by religious narratives that stem from a fear of losing identity and form a framework for understanding religion, society, people, and behavior that supports religious authoritarianism and bigotry.[2] The following are some of the underlying principles of these narratives:

1. Islam is under an existential threat.
2. The enemies of Islam include Western civilization, Shia Muslims,[3] India, and compromised Muslim leaders.
3. Hence good Muslims must defend their imperiled religion by all means possible, even violence.

In its most heinous forms, this defense evolves into violence against innocent civilians, schoolchildren, or persecuted minorities. Ibrahim's *jirga* conflated what might have been cultural and ethnic practices of the past with Islamic teachings. In fact, according to Ibrahim, he was taught to use violence against the West, women, other faiths, and Muslim minorities in the madrasa he attended for eight years, "but I know now that intolerance really has no basis in Islam." How a highly sophisticated and innovative network of Islamic madrasas—that gave rise to the finest universities and scholars—was transformed to produce graduates like Ibrahim was unfortunately easy: instill fear, teach that Islam and Muslim identity are under threat, allow grievances to build and fester. In response to these perceived threats, narrow sectarianism is taught in most of our madrasas. Madrasa students then become professional advocates of these rigid teachings and fan across Pakistan as mosque imams or madrasa teachers. This formation of religious identity at madrasas occurs in an ideological bubble. Dissent isn't tolerated. Critical thinking is largely banned. Questioning one's sectarian affiliation isn't allowed. Students and faculty form a community isolated from Pakistan's rich diversity of religious groups. In this insulated environment, students learn Quranic words in Arabic through rote memorization and are taught history and "correct" Islamic practices.

Madrasa students study and train hard, but their efforts are futile as they hardly comprehend the subjects and textbooks they study. They rely on what is passed on to them by madrasa leaders, their teachers, and rote memorization. They aren't exposed to other members of Islamic or other religious traditions. In a significant number of madrasas, the teaching materials instill religious perceptions, attitudes, and beliefs that call for the students to defend the faith—at all costs. Hence the graduates are convinced that they must aggressively defend an Islam under siege.

Students graduating from the sect-specific madrasas are expected to spread Islam by becoming a mosque imam or madrasa teacher or opening a new madrasa. Now surrounded by diverse Pakistanis of various Muslim denominations—including Shias, Sunnis, Sufis, Barelvis, Deobandis, Salafis, Ismailis, and Ahmedis—and different faiths, such as Hindus, Sikhs, and Christians, madrasa students experience culture shock within their own country. The ideas that students learned in isolation motivate them to vigorously defend their version of faith. A Pakistani from a different sect or religion is often viewed by a madrasa graduate as a foreigner or a foreign agent (Shia as an Iranian agent, Deobandi or Salafi as a Saudi Arabian agent, Hindu as an Indian agent). The students become community religious authorities, leaders, arbitrators, teachers, shariah judges, and opinion leaders. Then they pass on these same teachings to their students and communities.

But is intolerance and harsh treatment endemic to Islam? I'm a member of the minority Shia faith, which encompasses approximately 15 percent of Pakistan's 202 million people. The Sunni Muslims are a considerably larger group and form a huge majority, 80 percent. So when my parents sent me to a Sunni mosque to study as a child, why did I not experience any conflict, problem, or tension at all? How did the Shia later become perceived as enemies of the state and Islam? During my childhood it was normal for different sects to live harmoniously together. We were prepared to address the challenges of statehood as a united people of many ethnicities and languages and one *ummah* (Muslim community) with a rich diversity of Islamic beliefs and traditions. Why did my majority Muslim friends later abandon me and no longer accept drinks or snacks from me? One explained, "Shias spit in drinks and add unclean things in their food. That's why we are told by our parents not accept food or drinks from you."

Hence my challenge as a member of a marginalized Shia minority: How can a perceived adversary promote tolerance and meaningful change in an isolated and conservative traditional environment?

In this chapter I will briefly explain my personal faith journey within the context of huge changes that were occurring in the Islamic Republic of Pakistan. By understanding recent history, you will learn how a traditionally tolerant society quickly became intolerant and how and why our workshops successfully promote change, tolerance, diversity, and hope. We use local customs, culture, and relevant Islamic passages. These are ideas and practices owned by our Pakistani cultures but cast aside due to political and geopolitical interests. Since 2005 the Peace and Education Foundation (PEF) has engaged with and provided education and training in tolerance, critical thinking, interfaith dialogue, sectarian reconciliation, and peacebuilding to more than twelve thousand faith leaders in Pakistan.

FOUNDATIONS

Pakistani History and the Long Arc of Islam

> "Ye are the best of Peoples, evolved for mankind, enjoining what is right, forbidding what is wrong, and believing in Allah."[4]
> —Al-Quran, Chapter 3 [Al-Imran]: Verse 110

Al-Imran is the third chapter of the Quran. It is named after the family of Imran. Imran is regarded as the father of Mary, Jesus's mother.

My interpretation of this verse is that Muslims are asked to distinguish themselves through their service to humanity. When Muslim educators and leaders are teaching new generations to harm others in the name of Islam, they are denying the kindness, charity, and mercy of Allah.

Madrasas should teach students to honor their denominational traditions but also instruct them in social sciences and modern history to enable them to serve humanity practically. When madrasa students are taught to serve humanity like this, they are learning pure Islam. Indeed, once engaged in our programs of education and professional development, madrasa teachers and imams have actively supported us by convincing other unwilling religious leaders to support our programs. But when religious education teaches intolerance and provokes violence, it should be stopped, examined, and reformed to be consistent with traditional Islam, which teaches that God is merciful, loving, and compassionate. By learning these traditional values, madrasa students will be "the best of peoples, evolved for mankind."

Sectarian violence in Pakistan occurs in often hostile, reclusive, and embattled communities that view Shias like myself as insufficiently Islamic. Contrary to the vision of Pakistan as a land of Muslim unity, today's defining feature is sectarian intolerance. Prior to General Muhammad Zia-ul-Haq's coup in 1977, we largely lived together in peace. The various Muslim groups exhibited astonishing shows of respect and appreciation toward diverse Muslims and other faiths. Pakistan was founded in 1947 by Muhammad Ali Jinnah, a Shia Muslim (now a persecuted minority at risk of being declared non-Muslim). Pakistan's first foreign minister was an Ahmedi (now a severely persecuted minority declared non-Muslim), and the first chief justice of the Supreme Court of Pakistan was a Hindu named Bagwan Das (another persecuted faith viewed as an enemy of Pakistan). At the founding Jinnah declared, "You are free. You are free to go to your temples, you are free to go to your mosques or to any other place of worship in this State of Pakistan. You may belong to any religion or caste or creed—that has nothing to do with the business of the State."[5]

The Zia regime lasted for a decade, during which he implemented an Islamization campaign to reform Pakistani Islam to fit into a single uniform sectarian identity. This coincided with numerous destabilizing political events in the region. Foreign actors, mainly Saudi Arabia, Iran, and the United States, played significant roles in introducing and promoting religious militancy and a foreign ideology better suited for Zia's single-sectarian-identity model than our traditionally tolerant subcontinental[6] Islam. This impacted me personally.

My Personal Journey

I am a Shia and a Syed. The Syeds trace their lineage directly to Prophet Muhammad, Peace Be Upon Him. My full name, Syed Azhar Hussain Abidi, links me to the first Shia imam and fourth Islamic caliph, Ali ibn-Abi Talib. Ali was married to the Prophet's daughter Fatima. My childhood was devoted to learning my family heritage and understanding my role as a Pakistani, a Muslim, and a descendant of the Prophet Muhammad (PBUH). I've spent much of my life outside South Asia. Consequently, Western cultural, social, and political currents have influenced me. My primary identity is as a Muslim born in a Shia family.

My family had an indelible influence on me. When we were kids, we once chased and harassed a poor dog. A close relative saw this and told me, "You are a Syed. You must never hurt living things." This had a huge impact and was repeated throughout my childhood. Once, an uncle took me to an even older relative who compiled the information for our family tree, or *shajra*. I watched as he carefully wrote down our names in a thick book. Then, by drawing lines, he connected our names to previous and subsequent generations that reached Ali. Then the old man asked me to write my full name in Arabic. Then he said, "You are the son of Imam Ali. Do you know your profession?" No.

"Your profession is to do what our ancestors did, to protect Islam by thinking and to do good to others. You will learn and gain knowledge because that will protect you. You will be successful in what you put your mind to, but you will be most rewarded when you choose to do something that will benefit others, because that is what is written for the Syeds."

He asked me to recite a specific verse of the Quran and instructed me to recite it each day; the verse signifies the absolute oneness of God: "Indeed, Allah does not forgive association with Him, but He forgives what is less than that for whom He wills. And he who associates others with Allah has certainly gone far astray" (Al-Quran, Chapter 4 [An-Nisa]: Verse 116).[7]

Though I never saw that elder again, in January 2016 I took a twenty-two-hour train ride from Islamabad to Karachi to add my two children to our living family history, now safeguarded by his eldest son in a stark weathered house on the outskirts of the city. Hence, the formation of my Shia religious identity was very important. Growing up thinking that my link to the Prophet was clear, unbroken, and superior profoundly affected my thinking, identity, and worldview. Two views emerged from this.

I prayed and learned a "correct" history of Islam that put other Muslims in their place—which I understood as below me. This led to a narrow-minded attitude toward other Muslim groups. I was indoctrinated with a sense of superiority that my mosque, prayers, history, and imams represented the correct version and that Muslims who deviated from or denied them were less Islamic. I didn't join an extremist group but succumbed to the same religious current that now causes turmoil in our Muslim communities the world over.

Shias have always been a minority in Pakistan but were never so embattled until Zia took over. Though I was aware of the rich Islamic diversity in Pakistan and respected other traditions, I shamefully placed Muslims on different levels of authenticity. But they were still undeniably Muslim. Though my neighborhood was majority Sunni, they participated in Shia festivals and religious holidays. We were a harmonious community. When Shia mourners filled the streets of Karachi to honor the martyrdom of Imam Hussain,[8] Sunni youths provided cold water and sweet milk for the Shia procession, at the direction of their elders. Sunni leaders even addressed the large Shia gatherings. When the time came for Shia to mourn loudly and self-flagellate, Sunnis didn't participate—but did show reverence.

I mentioned that I attended a Sunni madrasa. That was simply because it was closer to home. That's how harmonious our communities were. A Shia would easily attend a Sunni mosque. My mom even sent me with a special curry dish and rose-scented drink for the Sunni imam. Once, a Shia imam made an unflattering comment about Hazrat Abu Bakr, the first caliph, whose election to the post became the proximate basis for division that ultimately split into Sunni and Shia sects. When I repeated the comment, my father reprimanded me, and I was taken to a Sunni mosque weekly for months to pray behind the imam and to pray the Sunni way. At my father's urging, the imam explained the virtues of the early caliphs, including Abu Bakr, Umar, and Usman. Soon I secretly began to question the narratives of my own Shia *zakirs* (preachers).

General Zia-ul-Haq Turns Pakistan Upside Down— and Changes the Face of Islam

> "Say, the Truth is from your Lord, let him who will believe, and let him who will reject."
> —Al-Quran, Chapter 18 [Al-Kahf]: Verse 29[9]

In 1977 Zia overthrew the elected head of state, the secular Zulfikar Ali Bhutto, father of future prime minister Benazir Bhutto. Bhutto was hanged in

1979. The coup marked the end of an era in Pakistan. The nascent democracy ushered in by Bhutto was flawed, so Zia, with the support of conservative imams, seized power. Zia felt threatened by religious minorities. Consequently, in collusion with conservative imams, Zia introduced Islamization policies—guided, aided, and financed by foreign powers—that soon engulfed Pakistan in extremist Islamic policies.

According to Zia's Islamic reforms, I belonged to a heterodox sect. The newly empowered conservative clerics decided we Shias were heretics. It soon became common for my previously very friendly schoolmates to badger me, saying that Shias were untrustworthy and weren't genuine Muslims. This happened within a short time.

Children would recite a litany of charges against Shias with the same zeal and meticulous detail that I proudly used when describing my exclusive religious ancestry. Subsequently my honored and cherished religious identity was now seen as a contaminant—to be isolated, quarantined, and removed from true and authentic Islam.

Imposition of faith is prohibited in the Quran, where God instructs Muhammad (PBUH) to spread the message of Islam without harassment and compulsion: "The Messenger's duty is but to proclaim [the message]. But Allah knoweth all that ye reveal and ye conceal" (Al-Quran, Chapter 5 [Al-Ma'idah]: Verse 99).[10] And "Now have come to you, from your Lord, proofs [to open your eyes]: if any will see, it will be for [the good of] his own soul; if any will be blind, it will be to his own [harm]: I am not [here] to watch over your doings" (Al-Quran, Chapter 6 [Al-An'nam]: Verse 104).[11]

Soon the military regime called on citizens to practice "true" Islam, which meant strict obedience to a literal interpretation of Islam. Zia was a follower of the teachings of Imam Hanafi, locally called Deobandis. He was awestruck by the gulf countries' interpretation of Islamic traditions. Hence he imposed religious versions practiced by the Arab monarchies. Gulf countries sought to purge Islam of Shia, Barelvi, and Sufi[12] influences through a literal interpretation of Islam known as Salafi Islam. Traditionally, Saudi Arabians inherited a legacy of discord with their Iranian neighbors in a way inconceivable to culturally tolerant South Asians. A great majority of Saudi citizens are Sunni, and a great majority of Muslims in Iran are Shia.

Those who fostered the Arab-versus-Iranian (Persian speaking and non-Arab) cultural clash found sectarian differences a convenient way to continue historical rivalries. Pakistan became a pawn in the conflict between Shia Iran and Sunni Saudi Arabia. When the Soviets took over Afghanistan, the United States had a newfound interest in Pakistani religious leaders and their institutions, urging them to get rid of the "godless Soviets."

The Shia-Sunni split is mainly political and goes back fourteen hundred years to the time when Abu Bakr was named the first caliph (Islamic ruler) after the death of the Prophet Muhammad (PBUH). Though the split is often explained as political, conservative Shia clergy believe that it is theological. Shia claim that Muhammad's son-in-law Ali should have been appointed as first caliph. Shia believe that the Prophet Muhammad (PBUH) appointed Ali as his successor, and hence Ali was wronged, which resulted in Islam being deprived of its rightful Islamic leadership from the start. Therefore "fully genuine Islam" is not being practiced by Muslims. This narrative was further reinforced among early Shias by subsequent events. Ali, then the fourth caliph, was assassinated, his oldest son, Hasan, was poisoned, and his other son, Hussain, was martyred along with his family and companions in Iraq. The entire family of the Prophet Muhammad (PBUH) was systematically massacred by sitting Islamic caliphs to consolidate political power and deny it to Ali and his followers. This is the narrative believed by Shia scholars.

Sunni Islam largely accepts the same historical events but does not share the Shia interpretation that the Prophet Muhammad (PBUH) named Ali as his successor and that there was a deliberate effort by early Muslim caliphs to strip Islamic leadership from him. Shia have also developed elaborate ceremonies and practices to remind the Muslim *ummah* of the injustices against and oppression of the Prophet's family. Once, in a conversation with me, a senior Shia clergyman[13] described this phenomenon as a religious movement to purify Islam from oppressive regimes. In his view, until the Muslim *ummah* acknowledges the past oppression of and injustices done to the Prophet's immediate family and their followers, the majority of Muslims will continue to support autocratic religious leaders.

Back to Pakistan and Zia, the Sunni-Shia conflict has flared when rulers found it useful. Zia accepted billions from the West and Arab countries in exchange for making Sunni the state religion and marginalizing other sects, while becoming their Cold War ally in fighting the Soviet invasion in Afghanistan. Mosques, madrasas, and Islamic political parties were supported in waging jihad (holy war) in neighboring Afghanistan against the Russian invaders. Eventually, millions of Afghan refugees poured into Pakistan. Ironically, the West originally armed and trained the mujahedeen (Islamic fighters) it is now fighting. These Islamic combatants fought the Russians and eventually evolved into al-Qaeda, the Taliban, and now various other extremist groups.

Zia merged the interests of the West and Arab countries since both feared the spread of Soviet influence in Central Asia and Iranian influence in the Muslim world. Pakistan received modern military equipment and lavish funds to distribute to madrasas willing to accept the conservative version of Islam, send their students to battle the "godless Soviets," and of course support Zia's Islamization. Pakistan also received oil from Saudi Arabia for almost nothing. Plus, Pakistanis were invited to work as domestic servants, construction workers, drivers, and laborers in the Arab kingdoms. This soon accounted for 80 percent of Pakistan's total foreign remittances.[14]

National narratives spread *fitna* (discord) among Pakistanis. Shias and Barelvis/Sufis were accused of practicing *shirk* (polytheism), which contradicts Muslims' understanding of *Tawhid* (the unique and unparalleled nature of God), which is fundamental to all Muslims. Zia peddled this constant campaign of misinformation about the sacrilege of Shias and Sufis through the religious sector and the schools. Sweeping changes were made to the national curriculum that included concepts of jihad and ridiculing and dehumanizing religious minorities. History was rewritten to make Pakistan an ultraconservative Islamic state. The Shia and Barelvis were now in danger of being systematically excluded by a rigid new Pakistani Muslim identity defined and promoted by the states that adhered to ultraconservative interpretations of Islam. Muslim leaders imposing their version of Islam forget that the Quran also says, "Say, 'The truth is from your Lord': Let him who will believe, and let him who will reject [it]" (Al-Quran, Chapter 18 [Al-Kahf]: Verse 29).[15]

The primary output of the Arab Pakistani partnership was a network of mosques, madrasas, imams, religious scholars, university chairs and departments, and political and religious organizations designed to promote "true" Islam. This network created an aggressive and conservative religious milieu, powerful enough to suppress dissent from civil society and moderate religious voices. Many Barelvi religious leaders felt enormous pressure to conform so they started to align with (not adapt to) the state-sponsored, ultraconservative Islamic identity. They now took part in *takfir* (declaring someone non-Muslim) of the Shia.

The Islamization narrative has been designed to forge a common collective Muslim identity along militaristic lines, assimilating the many into one. However, a collective Muslim identity already exists that is strengthened, not threatened, by diversity. There is amazing diversity within the Muslim community. Muslim identity must accept and celebrate these differences, or it becomes yet another inquisition—a sect with an identity structure too rigid to include most Muslims. Muslims should model Islamic behavior but never force the rituals of Islam upon others: "We know best what they say; and thou art not one to overawe them by force. So admonish with the Qur'an such as fear My Warning!"[16] (Al-Quran, Chapter 50 [Qaf]: Verse 45). And, "If it had been thy Lord's will, they would all have believed,—all who are on earth! wilt thou then compel mankind, against their will, to believe!"[17] (Al-Quran, Chapter 10 [Yunus]: Verse 99).

Survival Identity in a New Pakistan

Living through Zia's Islamization jolted my religious identity. Though at home my identity became even more orthodox, outside I faced hostility. I overheard whispers in my family about our safety and learned about violent clashes between Sunni and Shia in Karachi. I was pulled out of the Sunni mosque, and my imam refused my mom's curry—a dish he had previously loved. My religious education was now conducted under a Shia imam. My schoolmates betrayed me; I felt humiliated and alone. The mutual trust and friendship of my parents and their friends began weakening and collapsing.

Traditionally the Pakistani Shia community was aligned with the Grand Shia Imam of Najaf, Iraq. This distanced the Pakistani Shia from the Iranian Shia. But after Pakistan's relationship with Saudi Arabia strengthened, the Shia community tilted toward Shia religious scholars in Qom, Iran. The Pakistani Shia community began to sympathize strongly with and support the Iranian revolution of Ayatollah Ruholla Mussaui Khomeini, and Iran rewarded Pakistani Shia with resources and favors. Once just curious observers of the Middle East's sectarian conflicts, the Pakistani Shia began expressing open solidarity with Iran and started to organize political rallies demanding *Nifaz-e-Jafferia* for Shias (a Shia system for the Shia community). Zia now saw us as a potential threat. We became viewed as foreign agents with revolutionary aspirations. We had quickly become adversaries of the state.

During my last years in Pakistan, my mom sent her three sons to different places to observe Shia events. I later learned my mom feared violence and didn't want all three of us to die in a single attack. If a place was attacked or bombed, she'd lose just one son, not all three. Soon, we decided Pakistan was unsafe, and we left.

Immigrant in the United States

In 1970 my eldest brother was offered permanent residency in the United States. At first, my father angrily rejected this because he had sacrificed everything to come to Pakistan when Pakistan separated from India, and he expected his children to help build their new country. However, just as the paint began to dry on a pluralistic and inclusive Pakistan, it began chipping and fading. The climate was changing and the future darkening after the war with India in 1971 and the separation of East Pakistan, which became Bangladesh.

Hence my parents reluctantly gave my brother permission to emigrate. After the Ahmedi sect (founded in 1889) was legally denied Muslim status in 1974, my father, now completely hopeless, asked my brother to sponsor our family's emigration to the United States. My father wrote, "I see no safety for us, for your brothers or sisters. . . . I see increasing sectarian and ethnic prejudices will turn this country into a war zone. . . . You must do everything to bring my children to America. . . . No matter what happens we must always try to do something for this country. . . . When my children are educated let them come and serve Pakistan."

My father tragically died the day he wrote that letter. Characteristically his final thoughts were devoted to the safety of his family, fear of an uncertain future, the education of his children, and a reminder of our obligations as Muslims and Pakistanis. The work I do with my foundation today honors my father's last wishes and legacy. Soon after my father's death, a close cousin was shot and killed outside his home in a targeted killing by two religious extremists on a motorcycle. The shooters asked for his name and shouted, "Shia shia kaffir shia" (Shias are infidels) as they shot him. My family emigrated to the United States a few months later.

We settled in cold Rochester, New York, and I was overwhelmed by the social differences. Ironically American pop culture, miniskirts, and democracy were far less threatening than facing the loss of my Islamic identity in Pakistan and the constant burden of proving myself as a Muslim to the majority Sunni Muslims. American Muslims didn't care about my lineage and Shia identity. I was a Muslim. That was all that counted.

Sadly, I continued hearing about Shia doctors and professionals being targeted and murdered in Pakistan. I was drawn to identity issues and how Islam shapes understanding of the world. I pondered why Islam couldn't accept its own diversity. I prayed in numerous mosques and made friends with fellow Muslims from more sects than I knew existed. At Rutgers University in New Jersey I joined the Islamic Student Association and simultaneously lived in a Catholic House called Newman Center with two priests and three brothers training to be priests. I soaked up the diversity and often joined the brothers for church services.

In the United States, I freely practiced my Shia faith. I was again welcomed graciously and warmly in Sunni Muslim mosques. Meanwhile in Pakistan, a Shia would be taking his life in his hands by praying in a Sunni mosque. Hence it was remarkably refreshing not seeing the toxic divide among Muslims in the United States that I experienced in Pakistan. In the United States I was exposed to Muslim diversity and community. Subsequently my understanding of Muslim diversity grew exponentially.

I'd read the Quran in Arabic a few times but understood few verses. In the United States I read the Quran in English and gained a much deeper and broader understanding. Intrigued after reading about "people of the book," I joined a diverse group that met weekly to study the Torah and Bible. The futility of sectarian superiority was affirmed through Quranic verses like "Let there be no compulsion in religion: Truth stands out clear from Error"[18] (Al-Quran, Chapter 2 [Al-Baqarah]: Verse 256).

CHALLENGES

"Religious seminaries are not significant due to the number of jihadis they produce but are central to the production of the ideology that feeds the jihadi,

even if said jihadi is in fact educated in public schools and universities. The madressa denotes an essential power base that contributes ideology and the sustained supply of a narrative into society, which in turn, feeds both radicalism and militancy in Pakistan."[19]
—Dr. Ayesha Siddiqa

After establishing myself in the United States, I couldn't forget my heritage and my father's dying wish for me to return to Pakistan and contribute toward establishing a more peaceful and tolerant society. I wanted to accomplish this in the mosques and madrasas. To do this I had to overcome the following:

1. My own deeply held sectarian intolerance
2. Institutional intolerance in madrasas stemming from Western/secular demands for change
3. Macro-level sectarian intolerance created through Islamization

I had an awakening in the United States and discovered an Islam that embraced all sects and other faiths. Subsequently I consulted Sunni and Shia scholars in the United States for advice prior to engaging religious actors in Pakistan. I also consulted the Quran since I believed solutions must already be embedded in Islam and in Pakistani culture. I read as many reports and books on madrasas in Pakistan as I could and found most studies concluded that madrasas were extremist, backward, and sponsors of terror.

In Pakistan, I entered a society where students had been trained to correct perceived religious transgressions. In some areas students caught clean-shaven men and beat them up for not having a beard. Barbershops were attacked. Women drivers were sometimes dragged from their cars and beaten because they were driving. Music shops were burned. Targeted killings of Shia professionals continued. Sufi shrines were bombed. Large-scale attacks on Shia mosques and suicide bombings of communities by well-organized terrorist groups like Lashkar-e-Jangvi (a Sunni supremacist and jihadi militant organization) and Sipah-e-Sahabah (an extremist Sunni organization) occurred. My extended family in Pakistan was targeted. Almost every relative of mine lost a son in targeted murders. Many of my wife's cousins were murdered by Sipah-e-Sahabah in Karachi during the 1990s.

Mosques and madrasas that promoted intolerance were rewarded. Those that promoted peace and tolerance were shouted down or silenced. Religious leaders who attempted reconciliation were excluded and accused of being Western or Iranian sympathizers. Soon extremist groups roamed openly since no one dared counter their violent interpretation of Islam.

I saw how madrasa leaders felt threatened and understood their feelings of being used by their state and other nations. Religious institutions were isolated and abused by the British colonial powers and treated by their own country as second-class citizens. They were compelled to fight Russians in Afghanistan and Indian military in Kashmir. Madrasa students and religious leaders were rewarded by the United States and Saudi Arabia as long as they supported their strategic and ideological goals. Particularly, the United States provided enormous support to arm and finance Islamic madrasas fighting in Afghanistan during the Soviet invasion (1979–1989).[20] To say that madrasa leaders hold grievances toward their own government and international community would be understating the depth of angst they feel. With no confidence in their government and repeatedly exploited by Western governments, madrasas turned inward and became staunchly independent. They not only mistrust their own government but actively teach their students never to trust outsiders (politicians, international governments, nongovernmental organizations).

In order to maintain their independent status, madrasas refused any sort of Pakistani state funding or oversight, relying on donations from the public, foreign financial support from different Islamic countries through different channels,[21] the *zakat* tax (collected to support the poor), and other charitable gifts, a practice of financial independence from the government that has continued to this day. Thus, the madrasas became independent institutions trapped in time by their own insular theology, generally incapable of producing graduates able to relate to the ever-evolving context in Pakistan and the outside world. Furthermore, sectarian ideologies are often taught in a way that leaves little room for the understanding or acceptance of other sects, religions, or cultures. This approach tends to produce graduates who are ill equipped to deal with the challenges of modernity, have few economic opportunities, and may be susceptible to manipulation by violent ideologues.

What if I tell you that religious institutions, including madrasas, are not backward and extremist? Can all this stem from outrage against Western elites and like-minded people who have been responsible for so much unfairness and have alienated so many via their foreign policies, manufactured wars, and large-scale scapegoating of Muslims as violent?

Religious militancy was first introduced into the madrasa curriculum and education system during the late 1980s and early 1990s at the Education Center for Afghanistan, located in Peshawar, Pakistan. This center, operated by the mujahideen (holy warrior) groups fighting against the Soviets in Afghanistan, published a series of textbooks that aimed to indoctrinate a new generation of holy warriors to wage war against the perceived enemies of Islam. With the support of the University of Nebraska at Omaha's Education Sector Support Project, funded by the United States Agency for International Development, the center made a significant contribution to the Afghan education system both in Afghanistan and in refugee camps in Pakistan by developing a curriculum for primary levels (1–12) and training the teachers.

Craig Davis[22] has documented the systemic fusion of hatred and militancy within the madrasa curriculum, observing that the promotion of violence was not confined to ideological sections of the curriculum but was also present in subjects such as mathematics and the study of language. As an example, he quotes the following excerpt from a fourth-grade textbook taught in Pakistani madrasas: "The speed of a Kalashnikov bullet is 800 meters per second. If a Russian is at the distance of 3,200 meters from a mujahid [fighter], and the mujahid aims at the Russian's head, calculate how many seconds it will take for the bullet to strike the Russian."

Historical wounds, perceived injustices, and Western colonial subjugation[23] have created a "culture of victimhood" that has effectively isolated madrasa leaders from much of the outside world. Fearful that new ideas and interacting with others may lead to the loss of their religious and cultural identity, some instinctively reject modernization and the concept of coexistence as a form of Western imperialism. Conditioned by decades of fear, many madrasa teachers and administrators have reached the point where opposing others and living in conflict have become an integral part of their identity. This environment of hostility is preserved as these ideas are passed on to the students and their communities.

In the United States I see indignation from women, immigrant communities, and Black Lives Matter protesters. As the West with its excesses begins to victimize its own citizens, we ought to ponder extremism brewing in the American homeland. Then perhaps we can start to grapple with the madrasa leaders' reluctance to imitate Western-style ideals of modernization.

In more than ten years of working with madrasa leaders, I have found that most religious leaders, unlike the common perception, understand the need to improve madrasa education, but they are unwilling to take Western dictation on these matters. Instead, they support an internal reform process for promoting peace and tolerance and for improving education standards in madrasas. For any genuine change to happen in madrasas, the religious leaders are the ones who must bring that change. All we can do is to find ways to engage them in a discussion, in a process that can reduce their fear of being "used" for political purposes by the West and by their own "secularist" countrymen.

RESPONSES

Recapturing a History of Excellence

Not so much time has passed since Islamic educational institutions, including madrasas, mosques, and universities, achieved countless and notable accomplishments. Madrasas from Andalusia (the southern region of Spain) to the Indian subcontinent trained great thinkers in science, math, philosophy, and medicine while maintaining a firm religious base. These institutions were also centers for preserving and promoting the knowledge and works of the great classical empires of Greece, Rome, Persia, and Gallic Spain. Encouragement of independent reasoning, or *ijtihad*, was a main characteristic of those madrasas.

Many of the great innovations came from Middle Eastern madrasas during the Abbasid period (750–1258), including early ideas on evolution, important contributions to the philosophy of science, the first forms of non-Aristotelian logic, and the introduction of temporal, modal, and inductive logic. Such advances played a central role in the subsequent development of European logic during the Renaissance. Indeed, throughout the Middle Ages, Christian scholars traveled to the Islamic world to study the advanced knowledge available in the madrasas. The very first college in Europe, that of Paris, was founded by Jocius de Londoniis, a pilgrim newly returned from the Middle East.[24]

Al-Azhar University in Cairo, one of the oldest and greatest madrasas, has good claim to being the most sophisticated institution of learning in the entire Mediterranean world during the early Middle Ages. The very idea of a university in the modern sense—a place of learning where students congregate to study a variety of subjects under many subject-matter teachers—is generally regarded as an innovation first developed at Al-Azhar. Even concepts such as having "fellows" holding a "chair" or students "reading" a subject and obtaining "degrees," as well as practices such as inaugural lectures, the oral defense, and even mortar boards, tassels, and academic robes, can all be traced to the past practices of madrasas.

Madrasa Al-Quaraouiyine, now Al-Quaraouiyine University, in Fez, Morocco, established in 859 by a woman named Fatima al-Fihri, was the first degree-granting institution in the world, according to the United Nations Educational, Scientific, and Cultural Organization[25] and the *Guinness Book of World Records*.[26] The great Jewish scholar and reformist Maimonides was an alumnus of Al-Quaraouiyine. Given the distinguished history of the madrasa education system, it is not too late to recapture its excellence.

How We Do What We Do

I established the Peace and Education Foundation in Pakistan because the religious leaders of Pakistan are the key to bringing peace to this region. Thus far we have been able to engage more than twelve thousand religious leaders in Pakistan. And demand for our programs exceeds supply by a huge margin. Given adequate resources, we believe madrasas could be put back on the path of their historical excellence.

The PEF effort to enhance madrasa education and promote social change in Pakistan is based on the following assumptions:

- Building relationships of trust and understanding different perspectives is more important than changing minds and hearts.
- It is necessary to faithfully develop a holistic approach of proprietorship (buy-in) within Pakistani religious leadership, integrating modern disciplines by applying Islamic principles of tolerance, critical thinking, and scholarship.
- Based on past experiences and perceptions, Islamic religious leadership in general mistrusts the West and secular reform approaches to Islamic institutions.
- Social change will be more sustainable if the individuals and communities most affected assume a high degree of ownership in the content and implementation of new programs and policies.
- Despite the trust deficit created by Western interventions, genuine engagement and exchanges of coreligionists (Muslim scholars and clergy) from the West and Islamic countries can support better understanding between Islam and the West.

The PEF madrasa education model is simple. We ground all our programs in understanding the historical accomplishments of Muslim scholars and their contributions to the modern world. In our first session, we celebrate the magnificent triumphs of Muslims who benefited the world—and even helped transform Western civilization—as described above. We delve deeply into Islamic history with the madrasa leaders in Pakistan and elicit key elements that were present in creating the environment that produced influential scholars and great institutions of learning. Madrasa leaders quickly highlight many of the same virtues we find in "modern" societies, such as independent thinking, reflective and critical thinking, and exposure to other scholars, cultures, and languages.

Our next session is a discussion about education in the Islamic world today. Madrasa leaders are, at this point, eager to talk about the weaknesses in their curricula and institutional and management systems. They want to know how they can bring back the qualities present when Islamic education was creating great scholars and innovations. One madrasa leader commented in a consultation meeting with PEF held in Islamabad, "We will be modern if we go back five hundred years." We then move into activities that explore the definition of education and discuss critical thinking skills, teaching tolerance to students, conflict transformation, religious freedom, and Islam and diversity. Madrasa leaders and teachers are asked to create realistic action plans that will enable them to transfer what they have learned to their students. The majority have already started teaching English, math, and social sciences.

Madrasa teachers and religious leaders who took our workshops said they wanted to understand Pakistani religious minorities and their grievances:

Christians, Sikhs, and Hindus. We created an interfaith dialogue project and have conducted more than fifty interfaith workshops, which trained over two thousand leaders in Pakistan. We have created twenty-five teams of Interfaith Champions, involving Muslim, Hindu, and Christian clergy. Together they conduct interfaith dialogue workshops within their communities, celebrate Christian Christmas, Hindu Diwali, and Muslim Eid festivities in each other's places of worship, and serve as a preventive team against interreligious/ intersectarian conflicts. These clergy have also intervened in more than ten violent outbreaks of interreligious conflicts where Muslim mobs have advanced toward Christian or Hindu communities. In the past, similar mobs have burned down minority villages and slaughtered minorities.

After participating in our interfaith dialogue workshops, madrasa leaders and teachers have asked us to provide them with opportunities for further professional development similar to that offered in universities. Based on their requests, we have set up the University Teachers Training Certificate Program for Religious Educators. The forty-eight-hour certificate course is now being taught in six universities across Pakistan. Our alumni also insisted that PEF create a peace textbook that teaches madrasa students peacemaking, tolerance, and interfaith dialogue skills. We created a team of religious leaders and developed a textbook called *Peace Education and Islam*.[27]

The textbook was endorsed by all influential madrasa boards, including Shia, Barelvi, Deobandi, Salafi, and Jamat-e-Islami, covering twenty-six thousand madrasas and 3.2 million students. Further, because our alumni consistently urged PEF to engage the top madrasa leadership, we began to work with those same madrasa boards toward longer-term collaboration. Only those boards can systematically change policies to integrate modern standards, provide teacher training, and reform curricula. Thus, we have worked together with the madrasa boards to create the Best Practice Madrasa Enhancement Project. Through this project, the capacity building of madrasa teachers is being enhanced in classroom management, critical thinking skills, leadership and management skills, conflict resolution, and resilience against extremist narratives.

We partnered with Turkish and Egyptian governments and religious bodies and exposed Pakistani madrasa board leaders extensively to the Egyptian and Turkish religious education systems. Based on this work, the madrasa boards agreed to train their religious teachers in teaching modern subjects, by setting up teacher-training centers within each board headquarters. The training centers will be used for professional development of religious teachers and imams based on the rigorous standards being created by a committee of religious leaders and the PEF. The madrasa boards also requested that we start an Imam Professional Development Project, through which more than one thousand imams have been trained in intra- and interfaith reconciliation, resilience, messaging, peaceful sermons, and our peace textbook.

CONCLUSION

The enemies of *ummah* (the Muslim community throughout the world) are bigotry, isolation, ethnocentric attitudes, and the lack of continuous dialogue—not diversity or disagreement. The preeminent Shia religious authority, Ayatollah Ali al-Sistani, said, "Islamic education does not consist of any one or more subjects. Islamic education is every subject that enhances knowledge, serves humanity, and advances societies."[28] He goes further to say, "If teaching *deeni talim* [Islamic subjects: Hadith, *fiqh*, Islamic jurisprudence, etc.] leads to conflict, does not contribute to positive social development or destroys peace with others, then those cannot be considered *Islamic subjects*."

Madrasas in Pakistan safeguard their Islamic identity from Western exposure because of historical grievances, colonial subjugation of Muslims and their lands, and their perception of the West as a continuing threat for Muslims and Islamic identity. While Pakistani madrasas have come under great criticism, particularly in the West, for spreading radicalization and broadcasting anti-West sentiments, they have demonstrated an openness to change and a desire to incorporate thoughtful modifications into their curricula to include social sciences, critical thinking, and peace studies with our project of madrasa enhancement in Pakistan.

Western policymakers interested in working with Islamic religious leaders and their institutions should create pathways to sustain engagement in a manner that genuinely exhibits Western respect for Muslims and their faith; this can occur at Western diplomatic missions in Islamic countries. While madrasa leaders are very cautious about direct Western approaches, they welcome meeting with coreligionists from the West. The United States and Europe can bring together madrasa leaders from Islamic countries to meet and share best practices with Islamic scholars in the West and eventually expand that engagement to Christian, Jewish, and other faith leaders. Theology departments of Western universities can also sponsor exchanges with madrasas and expand that to interfaith collaboration efforts between the Islamic world and the West.

Perhaps the most important aspect of building long-term trust with Islamic leaders and madrasas would be for Western countries to champion the rightful aspirations of Islamic madrasas to educate Muslim generations to be good Muslims.

NOTES

1. Holy Quran, Yusuf Ali Translation (London: Wordsworth, 2000).
2. This chapter explains how religious identities were pitched against each other for political reasons and to satisfy foreign interests. My views are general and at times sweeping because

they reflect a highly complex historical context through the lens of my own experience. However, I am not certain that the situation in Pakistan would differ if the demographics were reversed, such that political power and resources were controlled by Shia Muslims. A Shia majority might also have the potential for intolerance.

3. Shia is the second-largest branch of Islam.

4. Yusuf Ali Translation.

5. "Muhammad Ali Jinnah's First Presidential Address to the Constituent Assembly of Pakistan (August 11, 1947)," Columbia University, http://www.columbia.edu/itc/mealac/pritchett/00islamlinks/txt_jinnah_assembly_1947.html, accessed May 17, 2017.

6. "Subcontinent" refers to India, Bangladesh, and Pakistan.

7. Sahih International Translation (https://quran.com, accessed May 29, 2017).

8. Imam Hussain is the grandson of the Prophet Muhammad (PBUH). He is the son of 'Ali ibn Abi Talib (the fourth Rashid caliph of Sunni Islam and the first Shi'a Imam) and Fatimah, daughter of the Prophet Muhammad (PBUH). Imam Hussain was martyred in Karbala along with his family, children, and companions.

9. Yusuf Ali Translation.

10. Ibid.

11. Ibid.

12. The Barelvis are Sunni Muslims who follow the Hanafi school of jurisprudence and are influenced by Sufi mystical practices. Though they are Sunnis, some Barelvi practices are seen as closer to Shia religious practices.

13. Name withheld out of respect for the individual.

14. Muhammad Sohaib, "The Contributions of Our Workers Abroad," *Express Tribune*, April 14, 2013, https://tribune.com.pk/story/535577/the-contributions-of-our-workers-abroad, accessed January 20, 2017.

15. Yusuf Ali Translation.

16. Ibid.

17. Ibid.

18. Ibid.

19. Dr. Ayesha Siddiqa, "The Madressa Mix: Genesis and Growth," *Dawn*, March 30, 2015, https://www.dawn.com/news/1166039, accessed February 28, 2017.

20. Peter Bergen, *Holy War Inc.* (New York: Free Press, 2001).

21. Khaled Ahmed, *Sectarian War: Pakistan's Sunni-Shia Violence and Its Links to the Middle East* (Oxford: Oxford University Press, 2011), 132.

22. Craig Davis, "'A' Is for Allah; 'J' Is for Jihad," *World Policy Journal* 19 (2002): 90–94.

23. As a result of colonial subjugation, many popular Islamic scholars who lived through Western colonial imperialism, such as Abul A'la Maududi and Hassan Banna, developed enormous Islamic movements through their Islamic scholarship and literature. Their overarching Islamic narrative—warning against the evils of secularism and Western-style modernity—still lives in the collective Muslim consciousness. Maududi and Hasan Banna, respectively, founded Jamat-e-Islami and the Muslim Brotherhood and were raised under colonial British rule.

24. William Dalrymple, "Inside the Madrassa, Part 2," *Interreligious Insight*, October 2006, originally published in the *New York Review of Books* 52, no. 19 (December 1, 2005), http://www.interreligiousinsight.org/October2006/Dalrymple10-06.pdf.

25. "Medina of Fez," UNESCO.org, http://whc.unesco.org/en/list/170, accessed April 5, 2017.

26. "Oldest University," Guinness World Records, http://www.guinnessworldrecords.com/world-records/oldest-university, accessed April 5, 2017.

27. See PEF publications at http://www.peaceandeducationfoundation.org.

28. "Special Address by Maulana Kalbe Sadiq—Aligarh Muslim University," video posted to YouTube by CPECAMI AMU, April 20, 2015, https://www.youtube.com/watch?v=In4-gJBR5Y8, accessed April 5, 2017.

Chapter Six

"Dili sayon ang pag sunod kang Kristo" (It is not easy to follow Christ)

The Road to Peace Is a Rocky One

Maria Ida (Deng) Giguiento with Myla Leguro

Challenge: How do you respond to actors who endorse the use of violence as a means to resolve their conflicts with other groups?

I am a Christian, a follower of the Prince of Peace. In my heart and mind, I do believe that a Christian should be a peacebuilder in his or her own way— big or small—that the way to reach the ideal "Christian peacebuilder" is a work in progress; it is never perfected, and that is why I pray always. I keep myself and others who work for peace in my prayers, day and night. Being a Christian peacebuilder opens my mind to other peacebuilders who are basing their work for peace also in their own faith traditions. Often, in their midst, I close my eyes and feel the Spirit in me.

So when I go and facilitate trainings, I know that I am doing the work for my God in creating a more peaceful world.

In Mindanao, located in the southern Philippines, this is where I really reflect on the words in the Bible: there is "a time for war, and a time for peace" (to everything there is a season, Ecclesiastes 3:8).[1] I have been work-ing for change since 1983. In the past, what I would fondly call "in my other life," I spent years as an activist who only knew one way of bringing about change—to topple those in power in an armed revolution. It took years of working and studying with the Mennonites and the Maryknolls to change my perspective. I saw working for change as the more challenging task of under-standing the "violent other" (in myself and in others), in talking rather than fighting, in managing anger and channeling energies from destruction to constructive engagements. In short, my perspectives and advocacies changed from engaging in and espousing violent armed revolution to bring about change to adopting nonviolent responses to violent situations.

In Mindanao, where cycles of war and stretches of peace mark our seasons, with a number of natural calamities thrown into our midst in between, I find myself always on my toes, ready to respond to any need of any of our partner communities—always wearing my "Christian peacebuilding trainer" hat in whatever scenario I am in. During times of war, I turn into a "phone pal," with my listening ear lent to my peace students coming from different sides of the conflict, partners in the field, and even community village officials. In times of peace, I turn into a mentor, accompanier, trainer, and process facilitator for those who are willing to learn, speak, and do peace. In times of calamity, I turn into an aid worker, always conscious of doing no harm to the people impacted by disasters.

I guess my biggest challenge in working in Mindanao is to always be attuned to what is happening and be ready to step in, in any role that would be of help to many of my people. This has meant working in close quarters with armed groups, including the military actors that I long avoided and feared. And this is difficult. The military is a sector that I avoid and fear because of the stories of killing and maiming that I often overheard when they came to visit my father. I heard their stories as they laughed and ate and drank beer, as if killing and maiming were normal. I also had an experience of being held at the point of military guns during the course of my work in the 1980s.

FOUNDATIONS

Early Days

My maternal grandfather had two wives—a Catholic wife and a Muslim (of the Maguindanao-Iranon tribes) wife. My mother is of the Catholic wife. I was born, baptized, educated, and raised as a Catholic. I hold my Catholic values and beliefs close to my heart. While this was true, as a young girl I had Muslim playmates. We would eat in each other's houses and respect each other's cultures. Teaching me the importance of respect, my mom used to say we had to boil all utensils, plates, bowls, and cups we had used before we could invite our Muslim friends to use the same. This was to erase any trace of pork or lard, in respect for the Islamic tradition of not eating pork. She learned this from her *Babo* (the Maguindanawon term for "aunt"), her father's Muslim wife.

I spent my elementary and high school days focused on my studies, reading through all the books in the library by grade five. I was allowed to borrow books from the high school library to keep my interest in reading. One particular event stood out.

During my last year of high school, I served as the year-level representative. I remember, together with some of the student council officers, leading a strike in the school run by religious sisters. It was simply over the fact that the school did not honor a practice that when a holiday falls on a weekend, the following Monday is declared a holiday. I remember, with the student body in assembly, waiting and waiting for an announcement from the school, but it did not happen. So we organized a sit-down strike from kindergarten to fourth-year high school to gain the administrator's attention. After the flag ceremony, we did not enter our classrooms; we sat on the field. I remember the sisters and teachers calling me aside and appealing to me to reconsider, calling the wrath of God on my head! I remember not budging, saying that God understood why I was doing what I was doing. One key person in the school, an elementary student who was the leader of the young girls, was a Muslim. We coordinated in managing to keep everyone sitting down and not moving into their classrooms, despite the teachers' urging. I remember that weeks after that event, we caught up in the school cafeteria, and we chatted like the strike was just "one of the things we had to do as students."

I also remember going to confession after this, and I remember the priest laughing and congratulating me. This was my first confusion about the teachings of the church and how the religious put different interpretations on these teachings. How come the sisters (religious sisters) scolded me for what I did and this priest (a religious priest) said I had done right? I decided to keep my relationship with my God private—between my God and myself.

After high school, I found myself taking a step back. I focused on my studies and finished my college degree. After passing the board exam, I asked my parents for a "year off" and stayed in the northern part of the country. It was still during Ferdinand Marcos's martial law days, and I wanted to be of help to the people who I perceived were being victimized by the state.

Practicing Resistance

In those days, the face of the state was the military. It was a very strong and fierce face. It was a very violent face. In those days, I felt that there was no way one could speak out—on the violent dispersal of rallies, the loss of lives, the disappearances, the signs of torture—and not fear for his or her life. And most often, the people being victimized by the state were the marginalized.

There I experienced working with the urban poor, the working class, the youth, the women. I experienced being with them in their homes, workplaces, and streets. Often there was no mention of God in our conversations. And yet, I felt the rosary beads in my pocket and whispered the prayer in my heart. During those times, when I was a young activist, the military and the political administration were often painted as "the enemy" for me.

One violent incident that made a huge impact on me as an activist happened when one of the labor leaders was stabbed. The wounded leader's family and I had to rush him to the hospital. His family had no money. Back then, the hospital wouldn't treat patients with no money. I ran to the nearest bank to withdraw money from the bank account where my parents deposited my allowance. I withdrew money and went to the hospital and paid some bills as a form of deposit. I remember my conversation with the wife after I did this.

> Wife: Where did you get the money? Did you steal?
> Me: No, I got it from my own bank account
> Wife: You have a bank account? Who are you? Why are you here?

I realized that I had not been totally honest with the family, because in the context of martial law, being honest meant risking discovery and arrest. I was nervous and lit up one of my seemingly endless cigarettes.

> Me: I have just graduated from college, and I want to experience what you are experiencing because I need to, I want to.
> Wife: No wonder you smoke too much. How much to do you spend for your smoking?

(Back then, I was smoking Philip Morris. I was consuming three packs a day, and each pack cost around twenty pesos then. A pack now costs eighty pesos or roughly $2.)

> Me: Between sixty and seventy pesos a day.
> Wife: That could feed my family three meals a day.

I quit smoking right there and then.

That evening, I remember sitting in front of the Blessed Sacrament in the tiny chapel in that urban poor area, tears falling down my cheeks as I grappled with the realities in my life. I had a nice home to go back to; I had support from my parents; I had a career in front of me. What about these people? The song of Brother Karl Gaspar kept running through my head:

> Ang hagit sa Ebanghelyo alang kanako [The challenge of the Gospel for me]
> Higugma-on ta ang atong isig-katawo [Is to love each other].

I refused to go on with the song because I did not like what the words were challenging me to do.

After that day, until the day I left their community, I would go to their home and give them my "smoking money" for their meal. I have never smoked a cigarette again to this date.

I knew in my heart I was becoming more and more involved with the issues of my people. I learned a lot about doing justice. I was strongly advocating and working for justice with indigenous peoples, with laborers and farmers, with youth. I knew about the work for justice, but I did not know how to build peace. And in my heart, I knew my God was asking me to work for justice and to help build peace.

Learning from Islam

One time, as I was spending some time with Muslim relatives during the month of Ramadhan, I felt humbled by their expression of their faith. They fasted, and they prayed five times a day. I knew that. I knew it was happening. But during that time, I asked myself if I was even half as committed as they were in religiously praying and fasting. I was fasting, yes, but my prayer life was still wanting. Then my *Bapa* (uncle) and I had a conversation after the *iftar*. He asked me about prayers. I showed him my rosary beads and told him I pray every morning and night. He nodded. Then he asked me some more about prayers. I said I went to mass every Sunday and on holy days and whenever I could. He nodded. He asked if I ever thought of praying not only whenever I could but really devoting time to prayer, consciously and with discipline. I kept quiet. He patted me on my shoulders and stood up. My uncle was a commander of the Moro National Liberation Front (MNLF).[2] He always held a gun, and he prayed a lot.

Since then, I have been keeping time in the mornings and evenings and even during lunchtimes for conscious prayers. I remember that I did that in the later part of my "other life," which clashed with the ideologies I held then.

One image that also kept coming to my mind is that of soldiers with rosary beads in their hands or around their guns when they go to the battle-field. I asked one why that is so. He said he prays that he will not be killed in the war, that God will protect him and bring him safely back to the camp, and if he gets killed, that God will forgive him for all his transgressions. This was when I realized that I had been bringing my rosary beads with me as a "talisman," like an amulet that wards off evil spirits. I realized that I had been relying on the rosary beads to protect me from any negative events, instead of relying on the love of the God I believed in. I began to change my prayer life. I began to seriously believe that I was doing God's work here on earth, and knowing that, I resigned myself to God's will and, if my life is taken, ask for God to be kind to me, his humble servant.

CHALLENGES

Buried in Books

In Mindanao, from the 1960s to the present, cycles of manmade violence involving the struggles of both Moro (Muslim) separatists and the Communist New People's Army, the ongoing effort to secure justice for indigenous peoples, and the regularity of natural disasters such as typhoons have made peacebuilding challenging. I grew up in a city where government soldiers used to pass by our house to go to war with the MNLF just across a river called Cacar, which was near our house. I grew up in a house full of guns. My father taught me how to fire guns and to fire accurately at targets. I grew up in a home full of my father's friends—generals and foot soldiers. And often, the conversation was about how one defeated the enemy in a gun battle, or what preparations were being made for another battle, or how to defeat the other in a political campaign.

I knew then that in many Christian and Muslim homes, this was not the norm. I had seen someone being tortured. I had seen two dead bodies tied to coconut trees. I had seen a cut-off leg being buried. I had seen brutality at a young age. My coping mechanism was to withdraw myself into my books. I buried my head in books and the world of make-believe. My comfort zone was sitting on a soft chair and reading a good story. I remember reading a book on St. Francis, and to this date I don't know why I was drawn to that book except that I earmarked the page where he gave his father everything and walked out naked into the streets, singing acclamation of the Lord.

Joining the Revolution

Violence had been part of my younger life and I believe also the lives of the young people in my city of Cotabato then. In school, we were cushioned, but outside school, in our homes and in our environment, there were tanks and guns. There was talk of how bad the "other" was, and thus the "other" deserved to be killed. The "other" for the Christians means the Blackshirts (who happen to be Muslims), and for the Muslims, the Ilagas (who happen to be ethnically Ilonggo-Christians).

Prejudice, hatred, and mistrust of the "other" were the dominant attitudes in society then. We were only friends inside the school. There we laughed and learned together, played and studied, and did class performances together, Muslims and Christians. Even our parents, when they came to school for meetings and social functions, would greet and chat with each other. However, outside the school grounds, I noticed that our families were merely civil to each other—they would seldom mix or socialize.

I felt so fortunate that I fell in with a group of friends who believed there was a need to respect, recognize, and reach out to the "other." I really felt that was the world for me.

It was for political reasons of course. Joining forces with the "other" could create a more potent political alliance against the Marcos regime. But then a number of religiously motivated people started thinking also in religious terms—empathizing, journeying with, experiencing the situation of the other—and the group Duyog Ramadhan (Joining the Ramadhan) for Christians was formed. It was composed of Christians who fasted and prayed with the Muslim community during the holy month of Ramadhan. It extended even beyond Ramadhan in the sense that when something happened to a Muslim community, this group of Christians would go and help in whatever way they could. I believe this paved the way for me to work both with state groups (soldiers and police, who happen to be mostly Christians) and non-state actors (who happen to be mostly Muslims).

Personal Trauma

I still can feel the cold muzzles of the guns pointed at my tummy, years back, in a dark place called the "killing fields," and the laughing faces of the guys in uniform with their names and ranks stripped from their uniforms, seemingly drunk as they told my companions to leave me behind. This happened when I joined a fact-finding mission organized by a nearby diocese. The team was trying to reach base while it was still daylight. One military contingent we passed on our way back delayed us until sundown by asking us a lot of questions. Then they let us go. We deliberated about whether to proceed or not, knowing we would be passing the strip of land with no houses around, known as the "killing fields." We decided to proceed and were asked to stop by uniformed men. They asked us to disembark. We assigned one person to negotiate for us, but unfortunately the person lost his cool. I pulled him back and put him in the middle of the team. When I turned around to face the men in uniform, that was when I felt the muzzles of the guns around my tummy. I still have nightmares about that night.

Still Seeking Healing

Now in the present, I ask myself, Are we peoples of Mindanao healed as a people? We do not openly express our biases and prejudices against each other. We have learned a hard lesson—if we are divided as a people, nothing good will happen in Mindanao. We have to be united. However, whenever a trigger goes off (a killing, an ambush, even the proposed Bangsamoro Basic Law),[3] biased statements and prejudicial actions rear their ugly heads. We have to recognize we are not yet totally healed. We have to recognize we are all works in progress. We have to recognize we have to help each other heal.

It is easy to pick up a gun and shoot. It is difficult to restrain one's self, sit patiently, and talk through our conflicts.

RESPONSES

The Mindanao Peacebuilding Institute Experience

In my work as a trainer in peacebuilding, I have had the opportunity to train men and women in uniform (state actors) and others (nonstate actors). As a facilitator at the Mindanao Peacebuilding Institute (MPI),[4] I was involved in training armed people from different sides of the conflict in peacebuilding from 2005 to 2010. I was also involved in training trainers to build more capacity for other organizations to do this kind of work. State and nonstate actors participated alongside other peacebuilders in some trainings, and some trainings were done exclusively for one group.

The openness of the government, under Gloria Macapagal Arroyo, in supporting the peace talks between the government and nonstate actors facilitated the engagement of civil society organizations in promoting an environment of dialogue with armed groups. We at MPI made a conscious decision then to help our own people. It was not for the soldiers; it was not for the nonstate actors. It was for our own people—so that they would not be pulled to the left and to the right when a battle was fought between armed groups. We knew that in order to do that, we also had to deal with our own fears, biases, and prejudices and directly engage with these two groups. I was assigned, as the senior peacebuilding trainer, do lead this endeavor.

And it was a challenge. I had to face my own fears and deal with my own trauma at the hands of the military. There was also the challenge of being accused of collaborating with the rebels if one engaged with them. At that time, many people thought we were a bunch of crazy folks: "Soldiers are primed to kill. Do you think you can turn them into peacebuilders?" At one training, I had more than a hundred chaplains (from Catholic, Protestant, evangelical, and Islamic faith traditions) in two batches. Here I was confronted with the statement "I am a soldier first and foremost, before I am a chaplain." This statement made me feel so sad that I cried. The bishop-ordinary cried with me.

My first engagement with government armed forces was within the "safe space" of the Mindanao Peacebuilding Institute. Officers enrolled in the classes that I cofacilitated. With their civilian classmates, the officers were relaxed and were seen and experienced as "just one of the students." As a facilitator, I would often put the soldiers in roles other than soldiers during simulations (in a kind of role-playing for at least two hours in a given conflict scenario). In one class, one officer became the head of the revolutionary group, while another was the media person. I remember during the debriefing session, when students were asked to express their first thoughts after getting their roles, how they prepared for their roles, and how they felt when they were acting out their roles, the officer who acted as the head of the revolutionary group shook his head and said, "Please, I don't want to share anything right now," and his classmates did not force him to talk. After the class, the officer came up to me and asked for some private time. We talked for at least an hour. He was crying, and I held his hand. What we talked about is private at this point in time. The impact on me was to see the human face of the armed man who is only seen as the one holding the gun and pointing this at another.

The one who played a member of the media said, "I am finding myself opening up and beginning to be more tolerant towards the media. I often called them 'pesky flies,' but during the simulation, I began to understand why media had to get to the bottom of what is happening and why they expose things left and right."

Back and Forth

Juggling training schedules is difficult when armed groups request training in "conflict resolution." Their schedules are tight, so when they requested training on certain dates, we felt we had to grab the opportunity to spread the concepts and skills of conflict transformation, dialogue, mediation, and, yes, even peacebuilding. I remember cofacilitating a conflict resolution workshop for the mid-level leadership of a nonstate armed group in one area, when the government armed group sent a text message asking if I could be available for their workshop the following day. Our team had a huddle, and it was decided that I would do day one for the nonstate actors, leave the area toward the end of the day, and travel to the government camp. Then I would do the one-day training with the military. On day three, I would leave the military camp very early so that I could rejoin the team with the nonstate actors and resume facilitating on day three.

So on day one with the nonstate actors, they sat there, silently, folding their arms. I sensed that for everything that was presented, a man seated at the back of the room had to be consulted; when he nodded, they smiled and nodded back at me. The men were very eager, though, to play games (which I use to teach concepts). I remember asking someone during lunchtime, "Do you feel uncomfortable without your gun?" He smiled and shook his head: "We were assured that there was no need for our guns because we will be the only ones in this venue, and there are forces around securing us." Frankly speaking, that made *me* nervous.

Later that day, I traveled to facilitate the conflict resolution workshop in one of the military camps. I would be sleeping there for two nights. I remember the commanding officer commenting on my attire, which was a shalwar kameez (an Indian-style outfit featuring a long, loose-fitting tunic that fully covers my body and sometimes my head, which I wear out of cultural respect and modesty when working with Muslim groups in Mindanao). "Why are you so wrapped up?" he asked. I said that I had just come from a very cold place and jumped into the car without changing my clothes. I immediately proceeded to the room assigned to me and changed into a loose T-shirt and a pair of knee-length shorts before starting the preworkshop activities.

I remember I had difficulty sleeping that night, and I heard a knock on my door very early in the morning (when reveille was being sounded). The lady soldier assigned to be my aide-de-camp asked if I wanted to jog or walk around. I stood up from my bed, looked outside the window, and saw the silhouette of a cannon! I perspired, sat weakly on my bed, and said, "I think I will pass this morning. I would like to prepare for the workshop." I realized I was still scared of guns and cannons!

During breakfast, I shared with the aide-de-camp the real reason why I did not leave my room. She laughed and pulled me toward the area and . . . it was not a cannon after all! It was a plough for their fields! She said, "Ma'am, our commanding officer told me you are still scared of guns and so your room is very far from cannons and stuff like that. You still do not trust us, Ma'am?" I apologized.

The soldiers were asked to be in their "civvies" (civilian clothing). The commanding officer told me that was the only way they would participate in a workshop with no guns, and the ranks were blurred. I used the very same material that I had used the day before for the nonstate armed actors. There was no difference in the response of the government soldiers.

I remember facilitating the workshop and, at the end of the day, asking them to make a diorama of their dream place. They made six dioramas, and when the commanding officer came in to view their work, he had only one question: "Why are there no camps in your ideal villages?" There was silence. Then one junior officer spoke: "Because there is no more need for camps as we are safely in our homes, with our families. Soldiers will only be called to active duty when a foreign country threatens our sovereignty." The commanding officer smiled, looked at me, and shook his head.

At the end of the day, one soldier asked me, "Ma'am, why are you doing this? Why are you training us to be peacebuilding officers?" I looked at him while digging into my heart. I took a deep breath and told him, "Because I want to dream that you will be serving the country one day in a different capacity, and I want to prepare you for that. I dream of you being a part of the UN Peacekeeping force. I dream of you becoming the head of the National Defense or the Office of the Presidential Adviser on the Peace Process. I dream of you becoming an ambassador or envoy to some other places. And I would like you to have at least an orientation of how to build peace."

That evening, the commanding officer told me that he had briefed the guards at the gate that I would be leaving very early. The next morning, I got up at 3:00 a.m. and prepared to leave the camp at 4:00. I was "wrapped up" again in another shalwar kameez. The commanding officer was up and about; he wanted to see me off. He smiled when he saw me and said, "You going somewhere cold again?" I smiled at him as I shook his hand.

When I reached the area where the nonstate actors were, they were sitting around. They stood up and *the* man said, "Okay let's all organize ourselves, she's here, let's start our training." I laughed and said, "Please let me have my breakfast first!" He turned to me and said, "They did not feed you?" I looked at him puzzled, shrugged my shoulders, and washed my hands. Together with the driver, I sat down, gulped my coffee, and ate hard-boiled eggs with rice. Their leader, the man previously assigned to sit at the back and monitor my lectures and materials, sat beside me and said, "So, how are the soldiers in the barracks?" I remember choking on my coffee in surprise because I did not realize that he had known my whereabouts in the "enemy camp." Up to this day, I am not sure how he found out. He laughed as he stood up. After that, we were nodding friends whenever our paths happened to cross.

In both camps, there was one wish that the armed men expressed. Let me put it first in our language: "Sana marinig din ng kabila itong naririnig namin para marunong din sila ng peacebuilding" (We wish the other side is also hearing what we are hearing so that they too will know about peacebuilding). I would smile and nod and say, "In shaa Allah, God willing . . . it is going to happen."

Both nonstate and state actors look for other ways of solving the present conflict. Opportunities like peacebuilding workshops provide them with skills other than fighting.

During the course of my conflict resolution workshop with the first batch of chaplains, I prayed a lot and joined them during their prayer times. I was affected by their "being soldiers first and chaplains second," but I entrusted everything to God and just did my best. I worked with a team of soldiers who themselves were very committed to peacebuilding work as soldiers. They were my cofacilitators. We helped each other. After the one-week engagement, we received so much positive feedback:

- "I sent a text message to the other ministers to make sure they are coming! I said if they will not come, they will surely miss something that they will regret for the rest of their lives."
- "I sent a text to the others saying they must participate or they will miss 1/2 of their life!"

- "I am now sure that I am a minister first before I am a soldier."
- "I now promise to take care of my flock, not just during prayer days but in their everyday life as soldiers in the field."

And true enough, the second batch came, and on opening day, they sat full of expectations and energy to learn and engage and become chaplain peace-builders.

CONCLUSION: WHAT I'VE LEARNED

Embrace your own faith.

As a peacebuilding trainer for my organization, Catholic Relief Services (CRS), the word "Catholic" often raises the question of how one engages other religious leaders who are not Catholic. It is always good to find in my organization those who follow the guidance of serving especially those in need "regardless of religion, race, or gender." This is what I always share with our partners. By our building a spirit of partnership and trust with local community-based partners, they become our champions on the ground. In one instance, a politically powerful group questioned the presence of CRS in their area. One partner spoke on our behalf. "We have partnered with them for the past fifteen years, and we were never converted. They have even provided us with opportunities to increase our appreciation of our own religion."

Embrace your own faith: I have never denied being a Catholic in terms of my personal faith or in terms of the implications of my faith identity in the Mindanao context, and I believe that partners and community leaders have respected that. I have used that understanding in bringing across a strong message of solidarity that bridges the divide that can be caused by tribal and religious differences.

I have often said that the principles I espouse are influenced by my Catholic faith. But I also say that I have opened myself to other religions and the spirituality of the indigenous in their teachings about peace and justice.

Being open in learning and being humble in accepting that other religious/spiritual traditions also have peacebuilding tenets in them helped shape me as a Catholic peacebuilder. Showing openness to traditional and religious leaders has helped bridge the gap in engaging them.

I remember one particular instance when a community said it was okay to do a workshop in their village even though it was the holy month of Ramadhan. In my part of the country, working time is shortened in offices during this month, but regular work is encouraged during working hours. Some of the leaders showed signs of wanting to end the workshop. I asked if we could continue or if people were tired and wanted to go home. Some people said,

"We stop, you eat your lunch and we can take our nap, and then we resume after you have eaten." I smiled and said I was fasting. They looked at me, some in disbelief. We had a conversation.

How do I fast? I eat no pork during the season. I wake up at 2:00 in the morning, cook my food, say my Catholic prayers while waiting for my food to cook, eat my breakfast, take a bath, brush my teeth, and gargle before 4:00 in the morning. The whole day I do not eat or drink and refrain from bad thoughts, especially against the other. Then, depending on the time, I break my fast after sunset.

Why do I fast? It is a commitment I have made since 1983. But I was doing it off and on then. It was in the 1990s that I seriously stuck to doing it every year. Why? To show my solidarity with the Muslim world in the holy season. In my own way, I am one with my Muslim brothers and sisters during the holy month.

Have I converted to Islam? No, I am a Catholic and continue to be a Catholic.

I then asked them to take a nap. One elder person said, "If she, the trainer, can do this for us, we can stay and participate in the training for the rest of the afternoon." And we proceeded.

A key military personality can be a champion for peace in the institution.

Finding one or two key military personalities and one or two key personalities in a nonstate group to champion the cause of peace and support the building of capacities for dialogue and other ways of conflict resolution can help build a consciousness of peacebuilding in their institution or group.

Having a general champion peacebuilder went a long way in orienting other officers toward peacebuilding in the very much troubled Central Mindanao. During his term, civil society organizations and community leaders experienced almost zero atrocities by the military.

One nonstate group leader said, "There is a new configuration with a new set of men and women in position. There is a new head of the armed group. He knows how to go to war. He also knows negotiation and conflict resolution. He should, he was your student."

Face-to-face engagement in more neutral settings (trainings, seminars) between military and CSOs can help clarify perceptions of the other and start the process of trust building, which can lead to collaboration.

Training workshops are "safe spaces" when in the hands of experienced facilitators. I have experienced feeling the tension during day one when CSOs trembled and some even cried when they saw military men and women in the same room with them. One sultan stood up and walked out of the room, and when I went after him, he told me to my face, "You don't expect me to sit in that room with those guys, do you?" I told him, "Yes, I expect you to sit in that room with those guys. Remember what you read in the brochure when you applied to come and join the course? This course is open to all interested in seeking to learn about peacebuilding. They have as much right as you to sit in that room and learn."

A general sent me a text message: "What is happening in the room? My officers are feeling awkward and experiencing discomfort. They said that people are crying because they are in the same room with soldiers." I sent a text back: "General, when you were in my class, you trusted me. I ask you to trust me again with your officers."

This is the beauty of having a cofacilitator. My cofacilitator takes over the class, while I take on the task of dealing with the emotions and creating the safe space for everyone.

After a week of being in the same class, working with each other on their group tasks, sharing with each other their responses, getting to share snacks and meals, laughing and seriously talking about working on how to resolve a conflict situation, they have built some kind of bridge toward each other. In one particular case, after the course, one senior officer worked with a woman leader in presenting a more humane image of each other to their particular group/community.

Both the military and CSOs have one common goal, and that is to make the community a safe space/peaceful. They have to work with the community to come up with a plan of how that can be made possible.

This can only happen if members of the military erase the image in their minds that the community is a safe haven for "the enemy" and members of the community can erase from their minds the image of the military as "the invader."

Institutional and community efforts in peacebuilding involving the military as stakeholders can best benefit the communities they serve.

In the past, peacebuilding efforts in the community have not taken the military as key stakeholders. It is perceived as "the invader," not as a force that helps and protects. In cases where the relationship between the military and the CSOs has improved, communities experience some pockets of peace.

Clarifying one's motivation in working for peace (political? economic? religious?) helps one become more inclusive in the process.

I realize that even as I work with these armed actors and other religious leaders, I have to deal with my own negative experiences of the past. There are times I feel that I am backsliding in some efforts. I have to check myself and hold an inner dialogue. It is when I get in touch with my faith, connecting with my God who is the Prince of Peace, that helps me. As I said, I am a work in progress. And I have a long way to go.

NOTES

1. New Revised Standard Version Catholic Edition (National Council of the Churches of Christ, 1993), BibleGateway.com.

2. The Moro National Liberation Front was the primary Moro separatist organization in Mindanao from the 1970s to the 1990s. In 1996, it signed an autonomy agreement with the government of the Philippines, but some of the leaders and members continued their struggle under a new organization, the Moro Islamic Liberation Front. In some cultures, *moro* is considered an insulting term, but that is not the case among the Bangsamoro (Muslim) tribes of Mindanao.

3. Adopting the Basic Law would bring about the implementation of the Comprehensive Agreement on the Bangsamoro between the government of the Republic of the Philippines and the Moro Islamic Liberation Front. If enacted, it would create a new autonomous territory for Bangsamoro people within Mindanao.

4. The Mindanao Peacebuilding Institute is a training center for Asian peacebuilders. It was founded through the collaborative efforts of Catholic Relief Services, the Catholic Agency for Overseas Development, and the Mennonite Central Committee. In 2009, the institute became an independent legal entity working with a broad network of Filipino and international partners. See Mindanao Peacebuilding Institute (https://www.mpiasia.net, accessed August 24, 2017).

Part III

Engaging Policy

Chapter Seven

Deconstructing and Reconstructing Secular Approaches to Religion in Multilateral Settings

Azza Karam

Challenge: How do you engage policymakers on sensitive issues that are religious or perceived to be religious?

Working on faith issues as "a faith warrior" is a challenge on many fronts, including within faith-based institutions themselves. But working as a faith warrior within an entity that encompasses all the world's governments and is built on secular values—and cannot but be as such—is, shall we say, a job and a half.

The United Nations is a secular organization. That is to say, this unique intergovernmental entity does not profess, belong to, adopt, or speak for any faith tradition. Its guiding principles and values, as enshrined in its own charter and the Universal Declaration of Human Rights, are derived from the best of all faith traditions, but they are secular values that are not attributable to any particular religion. And that is as it should be. Given the 193 governments that are members of the United Nations, and given the fact that all its staff are considered international civil servants, the secular character of the organization is both logical—to ensure unbiased attention and representation —and necessary. The fraught religious dynamics around the world today— whether in the form of politicized religious parties governing or in opposition—lends further wisdom to a convening and serving mechanism for the world's peoples that would not be hostage to the deepest sentiments and realties of religious identities. And if the staff members of this organization are supposed to work to serve without regard for their own national affiliation, then it follows that this service should not be swayed by gender, ethnic, class, racial, or religious affiliations either.

This secular character of the UN system has become part of the institutional identity and its worldviews as a whole. So, while most UN staff members may have particular faith traditions influencing their own lives to different degrees, as a body of staff serving at the United Nations, we may work together for decades, without necessarily even knowing what faith traditions our colleagues were born into, may have espoused, or, alternatively, perhaps distanced themselves from. And if it were not for the occasional person in the midst of a packed elevator wearing a symbol of his or her faith, most staff would remain blithely unknowing.

This is my professional world, where I spend an average of at least nine hours each day and which, like many others, also requires my attention on weekends and holidays and during any leave. This is the world I have dedicated my life to since June 2004, when I joined the United Nations after serving as a university lecturer in politics and development and as a program and policy advisor for other intergovernmental entities and NGOs, and after dedicating myself to human rights activism as a young, Egyptian, Muslim woman of faith. This world is one which has captured both my heart and my imagination. So, while I may constructively criticize in the lines to come, I do so with unadulterated passion and commitment to the UN system—and most significantly, to the ideals underpinning it.

I expected—and continue to both welcome and affirm—the secular nature of this remarkable entity of over forty thousand[1] staff, with on-the-ground presence in most developing countries, mostly headquartered in so-called developed countries, and with well over 120,000 peacekeepers.[2] But it nevertheless came as a significant shock when I first realized how the context of UN staff realities went beyond a principled secular attitude. In fact, in many instances, there is, at best, an almost blanket ignorance of the role of religion in people's lives and, at worst, a determination that can only be crudely described as one to work with religion only when necessary and on our own terms. Thankfully, this attitude is slowly, but surely, changing—thanks to the work I will describe in the lines to come.

FOUNDATIONS

But what inspired me originally to become "a faith warrior" and what do I mean by it? I grew up in an extended family where religion was part of everyday life and even the language. Every other word in an average sentence included (still does) a variant of *insha'Allah* (God willing), *masha'Allah* (praise God), or *alhamdullilah* (thank God). No matter where I lived within my father's house, wherever his diplomatic postings took him, faith was second skin, the friend who never changed and was always there for me. And yet precisely because big families contain diversities within them (from the very observant to the atheist), and because I lived in many countries (including multicultural India, Communist Romania, and diversely Catholic Italy), I realized that not everyone around me seemed to take for granted this business of God's existence.

I contrasted this to another reality: I came of age in an Egypt that was rife with tensions between socialist president (yet believer) Gamal Nasser and the Muslim Brotherhood; heavily influenced by a nationalism built on the wounds inflicted by decades of British and French colonialism and reopened during the Suez Crisis; and with a sense of deep humiliation from the 1967 Arab-Israeli catastrophic war that seemed inscribed into our DNA. Religion was always part of the political and civic search for meaning. In Egypt, and in our family, politics was the stuff of everyday conversations. Very often, jokes—a staple diet—revolved around the intersections between the personal, the social, and the political. Thus, for me, religion, politics, rights, and selfhood are my DNA.

My first career made me into a faith warrior when working on human rights brought me face-to-face with the interplay between religious fundamentalism, democratic governance, and women's rights. I learned the absolute necessity of "defending" my faith (and eventually all faiths) from those who would use it for political gain, those who would decry it as the source of all ills, and those who would claim a variant of it as "the only solution" to all ills. I learned how to be a faith warrior by appreciating that the Divine is within each and every living creation; that none of us have a monopoly over understanding this Power; and that to really live is to love the Divine in all its manifestations and work for this love and with this love.

CHALLENGES

There is no estimate, as of this writing, of how many UN resources have actually been spent either on working with religious organizations or communities or on matters of religion touching on development. But this is not odd when one considers that indeed it is difficult to come up with UN-system-wide estimates[3] of spending on any one constituency or specific issue set. Every UN agency receives its own budget and allocates its resources to its mandated areas as guided—and approved—by the member states sitting on the executive of that UN entity. Also, the work of the UN is diverse and huge in scope, covering human rights, peace and security, and sustainable development. Nevertheless, it is usually possible to get some idea, from consulting the annual reports of the operational UN development agencies, of the amount of resources spent on diverse program areas. On some occasions, there may even be some estimate of the resources directed toward civil society engagement. One would expect that within these frames of activity, some mention would have been made of religious elements of civil society, or programs involving religion, or religious actors. However, in reality, one has to scour the financial pages to find any reference to resources directed toward any matters of religion.

All this when the United Nations Charter begins thus:

> WE THE PEOPLES OF THE UNITED NATIONS . . . determined to save succeeding generations from the scourge of war, which twice in our lifetime has brought untold sorrow to mankind, and to reaffirm faith in fundamental human rights, in the dignity and worth of the human person, in the equal rights of men and women and of nations large and small, and to establish conditions under which justice and respect for the obligations arising from treaties and other sources of international law can be maintained, and to promote social progress and better standards of life in larger freedom.

This has to be juxtaposed against a backdrop of one fact: in 2012, a Pew Research Center study of 230 countries and territories around the world informed us that there are "5.8 billion religiously affiliated adults and children around the globe, representing 84% of the 2010 world population."[4] That is, eight out of ten of the "we the people" noted in the UN Charter affiliate themselves with one religion or another. So how is it that we cannot account for the UN system's spending on religion or religiously affiliated issues?

Arab Human Development Reports

When I first joined the United Nations, it was to coordinate the Arab Human Development Reports (AHDRs). The idea of the reports was a brainchild of an Arab woman who led the Arab Regional Bureau in the United Nations Development Programme (UNDP). Dr. Rima Khalaf, an effective administrator, articulate intellectual, and able political reader, decided to apply the template of the UNDP Human Development Report to her ever-turbulent region.[5] The first AHDR was launched in March 2002 and, entirely by coincidence,[6] landed in the midst of a furor of questions raised in an attempt to understand the calamity of the events of September 11, 2001. The report, which identified three critical democratic deficits in the Arab region (education and knowledge, governance, and gender equality), appeared to answer many of the questions that were raised. The 1 million hits on the UNDP's website to seek to download the first AHDR remains a record for attempts to access any UN document.

What is most noteworthy about the AHDR, for the purposes of this chapter, is that religious dynamics received relatively scant attention in the first of the series of annual reports reflecting the Arab world's most well-versed intellectual minds. Although religion is a fundamental part of political and social dynamics in the region, there is barely a discussion around this role in the first series of AHDRs. Having been part of the process for several years, I learned that this particular deficit of insight was not entirely due to the fact that the intellectual elite solicited were largely secular themselves. A large part of the reason for the relative oversight around religious dynamics was, I believe, due to the fact that the culture within UNDP at that time had little patience for anything religious. As my "superiors" in the hierarchy clearly told me, "We do not do religion."

I was mystified, frustrated, and completely fascinated by the fact that the institutional culture of the UN could "overrule" realities of life in an entire region and that it could do so with the full consent of the crème de la crème of the region's own intellectuals and the governments that form this global institution. Few government representatives stepped in to point out what was ignored. Instead, several did seek to "edit" the content of the AHDRs in those years, to curtail the already minimal references to religious dynamics. After all, for some of those governments, to have religion even mentioned as a worthy political opponent was then—and remains—anathema.

To have witnessed this reality unfold around the mention of religion in the AHDR, not once but nearly four years in a row, taught me, at once, the value of part of the reality of the UN: the UN has prestige, credibility, and indeed a certain power—all of which can conspire to create consent among many who will work with it. This strength exists in spite of the ceaseless deprecation of this institution's past, present, and, doubtless, future.

So UN headquarters was relatively "silent" about religion for some time. This does not mean that religious events did not take place. On the contrary, as later research (referred to as "mapping of activities") would show, at the country level many operational UN entities established partnerships of diverse kinds with different religious entities for specific purposes. How could they not have—for were they not ultimately having to work with the government in question, to serve "the people" of that nation?[7]

In 2001, another Arab woman, this one a Saudi, took her position as executive director of the United Nations Population Fund (UNFPA). Dr. Thoraya Obaid made it her mission to ensure that UNFPA under her leadership could prove that "culture matters" in international development. Interestingly, it was an idea made possible almost entirely through the support of a major European donor—the Swiss Agency for Development and Cooperation. She appointed an Iraqi woman, Meysoon Malak, to lead the work in this unit, working together with renowned Nigerian feminist Ayesha Imam. Malak studied how UNFPA enacted its development programs and proved that religion, as part of culture, was a "tipping point" for the success of development intervention. She developed tools to render programs more "culturally sensitive" by identifying the intersectionality of culture with community leadership, media, political, social, economic, and legal realities.

It should not have escaped anyone's notice that it was women who steered so much of the milestones referred to here—a fact that should be recognized as significant, given the stereotyped assumptions about Arab women that still prevail.

A Movement of Religions

I joined UNFPA in 2007 and was given a one-sentence order by Ms. Obaid: "I want a movement of religions in support of human rights from around the world, and I want them to be visible, as critical resources, to the entire UN system." Having come from the NGO world of multireligious collaboration around common developmental challenges, I knew which religious leaders were supportive of certain rights and where some of the toughest dogmatic obstacles were. I understood well, and had tasted myself, some of the bitterness of the tensions among religion, women's rights, sexuality, and gender. These tensions become exacerbated in attempts to bring together different religious leaders and multiple communities of faith.

I had learned, to my frustration, that girls' and women's welfare was clearly espoused by most religious leaders—as long as this revolved around ensuring girls and women were kept safe from violence, educated, able to work and access resources (nutrition, sanitation, employment), and so forth. But to translate this to what women can (or cannot) do with their own bodies (especially issues of sexuality, sexual relations, marriage [including early and forced], pregnancy, abortion, and total and full equality between the genders) revealed the contents of explosive tinderboxes. These were at the heart of the contentious terrains where many religious leaders will not go. Where there is a need to emphasize commonality among religious leaders to showcase "moral authority" on things like poverty, climate change, refugees, peacemaking, preventing genocide, and the like, the unwritten rule is to steer clear of "contentious issues." A multireligious movement that would agree to also come together on these very contentious issues was, therefore, a tall order indeed.

I had interacted with several religious leaders and religious organizations around the world and understood their respective strengths and relatively less strong points. I had also learned about the power of religious NGOs that deliver services to most of the poorest and hardest to reach individuals and communities. In spite of four years at UNDP, I originally underestimated the organizational culture of arrogance and deliberate silence around, and vis-à-vis, all matters religious. And I had yet to appreciate one of the biggest challenges I would confront within the UN system: that some of us in the UN may be prepared to sacrifice distinct gender interests in order to achieve the image of supportive moral authority leveraged "to save lives." In other words, some of us may be prepared to compromise on specific girls' and women's rights for more "urgent" or "bigger" causes.

Moreover, while I understood the world of religion and the continuum of religious politics,[8] I did not predict the Arab Spring and its near reversal—the eventual winning of actual territory that groups like Boko Haram and ISIL would achieve and eventually lose most of—or the resulting increase in waves of migration each of these developments would lead to, which in turn are rocking the very foundations of international norms and political discourse across Europe and North America.

RESPONSES

But here I run ahead of myself. Back to building a global faith-based movement for human rights—and trying to bring in the contentious domains.

Working within UNFPA

In July 2007, the High-Level Dialogue of the General Assembly on Interreligious and Intercultural Understanding and Cooperation for Peace's Informal Interactive Hearing with civil society, including nongovernmental organizations and the private sector, took place. UNFPA, together with the UN Alliance of Civilizations and the UN Department of Economic and Social Affairs (UNDESA), provided technical support and formed part of a "task force" convened by the UN's Office of the President of the General Assembly. Part of the emphasis of this effort was to ensure a broad-based and deliberate engagement of religious NGOs as members of civil society. At the same time as this hearing was being organized, UNFPA sent out a questionnaire[9] to all its more than one hundred country offices, asking four questions:

1. Are you working with religious leaders, faith-based health service deliverers, or any other religious institutions?
2. If so, why are you doing so and with whom are you working?
3. On what issues/areas are you working and how?
4. What would you say are the lessons you are learning in terms of programs, advocacy, mutual building of institutional capacities, or any other areas?

The answers that came back were very surprising. Few offices were not working with faith actors—in fact, over 85 percent were doing so. A further 10 percent said they were but preferred to keep this work "out of the official limelight." Why? we asked. Because, came the totally unanticipated reply, it is fundamentally about building relationships with specific religious leaders and religious institutions, to convince them to drop their opposition to certain sexual-health-related programs and projects, and in some cases, even to have their own health services refer patients to other health service providers who would provide contraception. Given the sensitive nature of this work, the religious leaders involved did not wish their particular stances to be made public. This was the case with some Catholic, Jewish, Hindu, and Muslim leaders in some countries.

All those UNFPA country offices that reported their engagement indicated that this form of outreach was a sine qua non of getting the programs culturally accepted and adapted to community needs. Many indicated that engagement with religious communities was key to beginning to talk about needed behavior change among communities, since religious actors were "cultural gatekeepers." Some, particularly in sub-Saharan Africa, noted that Christian health service providers were key counterparts to the governments themselves and therefore also to the work of the UN in strengthening health systems in local contexts. Others, particularly in the Arab-speaking region, were quick to point out that engagement with religious institutions went back to the 1970s and was rendered critical when the governments signed onto the Program of Action of the International Conference on Population and Development in 1994. The majority of UNFPA's country offices in Asia also came back affirming diverse degrees of engagement. Some offices came back with a particular retort: "But of course we have to involve religious communities in different ways as part of reaching out to civil society. Why is this even a question now?"

This question, and the fact that it was posed in different ways by so many colleagues from different regions in response to the survey, was itself a valuable lesson: there is a huge dissonance between UN headquarters offices and the same UN entities' country-level presences. This gap in realities is not unique to any one UN entity—indeed it is not unique to the UN itself but is replicated in NGOs, government offices/missions, and private-sector entities. But it was particularly noteworthy, given the positions of the headquarters offices, which often tended to lean toward what I referred to earlier as willful ignorance of religious dynamics—or, to be more tactful, the "caution" expressed by Western-based UN headquarters in New York, Geneva, and Rome vis-à-vis even the need to engage with religious entities.

Working with the UN System

In 2009, UNFPA convened faith-based organization (FBO) and civil society liaisons from UNAIDS, UNDESA, UNDP, UNESCO, UNICEF, and the World Health Organization at a Global Forum in Istanbul. These UN offices cohosted two policy roundtables in New York, inviting FBO partners to discuss mutual collaboration and outreach. One outcome was the first set of

Guidelines for Engaging FBOs as Cultural Agents of Change,[10] which UNFPA developed. My research indicates that these constituted the first set of consolidated guidelines for engaging religious actors in the UN system. It is incomprehensible how an intergovernmental entity established in 1948 on the basis of peace, reconciliation, and human rights did not develop guidelines for engagement with faith actors until 2008.

On November 12, 2008, world leaders met at the UN for a debate on the culture of peace. A draft resolution on "promotion of interreligious and intercultural dialogue, understanding and cooperation for peace"[11] was introduced by then Philippines president Gloria Macapagal-Arroyo. She maintained that one of the resolution's most relevant points was the affirmation that mutual understanding and interreligious dialogue were important components of the culture of peace. This resolution was especially relevant to the United Nations as the Secretary-General had issued a report on interreligious and intercultural activities for the first time in the organization's history. The resolution also asked that a United Nations decade be proclaimed for interreligious dialogue.

In 2010, the principals of the various UN developmental entities, including the head of the UN Development Group (UNDG), approved a UN Interagency Task Force (UN-IATF) on Engaging with FBOs for Development. In 2010, representatives of the various UN offices met officially as members of this task force and developed a mission statement and terms of reference, which continue to be modified to take account of learning among UN members, together with World Bank colleagues, and the evolution of the circumstances of the UN and the world of religious affairs.

What follows here is a critical review of how some of these UN engagements with diverse faith entities have taken place, some of the lessons learned, and some considerations for going forward.

In 2013, efforts to ramp up global consciousness around what would become the "new" development agenda began.[12] The "post-2015 deliberations" were in full swing at the UN Secretariat in New York. The main UN development agencies were recruited in this system-wide process to identify where the partnerships, outreach, and achievements around the Millennium Development Goals (MDGs) had succeeded, what the shortcomings were, and how to ensure that the process of identifying the post-2015 development goals could harvest some of the lessons learned and, more significantly, catalyze an unprecedented global engagement.

In this process, as the coordinator/chair of the UN-IATF, I was asked to help identify and convene the faith-based development partners who had partnered with the UN system in different ways to help achieve the MDGs. Drawing on its 500+ Global Interfaith Network and its years of hosting strategic-learning exchanges around religion and development, the UN-IATF hosted what would be the first of many seminars and policy debates among

UN agencies, academic and policy think tanks, and some of the world's largest and most well-established FBOs. The FBOs were thus effectively "roped into" the process of global consultations and asked to reach out to their multimillion constituencies in order to provide insights into what the remaining challenges of human development should be.

Post-2015 Process

So how could we "rate" the outreach to faith actors around the post-2015 process itself? I would say it was varied, given the huge diversity of FBOs themselves. At the global level, the "engagement" of FBOs with the United Nations has tended to be informed by the following dynamics.

The Size of the Organization

The bigger the FBO in question, the more it has been active in UN-related outreach with civil society. Of particular note are organizations that have long partnered with diverse UN agencies on specific issues, such as World Vision on child rights and maternal health and Islamic Relief on humanitarian and emergency relief.

Heavily Dominated by Christian NGOs

Christian NGOs have a relatively longer history of centralized organization and presence at the international level (and, some would argue, a longer track record of providing social services in countries other than their own, in many cases preceding or coterminous with colonial presence). They are thus the most visible at the international "policy tables," conferences, and meetings, including at the United Nations. My own research, undertaken between 2007 and 2012, indicated that out of all meetings conducted within and by New York–based UN entities with FBOs and referring to religion or religious issues, an average of 75 to 95 percent of religious attendees were of the Christian faith.

Dependent on the Responsiveness of the FBOs Themselves

Some FBOs consider the MDGs to be part of their own agenda setting and responsibilities. Some have been more willing to be engaged and have articulated the MDGs in their own strategic and policy frameworks. It is noteworthy, and possibly not a coincidence, that those FBOs are also the ones likely to be headquartered in the Western Hemisphere and also relatively more comfortable "taking on" human rights language and issues. Many of these international FBOs build and work through long-standing partnerships with local NGOs. In many cases (such as Tearfund and Bread for the World–Germany), the entire faith-based development model is to build the capacity of local churches and/or community NGOs. In contrast, many other FBOs, while serving large segments of the local populations at the most micro-community levels, have no interest in or resources for a presence in Western headquarters. They rarely feel the need to accommodate MDGs or human rights in their own agendas. And yet they are critical development actors. In some ways, FBO engagement with the global development agenda has been, arguably, almost class based. The "elite" FBOs are the ones at the table.

Dependent on the Outreach by the Different UN Agencies/Offices Themselves

Some UN agencies have sought FBO input, deliberately organized outreach to their FBO partners, included them in program rollouts, and developed some sort of guidelines for such engagement.[13]

Lack a Centralized Institutional Focus

There is no one office in the UN system that reviews all outreach to faith-based entities. While there have been plenty of efforts to advocate for such a mechanism over the years (largely by faith-based actors themselves), it has proved challenging for a number of reasons, some of which are the following:

- Outreach to the whole world of religious groups is difficult. Religious communities are large, complex, differently structured, and even more diversely led and represented. To attempt to engage with all of this world in a fair, equitable, representative, and efficient manner is not a simple matter.
- The world of the United Nations itself is complex, and offices for partnership tend to be focused on specific modes and themes of outreach—as per the mandates granted by member states—and even those are organized in diverse ways with different objectives. There are multiple existing offices that aim to liaise with broad civil society units, and they tend to be tailored to the mandate of the entity they are housed within.[14]

Challenged by Crisis Situations

Ebola is a most noteworthy instance of a crisis that challenged UN-FBO engagement. Even though advocacy for engagement with FBOs (and a long track record around health issues) had been in place for some years, when the Ebola crisis hit, no one in the UN or FBO community involved with these policy advocacy efforts appeared to be able to immediately provide a vetted and comprehensive list of accredited faith-based health-care providers in the three African countries affected. Similarly, the rise of ISIL presented both the UN and FBO partners with practical as well as moral dilemmas, not least of which included such questions as, Who are these "faith actors"? Should they be engaged? How and how not?

Shifting Sands of "In-groups" and "Out-groups" within the UN Staff

Raising issues of faith and religion and working with religious actors around the intertwined nexus of development-peace-human rights still evokes a myriad of often competing reactions within the UN system itself. These reactions have led to the creation of "in-groups" and "out-groups" among UN staff—which are not set in stone but rather shift with time. At UN headquarters, polarization remains between those who are unwilling to go beyond lip service about working with religious actors and tend to refuse to allocate resources to this area of work and, at the other end of the spectrum, those who deem it necessary to work with these faith-based constituencies in diverse ways.

In 2010, several members of the UN-IATF, including myself, felt that we were the "out-group" in our own organizations because we were engaged with religious communities and therefore outside the normal UN thinking and praxis. Over time, and commensurately with the rise of (allegedly) religiously inspired conflicts and extremist actions around the world, the interest in working with religious actors grew. With this interest came a shift in "in-groups" and "out-groups." As the need to understand religious dynamics grew, members of previous "out-groups" became more in demand within their own organizations. This rise in interest presented opportunities (together with some resources) to work on faith-based engagement. It is also noteworthy that, unlike the earlier exclusively women-led attempts that opened doors and spearheaded the creation of a UN-IATF, these efforts today are led by senior male leaders in the UN, who have stepped in to steward some of this outreach with religious leaders.[15] Therefore, today, it almost feels as if those of us (read: me) arguing that we need to be careful and deliberate about ensuring we keep the full spectrum of human rights (including gender-related "contentious issues") and inclusivity as our compass and guide in determining all faith-engagement may well be the new "out-group."

On the whole, I believe that the process of engagement of international FBOs as part and parcel of the broader UN outreach to all actors, and the FBOs' own willingness to commit their own diverse resources to being part of the global policy, advocacy, and outreach efforts played a role in ensuring that the Sustainable Development Goals are the relatively better-known priorities they are today. Not only that, but it is difficult not to see a link between the engagement of the FBOs in these processes and the increasing "normalization" of faith engagement across the UN system to date.

When UNFPA invited a group of FBO representatives to join the Civil Society Advisory Group back in 2009, this was deemed an "unusual" move. Today, at least two UN entities housed within the hallowed halls of the UN Secretariat—the UN Alliance of Civilizations and the Office of the UN Special Advisor to the Secretary-General on the Prevention of Genocide—are setting up advisory groups and networks composed of religious leaders. Moreover, the World Food Program, one of the largest UNDG entities,[16] at one point spoke of setting up an interreligious council to advise all the Rome-based UN food entities.[17] At the same time, the UN Environment Program is keen on renewing its outreach with faith actors, and UN Women is working with UNFPA and other entities to set up a platform of religious actors dedicated to gender equality. The tide has definitely turned. Today, we are doubtless witnessing the dawn of increasing engagement with faith-based entities.

REFLECTIONS ON ENGAGEMENT AND REMAINING PRIORITIES

So how can we assess, even if imperfectly, the lessons of the attempts to engage religious actors with a multilateral entity such as the UN so far? What follows is by no means a comprehensive or data-based review. Rather, these are my impressions, based on my participant observation since 2000[18] and as a convener of multiple discussions in forums inside and outside the UN system itself. I describe here some weaknesses of the current approach.

Overemphasizing Religious Leaders and Religious Leadership

There is no doubt that religious leadership is critical. But these leaders should not be made to exemplify all religious communities, actors, and organizations. The world of faith is vast, and even the process of identifying and "naming" leadership differs from one faith community to another. Not only that, but in fact religious leaders are largely men—only in rare cases are women assigned leadership roles.

So, to limit the outreach to religious leaders is, at once, to unrealistically burden religious leaders with the task of speaking for billions on all things; to overrepresent the religious representation of Christian elements (given the relative ease of identifying those "leaders" and institutions); to risk a gender-imbalanced representation of faith communities and human lives as a whole; and to effectively exclude and silence gender equality from the discourse of "common concerns." The fact is that religious leaders, when they come together across diverse religious groups and countries, rarely, if ever, agree to unabridged versions of "gender equality."

I am reminded of an experience where four years of research and many millions of dollars in investment led to a compilation of a unique database of over four hundred faith-based women's organizations around the world. The database was meant to serve as a development resource for organizations around the world, to identify religious NGOs run by women of different faiths, serving their communities on such issues as youth empowerment, girls' and boys' education, nutrition, health and sanitation, and so on. Once identified, these women of faith could then be contacted and, where possible, partnered with as part of their nations' civil society development infrastructures. The database was launched online in 2002, with a corresponding hard-copy publication listing the FBOs in a user- and reader-friendly format where they could be searched by issue, country, religion, and region. When this resource was made known to some Catholic religious leaders, a complaint was made to the management of the NGO producing this work, noting that one of the FBOs mentioned referenced itself as Catholic and yet was vocal about its pro-abortion stance. The ire of the male religious leaders who were part of the NGO's leadership led to this entire database being erased from the organization's website. In one fell swoop, contacts and documentation for over four hundred women of faith were erased from public record.

The overreliance on religious (male) clergy remains an "emerging market phenomenon." In a reality where women of faith make up the majority of the actual developmental and humanitarian service providers, where the number of religiously ordained women in many religions is relatively low, and where there is not a single issue in human existence that does not involve an impact on girls and women and gender dynamics, I continue to wonder how it can be legitimate to limit our consciousness and outreach to male religious leaders only.

"Overmoralizing" the Development Agenda and Partnerships

By seeking to give the world of faith a role that is primarily "moral" in nature and even labeling it as such, we are effectively reinforcing the role of religious actors as a "moral compass" in international development efforts. This may indeed be consonant with the role that religious leaders apportion themselves, but this does not necessarily lead to an affirmation of international human rights. In fact, by prioritizing "the moral" narrative of religion, we may risk compromising on the universality of human rights—for not all religious actors who would occupy "the moral" space would endorse the value, relevance, or indeed universality of human rights.

Why should affirming human rights be a priority for engaging with religious actors? Because, as mentioned earlier, we are all confronted by the serious threat posed by religious extremism (whether Muslim, Hindu, Buddhist, Christian, or Jewish), and many nations are also confronting intrareligious sectarianism. These dynamics are making civil and political discourse more contentious. Religions today are part of the social consciousness—in ways violent and terrifying, yet alluring for many youth.

Increasing Religious Rhetoric While Failing the Marginalized

Elevating religious morality, and those who speak in its name, is not the same as ensuring inclusive civic discourse, engagement, and equitable access. Religious actors perform myriad roles, as behavior changers, social influencers, and political power brokers, to name but a few. To seek to increase the recognition of the value of religion in public life is necessary in an international development culture characterized by a hegemonic secular Western ethos. This secular ethos has increasingly come under attack, and its upholders—invariably women's rights and human rights actors—are struggling to find a common ground between faith and rights. So there is little question that there is potential advantage to bridging between these discourses. But again, as the experience of the Middle Eastern region continues to demonstrate, an expansion of the space for religion is not necessarily an expansion of the public space for all. In fact, there are legitimate concerns that religious rhetoric, especially that upheld and characterized by some religious leaders in conflicted settings,[19] is about demarcating "us" from "them" rather than nonjudgmental inclusion.

The challenge with moral agency is that it does not automatically translate into providing for the less privileged, regardless of their race, gender, ethnicity, religion, and class. Faith-based development organizations and religious institutions uphold and invigorate a centuries-old tradition of actual social service to communities. In fact, the credibility of any faith institution is significantly enhanced through its social service community outreach.

As an international secular development and humanitarian community, the UN has a natural affinity for service provision—after all, that is what the UN works to enable and enhance. Thus, it would make sense that the emphasis on strengthening systems of service provision should continue to inform and guide faith-based outreach. In other words, we partner because it helps us to serve the gaping basic needs better and more efficiently. But that has to be distinguished from "we partner because you are moral agents." Both are important, but they are not the same. What needs to be avoided is the prioritization of moral agency over actual service provision. For who is to say that faith-based actors are better moral agents than all the other development agents? And why would secular actors cede the moral ground to religious agents?

Prioritizing the moral agency of faith-based actors runs a subtle but definite risk of "bringing God to the decision-making table," thus undermining the agency of other mere mortals to represent a spiritual "voice." Faith-based organizations and religious leaders certainly "do spirituality" in their own missions and ethics. This is an added value and strength of their work. But when it comes to partnering, that is, working together with international mechanisms to serve all people, I myself prefer to acknowledge that the terms of engagement rest on shared values and mutual strengths. In that space of engagement, no one entity should claim a superior status of speaking either for or on behalf of any deity or specific religion. Rather, all can speak to the needs of the communities of human beings they serve and the mechanisms they have at their disposal to serve with. Faith itself is the domain of all and the purview of none.

Potentially Compromising the "Chosen Ones"

It is a fact that in the shifting sands of contemporary geopolitics, multilateral mechanisms such as the UN are not as powerful—or effective—as they were intended to be. Even attacks against UN offices and officials are not uncommon.[20] While this relative loss of impact and stature of the UN is not universal, it should nevertheless be factored into an analysis of its role in a changing global landscape. In turn, whom the UN reaches out to in the larger and more complex world of religion has to be evaluated with the same level of realism. The UN needs to ask itself, Do we add value when we approach and elevate certain religious leaders and actors, or could we possibly be denting their efficacy? For instance, could they lose credibility within their own communities because they become associated with the international elite who travel abroad more frequently than they are home among their constituencies? By associating some of these local actors with a global institution like the UN—itself in the throes of transition and not without its share of ambiguity or opposition—could there be some "collateral damage" to being branded a UN partner? One Christian NGO representative reminded me in a meeting, to several nodding heads from other FBO representatives, "Do not assume that our faith communities automatically appreciate us working with the UN . . . we often have to spend significant amounts of time explaining why there is value in working with this institution."

Self-Reflexive or Changing the "Other"?

Some of the attempts at outreach to faith-based communities tend to be informed by a vague notion that "we" (the UN and other secular development actors) will succeed, somehow, in changing "them" (religious institutions). This also happens with some religious actors: "they" (the UN) will eventually see the light if "we" (religious workers) keep talking to/working with them. These approaches miss an important point: it is not necessarily about changing one another's ways. The point is that it ought to be about what we question and learn about ourselves—our own institutions, attitudes, perspectives, and approaches—through working together so that we can serve better. For we have little control over our own institutions, let alone over others'. But when it comes to accountability, each institution ostensibly has its own complex processes and mechanisms. So why attempt to change the other rather than look more critically within? After all, humility is a strength.

CONCLUSION: THE VIEW FROM THE "BOTH IN AND OUT" GROUP

Efforts around the UN and wider multilateral system to engage with religious actors continue to both intensify and multiply. I believe this is pivotal. At a time when some governments are taking matters into their own hands and taking action across their own borders, and with several nonstate actors (many of them ostensibly inspired by religion[21]) effectively transcending borders and challenging weakened governmental entities, the criticality of the United Nations today needs more endorsement than ever before. Faith-based actors are part of the civil society with whom multilaterals engage in order to mitigate atrocities and conflicts, negotiate peace, and bring humanitarian relief and development services to more people.

At the same time, this outreach to faith-based entities needs to be part and parcel of broader, better coordinated, and more coherent attempts to integrate issues of culture writ large in development processes. To situate the religious domain as a separate domain of development not interlinked with culture is to risk committing an error of omission that may prove difficult to rectify. A simple—albeit extreme—example of why religious actors have much to do with culture lies in the cold-blooded efforts of ISIL to sell some of the world's oldest cultural artifacts to finance its own existence. It is destroying centuries of humanity's cultural heritage to support its efforts to wage war, maim, kill, and terrorize—supposedly in the name of religion. So how can we, with any level of integrity and seriousness, witness this and say that religion and culture are not connected?

The process of engagement with faith-based development and humanitarian entities provides us with a comparative compass about how we, as global peacemakers, are building a culture of peace. The UN has its own moral compass enshrined in the Universal Declaration of Human Rights and over seventy years of enactment. Faith-based actors have their moral compasses enshrined in multiple holy books and centuries of praxis in communities as well as significant transnational networks. Both sets of diverse actors work "for the people." Working together provides both with relative strengths. This increased engagement demands the systematization of principled approaches of partnership, knowledge building, and management, as well as pragmatic risk-reduction strategies, linked to clearly agreed timetables of mutual obligations—to which all sides need to commit.

How will we know whether a culture of peace has been realized as a result of this religious-multilateral outreach? We will recognize the signs of peace, but I am not sure we will be able to identify a single set of partnerships and efforts as the cause. Nevertheless, here is what I believe: building a culture of peace requires reaching every heart, mind, body, and spirit. If some form of faith is professed by 80 percent of the world's people, then working only with the remaining 20 percent will not bring about much peace. Nor will it be constructive to work with the 80 percent on their own in separated silos—another trend that should be avoided. At the same time, how we work with and for the 100 percent requires constant learning, determination, inclusion, and humility. Within the UN system this means we should seek to actively harness and build on the learning we have worked hard to realize over the last decade, rather than seeking to reinvent the wheel or to work only through a new elite or "in-group" that we create—or celebrate— "in our image."

NOTES

1. "Where We Are," United Nations, https://careers.un.org/lbw/home.aspx?viewtype=VD, accessed February 28, 2016.

2. "Peacekeeping Fact Sheet," United Nations, http://www.un.org/en/peacekeeping/ resources/statistics/factsheet.shtml, accessed February 28, 2016

3. For an overview of the structure of the UN, see "Main Organs," United Nations, http:// www.un.org/en/sections/about-un/main-organs/index.html, accessed August 24, 2017.

4. https://projectworldimpact.com/causes/view/ReligiousFreedoms?gclid=COumzdnZm8 sCFQIfhgod6o4CCw, accessed February 28, 2016.

5. Khalaf was strongly supported by the then UNDP administrator and undersecretary general, Mr. Mark Malloch-Brown.

6. It is important to stress that this AHDR was already "at the printers," so to speak, when the event of September 11, 2001, unfolded.

7. In 2000, then Secretary-General Kofi Annan convened almost a thousand religious leaders and organizations to mark the new Millennium Development Goals (MDGs). This marked a turning point, insofar as it visibly showcased the UN convening religious leaders in the same forum where it regularly convenes the political leadership. Yet this was, notably, a one-off event. It did not mark a change of institutional culture on religious engagement—yet.

8. See Azza Karam, ed., *Transnational Political Islam: Religion, Ideology and Power* (London: Pluto Books, 2004).

9. The results were published as *Culture Matters: Lessons from a Legacy of Engaging Faith-Based Organizations* (New York: UNFPA, 2008), http://www.unfpa.org/publications/ culture-matters.

10. See *Guidelines for Engaging FBOs as Cultural Agents of Change*, UNFPA, http://www. unfpa.org/sites/default/files/resource-pdf/fbo_engagement.pdf.

11. See UN resolution A/RES/63/22, adopted December 16, 2008, at the UN's 63rd Session of the General Assembly, UNESCO, http://www.unesco.org/fileadmin/MULTIMEDIA/HQ/ CLT/dialogue/pdf/UN_GA_RES_A_63_22.pdf.

12. The MDGs were designated to run from 2000 to 2015. Hence the next international development goal targets would be referred to as "post-2015" and eventually came to be known as the Sustainable Development Goals, or Agenda 2030.

13. Notable in this regard are the more operational agencies, such as UNICEF, UNAIDS, UNEP, and UNFPA. Other UN offices have, at different moments, selectively reached out to some religious leaders and engaged them in certain advocacy efforts or mediation initiatives—when deemed advisable. Here UNDP, UNESCO, UNHCR, the UN Office for the Prevention of Genocide, and the UN Alliance of Civilizations feature.

14. For instance, the Partnerships Unit, UN Department of Public Information, the ECO-SOC-related unit in UNDESA, UN development agencies in their plurality, the UN Alliance of Civilizations, the post-2015 groups, the UN-IATF, and so forth. To date, the UN-IATF is the only UN system-wide entity that convenes multiple UN offices, bodies, and development agencies specifically around engagement with faith actors.

15. Namely, the president of the General Assembly, Nassir al-Nasser, who is now the High Representative of the Alliance of Civilizations, and Mr. Adama Dieng, the UN Secretary-General's Special Advisor for the Prevention of Genocide.

16. For more information on the UNDG, see https://undg.org/home/about-undg.

17. Together, these agencies operate a budget of well over US$6 billion.

18. This dates to my work at Religions for Peace, which describes its mission thus: "Multi-religious cooperation for peace is the hallmark of *Religions for Peace*." "Mission," Religions for Peace, http://www.religionsforpeaceinternational.org/vision-history/mission, accessed August 24, 2017.

19. Thinking here of certain Muslim and Jewish political leaders in the Middle East.

20. Sadly, attacks against non-UN humanitarian and development officials also take place.

21. For instance, Boko Haram and ISIL.

Chapter Eight

Tightrope Walking

*Reconciling Faith Convictions
with Impartial Peacebuilding*

Peter Dixon

*Challenge: How do you remain true to your own faith convictions while also
cooperating and working with those who think differently?*

INTRODUCTION: THE CHALLENGE OF NEUTRALITY

Seven years ago, I joined a Christian worship service at the Anglican Cathedral in Juba and watched singing children processing joyfully down the aisle. It was a moving spectacle. The children had been born in the midst of a civil war and were now at peace. On the previous day, I was sitting under a thatched straw roof in the South Sudanese capital, reflecting on the newly peaceful environment that surrounded me. Four years had passed since the peace agreement between Sudan and South Sudan had been signed, bringing two decades of civil war to an end. There were still two years to go before the South Sudanese would vote overwhelmingly for independence and in 2011 form the newest of the United Nations' 193 states. Yet, as those who have followed the story will know, a new civil war within South Sudan soon broke out, while violent conflict within Sudan has restarted too.

Looking back at the Sudanese conflicts and at the peacebuilding role played by Concordis International, the organization I led from 2003, raises questions about success and failure, about short- and long-term horizons. We had contributed to making the peace agreement possible, we continued to lay the foundations for implementing it successfully, and the organization still works to build peace among the Sudanese. However, as the conflict continues, how should we assess the success of our work?

As important, though, and the subject of this chapter, is the question of taking sides. South Sudanese friends were always ready to see the "hidden hand" of Khartoum in every misfortune that befell them. It was easy, then as now, to describe the Sudanese conflict as one between Muslims and Christians. Should I, as a Christian, take the side of the predominantly Christian South Sudanese or, as a peacemaker, remain neutral? Yet even that question is simplistic. Over a decade of engaging with the politics of these conflicts persuaded me that the causes of the conflicts, as elsewhere in the world, were always much more complex.

Many peacebuilders are motivated by strong religious conviction that may be assumed by definition to compel them to take sides, particularly if religious identity is a factor in a conflict, but they nevertheless may wish to engage in impartial peacebuilding. There is a tension here. Does one have to set aside a strongly held personal or organizational commitment to religious truth in order to be an impartial peacemaker? I do not believe one does, and I offer in this chapter a suggestion for how this dilemma may be solved.

Some voices in the peacebuilding community suggest that an impartial approach is in any case inappropriate,[1] either because they favor an "insider-partial" approach or because they think it is "wasting time" without actively transforming society. Moreover, many suggest that activities on a spectrum ranging from human rights advocacy through building state institutions to conflict-sensitive development can be called "peacebuilding."

Sustainable peace may need foundations built on this wide range of activity, but such a broad view of peacebuilding can become open-ended and the word can lose its meaning. I find a narrower definition to be more useful in answering the immediate question of what individuals and organizations can do. I see peacebuilding as helping divided societies find peaceful solutions to their differences, whether in preventing violent conflict, achieving a settlement of a conflict, or consolidating the peace afterward. Even within this definition, though, peacebuilding can take many forms: mediation; dialogue facilitation; support of local peacebuilders and a "peace constituency"; conflict-resolution training; trauma healing; and "dealing with the past" through truth-telling, justice processes, apology, and forgiveness.

Which of these activities may be considered "faith-based"—the focus of this book—is an open question. The supposed "secularization" of international affairs and, in parallel, of conflict-resolution practice since the 1960s—that is, the assumption that religious points of view are no longer significant—no longer holds water.[2] Nobody today can claim that religion is not relevant. This "desecularization," though, is often a view of religion as a whole studied "from outside" through a secularist lens. The "objective" view, it is assumed, does not allow for personal faith. In this view, "faith-based" might include engaging with religious leaders and constituencies or the work of explicitly religious organizations. Yet the underlying motivation of the individual peacebuilder also comes into play, even if not working on behalf of a "religious" organization or faith tradition. To me, "faith-based" encompasses the work of people of faith whatever their organizational affiliation.

My experience lies in the field of inclusive dialogue, often called "Track 2" or "Track 1.5." While definitions vary, unofficial or "Track 2" diplomacy brings nonofficial but influential individuals from both (or all) sides of a conflict together to seek constructive ways forward, in parallel to official "Track 1" diplomacy. Dialogue that brings official and nonofficial people together is—not surprisingly—often called "Track 1.5." These unofficial "tracks" have the disadvantage of not necessarily leading to a signed agreement, of course, but also the many advantages of a more open context where positions do not have to be taken, relationships can be built, and options can be explored. Those who facilitate such dialogue need to provide an atmosphere where every faction or viewpoint is treated with equal fairness and any understandable tendency to mistrust the third party is reduced to a minimum.

Given my field of work, then, it is no surprise that I see not taking sides as essential for mediators and facilitators of dialogue. Yet I have approached the work of peacebuilding primarily as a convinced Christian attempting, however inadequately, to put into action the call implied in the phrase "blessed are the peacemakers" (Matthew 5:9).[3] I have sat as a facilitator for days on end with different groups of Muslims, helping them to find creative ways out of violent conflict, and in general have been seen as an impartial third party. How is this possible? Is being a Christian compatible with not taking sides? How can one hold firm views and still act impartially? Herein lies the dilemma addressed in this chapter: Does one have to set aside strongly held personal or organizational commitment to religious truth in order to engage in impartial, effective peacebuilding? The question is no doubt relevant to all faith traditions in different ways, but this chapter necessarily takes a Christian viewpoint, being based on eleven years' personal experience of leading a peacebuilding organization with a Christian heritage and ethos. At times during the past decade or so, I have felt that I was walking a tightrope, like a circus performer trying not to fall off to one side or the other.

So this is the question I try to answer in the remainder of the chapter. I first lay the foundations of the edifice by explaining how I came to be facing this challenge, before describing in more detail how the apparent conflict between impartiality and conviction has presented itself in my experience. I then suggest some potential solutions to the dilemma that I have found authentic and therefore helpful in keeping balance on the tightrope. Finally, I conclude by suggesting ways in which engaging with this challenge has broader relevance.[4] I illustrate the ideas with a few examples from experience, much of which relates to Sudan and South Sudan.

FOUNDATIONS: CHRISTIAN PEACEBUILDING

I approach the question as an individual Christian involved in peacebuilding rather than as a representative of a particular denomination or "religious" organization. What do I mean by Christian? In the contexts in which I have worked, it is often assumed that "if you come from the West you must be Christian." Indeed, as a label for social identity, this is understandable. However, for this chapter the word has a deeper meaning. A Christian is someone who follows Christ and adheres to the mainstream tenets of the faith based on the life, death, and resurrection of Jesus, through which a restored relationship with God and neighbor brings a responsibility to work for the welfare of others, in particular for justice and peace. This short distillation may beg more questions than it answers, and there is much more to Christian practice, pervading all areas of life; however, this is not the place for theological debate.

This chapter is not necessarily about explicitly Christian organizations, churches, or denominations. Just as there are Christian dentists, engineers, and academics, many leaders and members of peace-focused organizations profess the Christian faith and other religious beliefs. To label the organizations in which they work as "secular" would suggest a division that exists more in theory than in practice. The idea that one's faith should pervade all of life—including work, community, and politics—is more acceptable in other faiths than in modern and postmodern Western Christianity. Yet it is intensely relevant here.

I am perhaps an unusual peacebuilder. The identity of many in the field is rooted in either "technical" psychosocial conflict resolution or pacifist peace campaigning, or, more likely, a mixture of the two. In contrast, I came to this field after some thirty years as a pilot in the United Kingdom's Royal Air Force. My new colleagues in the peacebuilding community did not find it easy to accept that even the military, in some of its roles, sees itself as building peace. Consequently, I found myself challenging some of the political and moral assumptions I came across, or at the very least sitting outside the comfort zones of some whom I met.

The last few years of my government service involved more than a little international dialogue, and in my final tour of duty, I worked on dialogue between military and security officials and on confidence- and security-building measures, with a particular focus on the Balkans. Thus I had some background knowledge when I was invited to build the dialogue initiative of an existing nonprofit into the independent peacebuilding charity that became Concordis International.

Building on experience in South Africa and Rwanda, in the early days Concordis specialized in policy dialogue in Sudan, with the motto "Building Relationships for Sustainable Peace." The aim was to provide space for an inclusive group of key influencers of policy from a conflict-affected society to work together on conflict causes, with expertise and experience from elsewhere if desired but without imposed solutions. Concordis now also does community-level work in Africa, not least because the policy-level dialogue with which we started has proved much harder to fund than work that donors see as contributing directly to development. Of significance for this chapter is that Concordis has its origins as an initiative of a Christian social reform charity (the Jubilee Centre) and has derived much of its support from Christian churches, foundations, and individuals. While not in regulatory terms a religious organization, it has had a strong Christian ethos. But more on Concordis later.

THE CHALLENGE: CAN "RELIGIOUS" ALSO BE IMPARTIAL?

Some would not understand the work just described as religious peacebuilding, which would include interfaith dialogue and the peace-focused activity of religious organizations. Indeed, I find a dichotomy between religious and secular peacebuilding an unhelpful one. In practice, the distinction between secular and faith-based is not so clear. I was struck by the list of conflict-resolution "tools" employed by a pastor and imam from Nigeria[5] when we invited them to share their experiences of interfaith peacebuilding with Sudanese religious leaders in Khartoum. Any conflict-resolution practitioner would have recognized the activities as "secular" techniques and processes with which they were familiar. Similarly, in my own attempt to help Christians better understand how to put "being a peacemaker" into practice,[6] I relied heavily on lessons I had learned from self-identifying "nonreligious" colleagues. Even in apparently "pure" faith-based peacebuilding like interreligious dialogue, I am far from convinced that the process differs greatly from political "Track 2" practice. This is one of the reasons I have been uncomfortable with branding Concordis as either a secular or a religious organization and happier to focus simply on being peacemakers. Paradoxically, not being a religious organization does not define it as a secular one. That would be to roll over and accept the secularist assumptions prevalent in the academic and policy worlds. To stretch the metaphor, peacemaking involves walking a tightrope between two opposite sets of assumptions.

But why is the tightrope necessary at all? The answer lies in pressures on individual and organization from two sides. The first is the practical and legal pressure both to conform to constraints imposed by secular regulatory authorities and to meet the expectations of secular institutional donors whose funding may enable the work to proceed. The regulatory constraint manifests itself in limitations on how the charitable objects of the organization may be formulated, in antidiscriminatory employment law, and in constraints on the charity's governance and practice. Most countries regulate the work of not-for-profit organizations. Coincidentally, Concordis was a "test case" in 2003 for the United Kingdom's Charity Commission, in preparation for future legislation, as to whether conflict resolution could be a "charitable object" for an organization. As a result, the organization was tightly restricted in how the objects could be formulated and any suggestion of political—or religious—bias would probably have resulted in refusal of registration.

The bureaucracy in the home country is not the only regulatory hurdle to be overcome. In the "host" country, too, we can find ourselves walking on eggshells in order to be permitted to operate. Concordis's office in Khartoum was closed down by the Sudanese government's security service in 2013, and while the reasons were never disclosed, the event demonstrates a political sensitivity that can be vastly increased by any hint of religious bias.

The practical financial constraint is subtler but no less significant. Many funding authorities base their decisions on secular assumptions, whereby building institutions of democratic governance, encouraging civil society, or delivering development aid will bring stability and peace. These are of course important, but space within this discourse for a concept of peace that includes dialogue, relationship building, and reconciliation can in my experience be limited. The language of religion fits even less comfortably within this framework.

The opposite area of pressure comes from Christians of influence who strongly believe that peacebuilding and conflict-resolution work should be practiced and presented as explicitly Christian, or at least Judeo-Christian. These people might be donors or people involved in the governance or historical development of the organization. They may be deeply committed to the peacebuilding aims but perhaps see "spreading the faith" as of key importance. If not intimately engaged in the everyday issues and problems that face the organization and its people, they may find it difficult to empathize with those directly involved and to understand why the Christian basis of the work is not more strongly emphasized. As an example, some have in my experience found it difficult to accept the legal constraints and the "good governance" reasons that prevent leadership from employing only Christians. The controversy that results can not only distract from the main task but easily damage an organization's reputation among current and potential supporters.

A similar dilemma may be faced by Christian relief and development organizations like Tearfund and World Vision, but I suspect that the issue may be less acute. Delivering humanitarian aid in the name of Christ, but without proselytizing, offers a somewhat clearer distinction, is at least in theory much less politically controversial than peacebuilding, and is therefore a less sensitive "proposition."

For peacebuilding, as I have understood it, the reasons for a neutral approach are not only pragmatic, political, and historical but also principled.

The pragmatic and political issue arises in the everyday practice of leading an organization and trying to be effective in a tense and potentially hostile conflict environment. Given the identification of "Christian" with "Western," local assumptions about the organization's political bias—especially if one or more parties to conflict are Christian—and even suspicion of intelligence gathering abound. This brings with it risks.

The duty of care for staff and local partners must be a paramount concern. Whatever their religion or lack of it, those associated with an organization that is seen to be part of a foreign religion may find themselves in a hazardous position. This cannot be solved simply by placing them in secure compounds where they are isolated from the people with whom they need to work—what Mark Duffield memorably called the "international archipelago."[7] We have generally thought that safety is achieved as much through acceptance by the people as through security. However, I recall a particular instance that occurred in central Sudan, where a Concordis-facilitated dialogue degenerated into acrimony, and both sides turned on the third party. Staff members were threatened by local authorities and in some actual danger because they were accused of being British spies. In my experience, such an occurrence was rare in Sudan, though. Sudanese contacts had no difficulty in collecting me from the Christian church in Khartoum after the Sunday evening service to enjoy a meal together, seeing me and many colleagues as "people of the book."

Nevertheless, effectiveness in facilitating dialogue requires not only the building of trust between the parties but also earning their trust for oneself. There are always barriers to trust building that need to be overcome and one is never starting with a clean slate. Historical assumptions and causes of mistrust, whether dating back to the Cold War or to the Crusades, take time and effort to overcome. The evidence that the only aim of the organization is to help build lasting peace must be clear, transparent, and true.

These are the pragmatic reasons for a neutral, nonpartisan approach. More importantly, it may simply be the right thing to do in the circumstances in which we find ourselves. There may be loud and critical voices calling for human rights, democracy, and freedom, and perhaps justly so. Yet such voices may simply be drawing battle lines for future violent conflict. An example is the defiant solidarity in Sudan sparked by single-issue campaigns like that in the West about Darfur and the associated indictment of the Sudanese president by the International Criminal Court.[8] If our role is to provide space for a conflict-affected society to find its own route toward a just and sustainable peace, public denouncements of one local party, policy, or action may satisfy our own desires but are likely also to destroy trust. A less confrontational approach may ultimately be in the interests of those impacted by violence.

All of this plays out not only for organizations but perhaps even more acutely for the individual, whether working in an explicitly religious organization or not. We may differ radically in our doctrinal conviction from those with whom we engage or cooperate; the clash between this commitment and the wish not to take sides poses a genuine dilemma. Belief systems are normally not generically "religious" but comprise deeply held convictions. Even though common ground in contrast with secular thinking may be substantial, commitment to vague spirituality may not suffice.

Thus the challenge I have described impacts the effectiveness and integrity of peacebuilding both at an organizational and an individual level. But does personal or organizational commitment to Christian truth actually have to be set aside in order to engage in impartial peacebuilding? Not at all. As I suggest in the next section, "walking the tightrope" consists of finding effective ways to support conflict-affected societies in their journey toward "just peace"[9] while not compromising our own faith convictions—and sustaining this ultimately creative and rewarding tension in the long term.

RESPONSES: KEEPING A BALANCE

A Christian View of Peace

To develop a response to the challenge I have described, it will be helpful first in broad terms to revisit a Christian view of peace. This will help to clarify what we are aiming for, so as to ground the subsequent discussion, which—as a response to the dilemma outlined above—looks at the principles at least some Christians might bring to a conflict situation and considers the application of those principles to practical, everyday peacebuilding. The particular view of peace I suggest, while not held by all, is helpful in that it enables a pragmatic approach to particular conflicts, without assuming that a nonviolent approach is always right.

The teaching and example of Jesus have been interpreted in widely divergent ways over the centuries in their application to violence and war. Two fundamental viewpoints have predominated. The first approach applies "turn the other cheek"—a nonviolent response—not only to insult and violence against the individual but also to a state or nation's response to violent threat. The alternative suggests that government's responsibility for the security of the state and its citizens may require the use of force but that it must be constrained by rules and principles.

The development of the just-war tradition over two millennia consolidates this second strand. While I respect pacifist viewpoints, their increased influence among Christians of many denominations, particularly in Europe, has in my view caused churches to abdicate from "ownership" of just war, leaving a vacuum to be filled by secularized versions based on communitarianism, natural law, and human rights.[10] Although the tradition has often been misused and interpreted for self-justification—and is rejected by many Christians—I am personally convinced that it remains a valid standard. This is particularly the case when just war is used as a framework to guide difficult judgments for our own actions and not simply as a checklist to justify self-interested decisions. Moreover, the extension of the just war tradition to principles for what happens after hostilities have ceased[11] forms a link with the Christian view of what peace means.

A holistic or "complete" concept of peace is a fundamental concept throughout the Hebrew and Christian scriptures. It is expressed most completely by the Hebrew word *shalom* and, without presuming that they are direct translations, by *salaam* in Arabic and *eirene* in Greek. The concept encompasses ideas of security, safety, prosperity, harmony, happiness, and reconciliation with God and with others. Its secularized equivalent, "positive peace," going beyond a peace agreement and cessation of hostilities toward a deeper stability, is today widely recognized by policymakers and practitioners as a goal, although something of the original has been lost in the focus on human security and human rights. Moreover, the idea of a "peace process" is still heavily weighted toward a negotiated elite political settlement, albeit with attention given in agreement texts to postconflict rebuilding of institutions and structures.

If, in contrast, we embrace the deeper meaning of peace, then the process of peacebuilding will extend to conflict prevention, broad and inclusive support of conflict settlement, and an extended process of subsequent consolidation and reconciliation. The question of how outsiders can support such a process becomes a much more profound question that cannot be answered by either purely secular or solely "official" responses.

A Christian Response

One Christian motivation for pursuing the goal of lasting peace is rooted in our compassion for the vulnerable victims of violent conflict, founded on God's love for them and for us as human beings. This compassion may have a more obvious application in international relief aid and development: feeding the hungry, housing the homeless. Yet it also applies to stability and peace, given the disproportionate impact of war on civilians and the legacy of hatred and suspicion it leaves behind for subsequent generations. Although the destination may be the same, this is a different route to peacemaking than that leading from a pacifist view of nonviolence as a principle in itself.

The Bible has many references to the compassion of God—his "mercy over all that he has made" (Psalm 145:9)[12] —and of our duty to emulate it. So if this is the fundamental motivation, how do we, as outsiders in a conflict, best put it into action? Even if some external interventions have been accused of neoimperialism and cultural insensitivity, it seems clear that we should not just stand by and let civil wars—today's most common form of violent conflict—continue if there is constructive action we can take.

If compassion for the victims of violence is our motivation, then directly relieving suffering may regrettably be a necessary response, but prevention of (further) violence is a far better way. This is our justification for undertaking conflict resolution and peacebuilding as effectively as we possibly can. Moreover, this is not fundamentally different from the goal of many other peacebuilders, whatever their religious or secular background. And the synergy of several strands of peacebuilding working with rather than against each other—"rowing the boat in the same direction"—will surely lead to more effective outcomes. Consequently, it is not only appropriate but essential for us to work with others: cooperation should be an essential part of our character. Sadly, differences in fundamental belief systems between peacebuilders working in the same situation often prevent or constrain cooperation.

We all have multiple identities associated with family, education, occupation, nation, and, most importantly, faith. This is of course seen as a cause of violent conflict, but it can also affect those who aim to build peace. There is a danger that our different identities will erect barriers, separating us both from those we wish to serve and from other outsiders, that will prevent us from being effective. However, knowing God's love and compassion for all humankind frees us to emphasize our common humanity rather than our separate identity. In other words, our view of other humans as made in God's image should trump any other identity with which we or they may connect.

This leads me to the conclusion that we should not allow our Christian convictions or identity to become a barrier to our effectiveness in peacebuilding. This is very difficult, requiring us to place the needs of those we serve ahead of our own need for self-expression and, more controversially, ahead of the call to share our faith. Yet this focus on immediate needs is not fundamentally different from the approach of Christian relief and development agencies. We can cooperate with those of other faiths or none, as the well-worn phrase goes, because we can respect them and their viewpoints without agreeing with them and without a postmodern pretense that "your truth is true for you."

The Christian Contribution

What distinctive insights and approaches can a Christian organization, or Christians in an organization, bring to peacebuilding? First, mainstream Christian thinking leads to a realistic view of human nature, protecting us from a "liberal peace" utopianism that suggests the societies in which we live can be made perfect.[13] We have to deal with self-centered and even evil attitudes and actions both in others and ourselves, so we should not be surprised if things do not go according to our plans.

Second, while this may also be true of others, it certainly should be possible for Christians to look beyond today's successes and failures. A confidence in God's sovereignty should enable us to press on despite our uncertainty regarding the effectiveness of our action. This is not to say that we can ignore outcomes or dispense with monitoring and evaluation! However, setbacks are inevitable, and our trust in God may enable us to carry on in the dark even if we cannot see the end of the tunnel. By the same token, many Christians feel very much at home with the long-term view of peacebuilding that is an inevitable companion of the holistic view of peace and reconciliation I have discussed above, even if this does not match the expectations of politicians and project-minded donors. As far as we can, we should seek resources that will allow us to commit to long-term engagement rather than merely short-term project grants.

Third, the Christian peacemaker—like those from other religions—is likely to be comfortable with understanding and engaging in conflict situations where religion forms a significant source of identity for one or more of the protagonists, where a purely secular viewpoint might have less traction. Two of many examples in which we at Concordis worked in this "religious" space related to Sudan and to the Israeli-Palestinian conflict. In working with Sudanese religious leaders on their role in encouraging reconciliation in Sudanese society, we focused much less on interfaith dialogue than on the symbolic impact of Muslim and Christian leaders working together in their communities on issues like land, justice, and governance. Was this "faith-based peacebuilding"? I think so, but it dealt with "secular" issues, bringing us back to the unhelpful dichotomy I discussed above. In the Israeli-Palestinian context, we facilitated dialogue between church leaders and activists representing the extreme poles of Christian thought about the Holy Land: Christian Zionists met those with sympathy for Palestinian victimhood and disagreed fundamentally but gained understanding of the other viewpoint. Both "sides" asked us to publish their dialogue within churches to increase knowledge of the issues. Was this "interfaith"? Even though it took place between Christian groups, I think it was.

Finally, in recognizing a deeper spiritual reality, as Christian peacemakers we should take a broader view of what a divided society needs. Not only is physical support needed, for example; we should recognize the need for prayer in the situations we encounter. Recognizing God's sovereignty should encourage us to commit our work to God in prayer with a genuine conviction that his intervention can make a difference to attitudes and relationships. We are, after all, to "act justly, love mercy and walk humbly with . . . God" (Micah 6:8). [14]

None of this is to suggest that Christian peacebuilders have a monopoly on ways of helping conflictual societies. Indeed, I have found in the past dozen years or so that we have much to learn from others, even if our pride may prevent us from doing so. However, we can bring our particular contribution to comprehensive change in the direction of peace. To do so, we need to work with others in a synergistic way. In the next section I suggest principles that, over more than a decade of practical, cooperative peacebuilding, I have found both consistent with Christian values and capable of being held in common with others. This is how we walk the tightrope.

Principles of Engagement in Conflict

If we are to have the privilege of being accepted as genuine by those engaged in or affected by conflict and of cooperating in our work with others who have similar goals but different belief systems, we need to express ourselves in terms that make sense to others. Quoting Bible verses and doctrine may make some sense to our fellow Christians, but for others we need to speak in terms of values that resonate with them.

The principles that I describe in this section are those we developed when the trustees and staff of Concordis International took the time to think through what should guide our work. The principles were already implicit in the mission statement:

> Concordis International works impartially alongside those involved in or affected by armed conflict, so that through dialogue they may build relationships of mutual trust and together develop and implement policies that improve human security and lay firm foundations for lasting peace. [15]

However, since the primary activity of Concordis was and is dialogue across conflict boundaries, we felt it essential to express our values explicitly to reduce any chance of misunderstanding in often tense political situations. During this review process, I was also aware that we should provide a means by which Christians and churches who wished to fulfill Jesus's injunction to be peacemakers could do so, by supporting a professional conflict-prevention and -resolution organization through prayer or financially. I therefore tried to demonstrate how these principles were either derived from or consistent with biblical values.

Our starting point was the organization's primary goal of pursuing lasting peace, motivated by compassion for the vulnerable victims of violent conflict and underpinned by a commitment to justice and reconciliation. Within this context, the mission statement emphasizes three main themes: the focus on relationships, a concern for human security, and an emphasis on laying the foundations for a peace that can be sustained. These three broad values led us to a number of explicit principles that, for many of us, translated biblical imperatives into an ethic that could resonate with others. While it is not possible to make a neat correlation of each of the principles highlighted below with just one of the three values, they are arranged in the following paragraphs according to their connection with relationships, human security, and sustainability, none of which is a stranger to most peacebuilders.

First, then, the derivation of *relational thinking*, as it has become known, from biblical roots stretching back to the Trinity has been thoroughly explored by others.[16] It will not be repeated in detail here, but the essence is that a fulfilled life for humans involves relationship with others, just as God is three persons in relationship with each other. In this spirit, Concordis seeks to strengthen relationships of trust, in a very practical and pragmatic way, between key individuals and between communities on opposite sides of political boundaries.

In dialogue, we provide an environment in which those involved in or affected by violent conflict can engage with each other productively. To make this easier, it would be tempting to select as participants those who are already willing to talk to each other. However, we have sought to ensure *inclusivity* in the dialogue we facilitate. The additional difficulties this creates "in the room" can to some extent be resolved by encouraging direct personal contact in a range of formal and informal contexts. An inclusive approach implies fairness by including the weak or those who represent them, including those most affected by armed conflict: women, children, and those whose poverty is exacerbated by the violence. Not least because policy dialogue is sometimes criticized as elitist, it is particularly important to include these excluded and disadvantaged groups and not to allow others to dictate who may and may not attend. Through our *independence*, we can avoid succumbing to pressure by third parties (including donors) to advance their own interests. This is fraught with everyday difficulty but is at the very least an ideal for which to aim. Also, recognizing the contribution of our relationships with other external officials and nonofficials to overall success leads to a determination to *cooperate* with other agencies so that, as far as it depends on us, all are working toward the same goals.

Second, the mission statement also stresses improving *human security*—a goal firmly linked to the biblical emphasis on the dignity and worth of every human being—through helping societies in conflict to develop policies that value the individual and the community in which he or she lives. This modern concept has deep historical and cultural roots; it is intimately connected to our commitment to a *complete concept of peace*, to shalom rather than just the cessation of fighting, encompassing ideas of wholeness, prosperity, justice, mercy, forgiveness, and well-being. That Jesus came "that they may have life, and have it abundantly" (John 10:10)[17] speaks of reconciliation with God but of much more besides. This has played out for us in practical terms through a sustained focus on issues of postconflict justice and reconciliation; incidentally, I much prefer this term to the more legalistic "transitional justice" often used for the process of dealing with the past in a postconflict society. We did this in many ways, but one example is the four-day consultation we facilitated for influential Sudanese from south, east, west, and north on justice and reconciliation, where the participants used experience from other countries to hammer out Sudanese answers to questions of justice, amnesty, apology, and forgiveness. I vividly recall the impact of the film *Long Night's Journey into Day*,[18] dealing with South Africa's Truth and Reconciliation Commission and the deep interest sparked by descriptions of the Rwandan *gacaca* community courts.

Also connected with human security and deriving from a "whole" concept of peace is Concordis's determination to *engage for the long term* and to unearth and understand all the complexities of a conflict. It is now widely accepted that a peace settlement is not the end of the story. Moreover, to seek in-depth understanding, beyond the one or two issues that reach media headlines, is a form of wisdom whose "price is beyond rubies" (Job 28:18). Just as important to this *strategic intervention* is the conscious focusing of limited resources in a sustained way, where they can do most good and where they will not lead to negative consequences. This is also part of the application of God-given wisdom and intelligence to *doing no harm*, often glibly cited but not always thought through in practice.

Third, it is a fundamental—and biblical—tenet of the organization's approach that laying the foundations for *sustained peace* needs policies that establish justice and fairness, developed together by all elements of a society. How does this translate into concrete principles for our intervention?

This returns us to the key question posed in this chapter. It seems clear that, in the context of violent conflict, *impartiality* is a crucial element of our service to those involved in or affected by war. It is often assumed that public advocacy is a natural part of the role of nongovernmental organizations. Yet public statements to justify a position can often increase hostility and mistrust. Tempting as it may be to make our position known, especially in defense against an attack against ourselves, a duty and attitude of service to those involved in conflict put the priority on their positions, needs, and aspirations. Such a service-oriented approach emulates Jesus. A corollary is a preference for quiet diplomacy over activism and advocacy; public statements can quickly reinforce preconceptions about bias. Think, for instance, of the negative connotations for Muslims of George W. Bush's use of the word "crusade" in initiating the "global war on terrorism." In practical terms, not least through avoiding making controversial statements, Concordis gained a reputation for independence, impartiality, and fairness that allowed it to be involved in difficult subject areas, like the role of religious leaders, without being seen as representing Christian churches or Western governments. This reputation is crucial to success as an intermediary.

Linking both to impartiality and to the "do no harm" idea mentioned earlier, it is often the case that harm done in conflict situations is the result of misapplied military, economic, or political power. Power differentials play a key role in conflict, so it is important that we ourselves are seen as nonthreatening. In a sense, our *power* consists in our weakness, a very biblical concept (see 2 Corinthians 12:8–10).[19] While power differentials in a society cannot be eliminated at a stroke, it is possible within a dialogue context to leave them "outside the door." Such a concern for the poor, weak, and powerless is entirely consistent with biblical teaching.

Our power is of course not only expressed through military force or economic superiority. It is also crucial to avoid the intellectual hubris of claiming we can bring solutions to others' problems. "Who is wise and understanding among you? Let them show it by their good life, by deeds done in the humility that comes from wisdom" (James 3:13);[20] according to the writer of the biblical book of James, *humility* is a wise option. There is, of course, a danger of being falsely humble like the Uriah Heep character in Charles Dickens's *David Copperfield*, but in the peacebuilding context, humility means not assuming that you have the answers to the complex problems facing a society in conflict. Rather, we look to those involved, who (collectively) know their situation better than do outsiders, to seek solutions that make sense to them. This commitment to "local ownership" does not necessarily mean stepping back and leaving the local people to sort out their own problems, but it does imply a very "hands-off" approach to dialogue facilitation. Expert advice may be brought in but offered as information in a spirit of service and not imposed.

Thus Concordis has been able to express an emphasis on the role of relationships, on the dignity and welfare of all human beings, and on sustainable peace in terms that are consistent with biblical values but shared by those whose philosophy derives from elsewhere.

CONCLUSION

The principles whose biblical resonance I have described above could have been developed or adopted by many individuals or organizations, whether they call themselves religious or not. And that is perhaps the point. If Christians are called to be peacemakers, they are called to be effective peacemakers. The principles by which they operate should not differ significantly from those of other practitioners, whatever their faith or philosophy. Whether one emphasizes that human wisdom comes from God or that modern Western ethics have Judeo-Christian origins, it should come as no surprise that an emphasis on long-term engagement for reconciliation, on comprehensive, cooperative peacebuilding, and on local ownership strikes a chord for almost all who seek sustainable peace. Indeed, shared principles form a basis for mutual respect without implying religious or even philosophical agreement and therefore provide a foundation on which those of any religion who wish to build peace can work together.

For Christians who feel the call to undertake or support peacemaking, there is an honorable biblical tradition. In his letter to the Ephesians, Paul says of Jesus, "He himself is our peace" (Ephesians 2:14)[21] and goes on to describe how Jesus brought together Jew and Gentile. Clearly this is addressing reconciliation with others on the foundation of reconciliation with God through Christ, but it is at the very least an example to follow. Taken together with our duty to the human victims of violent conflict and the call to wisdom described above, this biblical model seems to make the case for nonpartisan, service-oriented peacebuilding intervention. By expressing peacebuilding activity in terms of concrete principles with biblical foundations, it is possible to work effectively within a secular legal framework and avoid suspicion of religious bias, on the one hand, and to answer Christian accusations of secularization on the other. But it's not easy. It's a tightrope.

NOTES

1. Paul Wehrand and John Paul Lederach, "Mediating Conflict in Central America," *Journal of Peace Research* 28, no. 1 (1991): 85–98; Simon Fisher and Lada Zimina, "Just Wasting Our Time? Provocative Thoughts for Peacebuilders," in *Berghof Handbook for Conflict Transformation*, ed. Beatrix Austin, Martina Fischer, and Hans Giessmann (Berlin: Berghof Foundation, 2009).

2. Stacey Gutkowski, "Religion and Security in International Relations Theories," in *The Routledge Handbook of Religion and Security*, ed. Chris Seiple, Dennis Hoover, and Pauletta Otis, 125–35 (New York: Routledge, 2013).

3. New International Version UK (Colorado Springs, CO: Biblica, 2011), BibleGateway.com, accessed May 24, 2017.

4. The views expressed in this chapter, while based on my experience of leading Concordis International, do not necessarily represent the policies or views of the organization's board of trustees. I am grateful to Peter Marsden, Concordis program manager, for reviewing and commenting on a draft of this chapter.

5. Colleagues in the reconciliation work are presented in the film *The Imam and the Pastor*. See "DVD: The Imam and the Pastor," United States Institute of Peace, April 16, 2009, http://www.usip.org/publications/dvd-the-imam-and-the-pastor, accessed September 6, 2016.

6. Peter Dixon, *Peacemakers: Building Stability in a Complex World* (Nottingham, UK: Inter-Varsity Press, 2009).

7. Mark Duffield, "Risk-Management and the Fortified Aid Compound: Everyday Life in Post-interventionary Society," *Journal of Intervention and Statebuilding* 4, no. 4 (2010): 453–74. doi: 10.1080/17502971003700993.

8. David Lanz, "Why Darfur? The Responsibility to Protect as a Rallying Cry for Transnational Advocacy Groups," *Global Responsibility to Protect* 3, no. 2 (2011): 223–47. doi: 10.1163/187598411x5756852011.

9. John Paul Lederach and R. Scott Appleby, "Strategic Peacebuilding: An Overview," in *Strategies of Peace: Transforming Conflict in a Violent World*, ed. Daniel Philpott and Gerard F. Powers (New York: Oxford University Press, 2010).

10. Michael Walzer, *Just and Unjust Wars: A Moral Argument with Historical Illustrations*, 3rd ed. (New York: Basic Books, 2000).

11. Gary J. Bass, "Jus Post Bellum," *Philosophy and Public Affairs* 32, no. 4 (2004): 384–412.

12. New International Version UK.

13. Jean Bethke Elshtain, "Peace, Order, Justice: Competing Understandings," *Millennium—Journal of International Studies* 36, no. 3 (2008): 413–23. doi: 10.1177/03058298080360030201.

14. New International Version UK.

15. Concordis International (http://www.concordis-international.org, accessed February 1, 2014).

16. Graham Cole, "Christianity as a Relational Religion," in *Jubilee Manifesto: A Framework, Agenda and Strategy for Christian Social Reform*, ed. Michael Schluter and John Ashcroft (Downers Grove, IL: InterVarsity Press, 2005), 37–49.

17. International Standard Version (Bellfower, CA: ISV Foundation, 2011), BibleGateway.com, accessed May 24, 2017.

18. Deborah Hoffmann and Frances Reid, dir. *Long Night's Journey into Day* (DVD, Iris Films, 2000). See "Long Night's Journey into Day" (2000), IMDB, http://www.imdb.com/title/tt0236447, accessed September 6, 2016.

19. New International Version UK.

20. New International Version UK.

21. New International Version UK.

Chapter Nine

Peacebuilding as "Countering Violent Extremism"

Exploring Contradictions in Faith and Practice

Dishani Jayaweera with Nirosha De Silva

Challenge: How do you deal with the current tendency of some policy actors to link faith-based peacebuilding closely with countering violent extremism?

At a recent peacebuilding conference, I raised the question of our capacity to address the root causes of a conflict effectively, while at the same time being part of an agenda of countering violent extremism (CVE). CVE initiatives aim to prevent, disrupt, or interdict violent incidents motivated by extreme beliefs. While these are necessary and honorable goals, the CVE approach is limited by its narrow, state-centric understanding of security. When state mechanisms, as the driving force behind CVE initiatives, are also contributing to the "root causes" of conflicts in their societies, then it is problematic for peacebuilders to be associated with CVE. I explained to my fellow conference participants how I would be viewed as part of the root cause by our communities if I represented an initiative with a state-driven security agenda. I emphasized that one of our main tasks as peacebuilders is to address the root causes of a conflict, and being affiliated with a state-driven agenda renders us unfit to address many social conflicts effectively.

I questioned our functionality as peacebuilders to positively affect social change if we let the field of peacebuilding indulge in CVE-driven efforts, reversing the course of peacebuilding's purpose and distorting its face entirely. "If the terminology and tactics used contradict with the vision, strategies, and our interactions of peacebuilding, how effective could we be in a micro and macro level of the social change process?" I asked. My question was mainly left unanswered and was treated lightly by a couple of vague responses that disheartened me. We all agreed that these are undefined and untried role modifications that could alter the peacebuilding image in the long run. Strangely, I didn't witness much protest (to be precise, none at all!) from my fellow peacebuilders, who seemed to have already embraced the idea of "countering violent extremism" as engraved in trendy ideals of peacebuilding.

At the end of the convention, I was encouraged by the participants as well as the people who organized it to voice my opinion on the subject of CVE in the next rounds of discussions. I couldn't help but feel regret in my heart for my lack of capacity to have been an influential part of the prior rounds of discussions and decision making. I would have done everything in my personal power to stand up against this terminology of "countering" that we have inherited. These directives should have been discouraged and terminated in the idea's formation and initiation stages, instead of the frantic feeding and embracing of CVE in evidence today. If more peacebuilders who felt as strongly as I did had followed their intuition to protect our field, these initiatives would not have been born into our world today. I felt powerless and insignificant coming into the process at the latter stage.

I suggested that we rally to have a round of peacebuilding discussions on this issue, where the proponents of alternative strategies could come together to discover better solutions to this looming threat to/trend in our field of practice/community. I vowed to be part of such an initiative at my own cost, during my personal time, or on any of their terms, if we could reorganize to find solutions for better strategies. I was disheartened by the response I received, as none of the other peacebuilders viewed my suggestions as feasible.

How do we respond to the current tendency of many policy actors to link faith-based peacebuilding closely with countering violent extremism? As a spiritually and politically motivated peacebuilder, working with more than three hundred faith leaders representing Buddhism, Christianity, Islam, and Hinduism, with more than two decades of practice, I now find myself troubled by the growing emphasis on programs that aim to counter violent extremism embedded in peacebuilding initiatives. The concepts of peacebuilding and CVE are two distinct processes of seeing, understanding, and engaging with the world, but in practice, they are increasingly being fused, despite these fundamental differences.

My reflections and conclusions in this chapter are based on an in-depth understanding of peacebuilding theoretical concepts and practical exposure in the field. I believe that suggestions for peacebuilding to play a supportive role in countering terrorism undermine the already strained relationships between peacebuilders and the communities in which we work. The new role of peacebuilding was first defined to me by the CVE practitioners at two global conferences, namely, "Preventing and Countering Violent Extremism in South and Central Asia: The Role of Civil Society" in Istanbul in June 2015 and "The Ministerial-Level Regional Conference on CVE" in Astana, also in June 2015.[1]

Further, I draw on my Buddhist and multicultural heritage to analyze how peacebuilding and CVE concepts philosophically differ and, if merged, could harm field-based peacebuilding efforts, particularly interfaith or religiously motivated peacebuilding perspectives within diverse communities. In this discussion, I will explore the detrimental effects of merging state-driven CVE initiatives and civil society–based peacebuilding initiatives; these are two distinct notions that cannot come together without losing sight of their purposes and core values.

FOUNDATIONS

As a child, I grew up in a household with a strong moral base (based on Buddhist philosophy more than religious rituals). As a young girl, I was fascinated by people and what made them tick—including myself. I call it "searching for the deeper truths in us." Now, as an adult, I am mesmerized by the beauty of nature and the interconnectedness of the universe. In my youth, I witnessed two armed uprisings involving youth groups, majority Sinhalese Buddhists and minority Tamils, who represented the deprived social layers of the power hierarchy in Sri Lanka.

My upbringing unfolded amid the chaos of these rebellious youth groups being marginalized, terrorized, and defeated by state mechanisms, where senseless violence was used as an accepted form of solving social problems by both parties. I have also witnessed the highest human capacity to be courageous and compassionate to secure a dignified human existence for our people. My self-identity was shaped at a young age by absorbing these social ills as natural conditions of human existence and affirming the role-modeling behavior of good human qualities as the solution to them.

Growing up with war and destruction splattered around me as realities of day-to-day living, I have questioned the unjust structures that governed my country and racked my brain for just and fair solutions for Sri Lanka. I was a child who read literature containing accounts of the Russian Revolution, savored Leo Tolstoy's *War and Peace*[2] as a teenager, and tried to make sense of Karl Marx's *On Dialectical Materialism*[3] in my twenties. I studied law, thinking that the right path toward justice was siding with the law, and I felt disheartened at the end of my journey, finding myself at a loss. I withdrew to understand myself, taking long months of doing nothing but staring into space or sleeping peacefully, riding the uncertainty of finding my purpose in life.

At a time of self-doubt and fear I discovered "peacebuilding and conflict transformation," which spoke to my heart clearly and raised my capacity to heights where I contributed with passion. From then on, my life took shape with a force of its own. I cofounded the Center for Peacebuilding and Reconciliation (CPBR) with my life partner, Professor Jayantha Seneviratne, and today, close to two decades into my journey through an ordeal of self-discovery, I have shaped systems, structures, and the environment at CPBR to support justice and equality for the diverse Sri Lankan communities.

CHALLENGES: FLAWS IN MERGING PEACEBUILDING AND COUNTERING VIOLENT EXTREMISM

At the 2015 conference in Istanbul on "Preventing and Countering Violent Extremism in South and Central Asia: The Role of Civil Society," a few members of the peacebuilding community aired their reservations in closed groups, given the new expectations pressed on the peacebuilding role. We agreed that although peacebuilding could prevent violent extremism in communities through the proven strategies adopted, merging peacebuilding and CVE arbitrarily may not be a prudent solution to a complicated problem.

Universal peacebuilding concepts address root causes of conflicts, promote peaceful coexistence, strengthen inner and collective power, and build resilience, nourishing communities. Countering violent extremism is a field of policy, programs, and interventions designed to eliminate violence associated with radical political, social, cultural, and religious ideologies and groups. Originating from a security and defense standpoint, it is an evolving realm, facing challenges in its implementation and internalization within communities. In this context, there is a trend toward viewing peacebuilding, with its well-established community relations and well-versed conflict prevention and transformation strategies, as a vehicle to understand violent extremism, erase its imperfections, and build effective localized strategies.

Does the spoken language shape our thinking, or is it our social, political, economic, and cultural structures that shape our language, mirroring existing social ideologies? It is most likely that both are interlinked, and the language is integrated with our beliefs and interactions representing our philosophical and ideological base. For spiritually/religiously motivated peacebuilders, this terminology, especially the word "countering," creates contradictions. In that respect, when we adopt such terminology, it contradicts the peacebuilders' philosophical and ideological foundations.

"With a global North pushing to adopt vocabulary that does not sit well with the global South, where do the peacebuilders like us turn for clarity?" I asked myself. If the peacebuilding community feels that we are going in a direction that is harmful to the existence of our field, then why aren't more peacebuilders speaking on behalf of our integrity or disqualifying an entity that seems to drown out our voices?[4] If I had been there at the first round of CVE discussions, my response would have been absolute opposition, but I wasn't. I am placed at an impoverished level of the social order where I represent a third world country in South Asia that comes into focus only for the complexities of the problem of terrorism we have bestowed upon the world.

I did not have the role of "decision-making authority" or even come close to such an influence in these discussions. When I voiced my opinions, I was told that I had missed the idea's formation phase, and with the decisions made and strategies implemented, I was too late to change its course at the last stage. "We missed your expertise then, but now we cannot change anything." I was told that my views should have been noted and debated and might have altered the course of peacebuilding in the world today. I said that I failed to believe that other peacebuilders were unable to understand the gravity of CVE strategies, but if they didn't, I had my concerns about their capacity to protect the peacebuilding realm. I was informed (warned) that I was departing from the topic of discussion and the goals of our meeting. I declared that I shouldn't have been invited if they didn't want to hear my concerns. As expected, the end result was not fruitful, and I couldn't steer it in a positive direction.

The main target group in countering violence is the youth, and my argument is that more than countering extremism, we have to turn to creative solutions. My organization's strategic focus is using creative expression for healing and wellness, as an intervention strategy, benefiting communities affected by social ills. For example, the concept of the "healing capabilities of art" for individuals and societies is at least four thousand years old. Although it is not new knowledge, we can use it to create new strategies, instead of debatable ones such as CVE.

I will not dilute the spirit of the youth by promoting initiatives that tell them to conform to a subdued version of themselves or refrain from being who they were born to become. What I am promoting is being a distinctive personality in the mind of a spirited, nonviolent being. Instead of a gun to shoot as a form of an awakening, we give them a camera to shoot to capture their visions. Their identity as youth representing the future of the world, although trapped in a powerless dimension, is to bring justice to their community. Even the most rebellious of youths, once inspired and exposed to creative strategies for expressing their inner selves, gain immensely from our initiatives. Once they are on board, it is our responsibility to guide them to be socially responsible, belonging to a broader social identity where ethnicity, religion, social class, or political opinion don't determine their existence.

Instead of "I am a rebel. I have a gun. I stand up for the rights of my community. I am powerful," we introduce the youth identity of "I am a rebel.

I have a camera. I am a photographer. I am safeguarding my community through my artistic expression and ability to voice my innermost desires and vision for my future." It is the starting point of change where nonviolent strategies in the form of creative expression, compassion, and empathy embrace communities in healing transformation.

During our interactions with the Tamil minority communities, if we even mentioned the word "countering," the initiatives we were able to design would not have been possible, for we would have been treated as the "other" and the "oppressor." Our success lies in the pivotal area where we align strategic and creative avenues for Tamils to voice their problems, which wouldn't have been a possibility if CVE initiatives were around at the time.

In Thirrukkovil, I came across a unique village in the eastern province of Sri Lanka, with one boundary of the village controlled by the army and the other by the rebel Liberation Tigers of Tamil Eelam (LTTE). It was sandwiched between two distinctive power extremes, and villagers encountered problems very unique to their community. The youth in this village have acquired a distinctive self-identity, a hero image, either as a soldier or a rebel. I met three young male friends, inseparable and high-spirited—Shanath, Thushi, and Athisha—who breathed and yearned for the power of weapons. Their minds were shaped by the ideals of war and bearing arms. They would have qualified as the "culprits, suspects, or noted individuals" under a CVE initiative, but our workshops had a place for them and a positive impact on them. Our simple creative techniques taught them within a short period to look at violence as an unacceptable solution for civilized societies.

During the workshop activities, when asked to draw an object that represented them, all three of them drew guns, whereas the normal Sri Lankan youth in rural communities tend to draw objects like a cricket bat and a ball. Once they found an avenue to express themselves, they were the most committed photographers our workshops have ever created. We couldn't have transformed them that easily using an extremist agenda and terminology. They were in an identity crisis as freedom fighters and/or rebels, and with a CVE initiative, they would only be branded as "terrorists." I am in an identity crisis myself and have been for as long as I can remember, and for this reason alone, I understand why they perceive and act as they do. Instead of subduing their rebelliousness, I want to champion our youth by not suppressing their identity but understanding their struggles and giving them different tools and ideologies to function as responsible citizens.

Every extremist personality that I have come across—Tamil, Muslim, or Sinhalese—has trusted me as a peacebuilder for my capacity to give them clarity and hope. The community trust that I have earned is the most valuable gift and qualification I own as a peacebuilder. I am worthy of their trust because of my capacity as a human being to sense their contradictions, pain, and joy. I cannot go to them with one set of beliefs that limits me; I have to understand multiple personalities and identities to be empathetic to their individual and group dynamics. I cannot be bound by rigid CVE regimes that limit me in that effort.

Then again, CVE policy and global security efforts may seem to be a stronger stimulus for funding peacebuilding projects, backed by superior resources, authority, and powerful enablers. As all other institutions existing within social structures, NGOs can be easily manipulated by power inequalities when it comes to cultural, economic, and political pressure. Since the funding machinery is governed by a few powerful states that play a crucial role in shaping the cultural and ideological base of the world's NGO community, the peacebuilding and conflict transformation practitioners representing the NGO community and broader civil society are manipulated by these same mechanisms. Many get swayed by priorities and agendas of these hierarchical authorities while suppressing their values and belief in the concepts of peacemaking.

Even though this is the world reality, organizations such as CPBR have maintained their integrity and clarity, giving priority to needs on the ground emerging from the ongoing processes of peacebuilding. Today, there is a trend toward directing the majority of new funding toward programs supporting CVE. Civil society organizations and NGOs, relying on international funding, readily accept and internalize these flawed mandates set by the funding world without questioning the consequences.

In August 2016, while participating in the peacebuilders' summit in Germany,[5] I found myself engaged in a dialogue about integrating CVE strategies into peacebuilding with a fellow participant. She is a charismatic leader, excelling in her role, who can easily influence group dynamics. Knowing her beliefs on peacebuilding, I felt that she used the terminology and supported CVE and its initiatives too many times, to my bewilderment. When I inquired, she confessed that surrounded by a sea of viable funding prospects, she believed that it was sensible to use the terminology "they are looking for" to make them "hear us better." On many occasions, I have observed the same attitude toward securing funding and approaching funders in contrived ways. I remember asking her whether it was our purpose to speak in a language so they could hear us better or to make them hear what was best for our communities.

In the many international forums and retreats that I attended in 2016, the program agenda consisted of long sessions dedicated to discussions on "combating" or "countering" violent extremism. In such environments, it felt as if I were attending a state security meeting. Many participants approved these programs without a protest, even when that deeply contradicted their conscience. For the sustainability of their precious initiatives, peacebuilders are likely to accept programs married to CVE concepts against their better judgment, gradually becoming part of a repressive system. This concept of "speaking in a language they hear" slowly disheartened me and disconnected me from the peacebuilding community. As the facilitators who bridge connectivity and provide hope for marginalized groups, we must maintain a distinctive ideology, unattached to the ideologies of state and extremist groups.

Even if CVE programs bring about peaceful communities, the emphasis is on "countering" a problem as opposed to "engaging" a broader agenda and outcome. I believe the strategies that reduce peacebuilding to a supportive role to "counter" violent extremism are inadequate and diminish the peacebuilder's capacity to nurture and heal a community. The participants' perceptions of the facilitator's role and objectives matter in building trusting, long-term relationships. Framing these concerns in my role as a peacebuilder, belonging to the majority ethnic group with a Sinhalese Buddhist heritage, and hailing from and being educated in the capital of Sri Lanka, I have already sported the many hats of popular stereotypes of the "oppressor." Functioning under the banner of supporting CVE would incapacitate me indefinitely as a peacebuilder, exhausting my ability to work with minority communities and erasing their hard-earned trust in me, especially within the minority Tamil groups that I have worked with for decades.

Sri Lanka has endured thirty years of brutal war between minority LTTE rebels and the Sri Lankan government. Today we live in a country deeply wounded and bloodied, burdened by thousands of war-affected women, children, youth, and men from majority and minority communities. Now Sri Lanka is in the process of seeking to establish a value system in social, cultural, and political structures to bring justice, equality, and good governance.

Sri Lanka is a multiethnic and multireligious country where Sinhalese represent the majority ethnic group, and Tamils, Moors, Burghers, Malays, and indigenous people form the minority. Their religious breakdown comprises Buddhists, Hindus, Muslims, Christians, and others. I believe that the divisive war in Sri Lanka was a direct result of the limiting state-crafting systems adopted in our postcolonial era. As colonial rulers, we assumed a unitary system, based on principles of centralization, standardization, and homogenization. Under these systems, the Sinhalese Buddhist majority became the main ruling actors of the state and continued to introduce laws and acts to exclude the Tamil and other minorities from power structures. Using nonviolent struggles and tactics, Tamil politicians tried to bring their grievances and concerns into mainstream politics but failed in their attempts. As a direct consequence, desperate Tamil youth rebels rose against their government.

RESPONSES

Our Objective and Scope of Peacebuilding Strategies

Our peacebuilding exposure to understanding the complexities in Sri Lanka has proved the importance of aligning the "self" with "group" identity. Sri Lankan community groups are motivated by a unique mixture of Sinhalese, Tamil, Muslim, and other ethnic cultural definitions, religious influences, and political beliefs and attitudes. Our peacebuilding role in Sri Lanka concentrates on building individual identities to align with a broader peace-loving communal identity, instead of adopting strategies related to countering violent extremism that focus on a fraction of the society likely to embrace violence as a tool of conflict resolution.

A unique blend of "self" and "group" identities leads people to act on collective principles and beliefs rather than solely operating on their self-interest. For example, a radical religious mind of a Buddhist is ignited by spiritual beliefs collectively shared as well as the individual's own motivational factors. It is vital that we understand how these moral implications spread through a community to motivate only a small group to engage in violent actions. Promoting harmonious group values derived from the community's own social, cultural, and religious heritage, we have lessened these tensions in Sri Lanka. Looking through the lens of CVE tactics, we fail to address these distinctive issues.

Most religiously motivated exclusions and violations of civil rights in Sri Lanka do not reflect the common international stereotypes of religious extremism. The three decades of conflict between the majority Sinhalese and minority Tamil groups is not due to religious beliefs but rather to ethnic tensions between the Buddhist Sinhalese majority and the Hindu Tamil minority groups. Further, where religious extremism does exist in Sri Lanka, it is found in religious communities that outsiders typically assume to be peaceful. For example, many Buddhist monks contribute to divisive sentiments in Sri Lanka by thinking of Buddhist Sinhalese as the superior and privileged ethnic group, placed at the highest level of the social, cultural, and religious hierarchy.

Religion and Peacebuilding in Sri Lanka

Religious motivation springs from a collective spiritual experience. Violent extremism cannot be explained without understanding human nature molded by religious principles, defining aspects of a collective spirituality, and individual interpretations of religious teaching. In Sri Lanka, religion can be used as a powerful vehicle in reshaping troubled communities and transforming them into peaceful societies. How religion and peacebuilding cross paths is an important aspect needed to understand how to gauge their influence on each other. In my sixteen years' experience in fieldwork, journeying with grass roots and communities, I have realized that there is a clear gap between religious concepts and religious practice. As I am a spiritually motivated peacebuilder, my role entails supporting religious leaders and communities to lessen this gap.

Our initiatives have touched the lives of a substantial group of religious and community leaders who took part in our peacebuilding workshops and received training on conflict analysis, peacebuilding practices, reconciliation, and conflict transformation. We have created a safe place for religious leaders to discuss and find common ground on issues affecting their communities and regions while being open to others' values and beliefs.

Religion in Peacebuilding (and CVE)

Religion as a Driving Force of Violent Conflict

Religious division is deeply embedded in Sri Lankan history even though violent conflict in Sri Lanka was not religiously motivated. Many religious teachings and individuals' interpretations of religious concepts tend to devalue nonbelievers, removing them from moral obligation and concern and reducing them to an identity of the "other." A CVE agenda would only increase these detrimental effects of the nature of such religious influences on marginalized groups.

Religion as a Secular Version of Peacebuilding

I find that when religious teachings promote universal morals, the followers are more open to embracing other faith-based concepts, and they tend to respect and value human life over religious identities. CVE initiatives encourage divisiveness between religious groups, putting marginalized groups in danger rather than bringing them together.

Wide Gap between Religious Concepts and Religious Practice

The more I probe and embrace religiously and spiritually driven concepts, the more I realize how they are barely practiced in society today. There remains a clear divide between what is embedded as core in religious teachings and what is really being practiced. CVE advocates do not base their strategies on understanding this phenomenon and the potential of going back to the bones of religious thinking in peacebuilding. We have designed peacebuilding initiatives that lessen these gaps and encourage community-specific values, where commonalities of different religious philosophies, prophesies, and practices are outlined, embraced, and internalized as a group. Under a CVE agenda this is impossible to achieve.

This following story I am furnishing here happened in Galle, Sri Lanka, in 2003 in an era when most state power in Sri Lanka was in the hands of the majority ethnic group, namely, Sinhalese Buddhists. There was large-scale minority exclusion at play in the social, cultural, and political landscape. We were working with community groups in the southern regions as they played an important role as unwavering opponents of the rebelliousness of minority Tamil groups.

In this context, Buddhist monks, especially student monks, played a crucial role in the protests against rebels, state peacebuilding efforts, and any form of concession that the minority groups received under the government mandate. Both groups, namely the Janatha Vimukthi Peramuna (JVP) (Sinhalese youth rebels) and LTTE (Tamil rebels) bore arms against the state, during two different periods of time due to the repressive and restrictive social structures that only catered to and favored privileged community groups in Sri Lanka. When the JVP rebel power had been eradicated as a social concern, the proponents of the movement rallied against the Tamil rebels, although the rights they were fighting for and the root causes of social unrest remained similar. Both groups fought for similar rights against the same violator, but when the rebels became the Tamil youth community, they faced heightened effects of "double discrimination" because of their ethnic and religious identity differences.

During our peacebuilding and reconciliation work in the southern province, one of the prominent leaders of a Buddhist monk group, rallying against reconciliation efforts that favored the Tamil minority rebels, spoke about his experience after a series of workshops. As a Buddhist monk in Sri Lanka and a leader of a faith-based extremist group, he represented the highest level of hierarchical power available to a religious leader. According to religious rituals, a Buddhist monk receives extreme regard, where religious followers worship the monks who represent the Lord Buddha. This particular monk approached us with a humble demeanor and bowed in front of us, almost in a stance of worship. He said that his gesture was to show his highest respect, the way he would worship his religious leader. We were extremely taken aback by his sentiments.

He told us how he amassed, rallied, and swore animosity against peace talks between the government and rebels, how he walked right at the front of rallies, bellowing discriminatory slogans, believing that he was doing the right thing. He said that until the day he attended our workshops, no one had explained how he might be potentially harming and contributing to the extinction of minority rights. He confessed that after every uprising against the rebels, he felt a deep sadness within himself that he didn't quite understand, and after each such occasion, he had sat in front of Buddha and prayed for clarity and direction. Every day, he consoled himself in the truth he believed, that it was the Buddhist monk's role to save the country, especially when its sovereignty was at stake.

He believed during an era when the country was at war, as in the history of Sri Lankan colonization by European settlers, it was the monks' responsibility to side with the state to protect the country. He said he was motivated by the only identity that Buddhist clergy assumed that aligned with the religious history of Sri Lanka. He described the historical accounts of the monks' role during British rule and the war that led to Sri Lankan independence. He claimed that it used to be his life's purpose because he didn't know any better. The monk said, "My eyes are open now, and I know better ways of solving our problems. Now, I can go back to being a real Buddhist monk, and for this gift of vision you have given me, I am eternally grateful. I am worshiping you for giving me such wisdom." That was the day that I committed myself entirely to religious conflict transformation initiatives, although I had my doubts about our success in such a complex process. I told myself that if I can at least transform one monk at a time, I can be content with our progress.

My spiritual and universal responsibility to the world in peacebuilding was affirmed by the words of that young monk. He saw our basic goodness, as we did not represent any branding from groups such as CVE proponents or any other form of organized power behind us. Our connection only represented a simple human-to-human relationship that can be embraced by any empathetic person. When we operate in grassroots communities, we try to refrain from using organizational branding for the negative images attached to the name of peacebuilding. CVE initiatives represent the most extremist branding that we can operate under; therefore we have to stay away from initiatives that are harmful to our image. This is a clear example of how faith-based peacebuilding succeeded in a context of religious extremism. Operating under a CVE tag, we would have failed even before we started.

Challenges in Peacebuilding Associated with CVE

Linguistic Vocabulary of Peacebuilding and CVE

In peacebuilding concepts, words such as "engaging" and "transforming" are used in place of "countering" and "combating." Our linguistic vocabulary shapes a cultural ideology as well as the founding philosophy of resulting discourse. Words with a forceful meaning attached to them, such as "countering" and "combating," are derived from a state security mandate. Similarly, people give meaning to words that resonate with their thinking as products and victims of social violence. The peacebuilding community has given birth to many meaningful words and combinations of words, such as "conflict transformation," and the peacebuilder in me "engages" with the world to promote "harmony" and "human well-being." The ideology of a merger between security mandate and peacebuilding might engrave words in contradiction with the vision and nature of peacebuilding.

Ideological Differences and Contradictions

Peacebuilders interpret conflicts through a neutral and wider lens with a deeper understanding of the drivers of violent extremism. A peacebuilder imprisoned in the ideals of state security concerns offers a diluted approach. Being part of another set of ideals means being trapped in its agenda. We represent the change needed in the world, as we symbolize hope, a morality check, and a conflict resolution mechanism, tested and proven, in working with both state and civil society. As peacebuilders, we carry a fundamental responsibility to stay true to our course. We cannot be part of root causes that we stand against. It is an inner conflict I struggle with daily, trying to escape reins that keep me shackled and feeling extremely uncomfortable when others expect me to cater to ideals that I don't believe in.

Religious Beliefs and Heritage

The religious roles of Buddha, Jesus, Muhammad, and Gandhi in faith-based peacebuilding are examples of empathy, forgiveness, and compassion. It is my innate responsibility as a peacebuilder to open my heart to every person subjected to injustice through discriminatory practices employed by social and structural institutions and to forgive, empathize, and understand with a compassionate mind-set. It is my faith-based responsibility to practice nonviolent strategies to win the heart of the "other" that I inherited from my Buddhist religious heritage.

Objectives of CVE and Peacebuilding

CVE does not focus on root causes of conflicts; it only focuses on outcome. In peacebuilding, the fundamental element of finding a solution to a problem is through addressing root causes while engaging with the outcome. The purpose and objectives differ between the two, where CVE is focused on protection of social, economic, and political institutions, and peacebuilding is focused on conflict transformation while protecting humanistic and ecological well-being. In this context, CPBR empowers civil societies, builds resilience, heals wounds, and enhances tolerance.

Individualized and Internalized Specifics

As a Sinhalese Buddhist, representing the ethnic majority group in Sri Lanka and the key contributors to social conflicts, in my mind, I carry a heavier level of burden and responsibility for the violent extremism in our society than someone coming from a religious minority background. My vision for a peaceful society in Sri Lanka is about bringing justice and equality to people who have faced injustice for decades under ethnic and religious discrimination, rather than "combating" or "countering" those who are more likely to be the "victims" of extremism, not the "contributors." As a peacebuilder, I cannot stand shoulder to shoulder with armed forces, state intelligence strategy, war machinery, or an ideology behind a militarized mandate, supporting CVE.

Peacebuilding, Intimidation, and Threats to Person

In many instances when peacebuilding takes the state-driven security identity, the practitioners become susceptible to psychological, physiological, and institutionalized threats from external sources. Unless peacebuilding practitioners are truly open to seeing others as humans first, instead of dehumanizing groups as the "enemy of the state," we are unable to create and earn the trust of groups we work with. One of the core competencies nourished in ourselves to become effective peacebuilders is the ability to embrace and understand both the "victims" of violence as well as the "creators" of violence. When we take a stand to "counter extreme violence," we choose one group and oppose the other. We become the "enemy" of one movement, raising the risk posed to our lives in violent communities of the world today as we are not protected by a security blanket.

Controlled Framework Stifling Innovation

When we cage our thinking and scope into a controlled framework, we lose our capacity to think innovatively and fail to reach optimal results through human creativity. A rigid framework stifles innovation, and controlled frameworks act negatively, deterring much needed change. As a peacebuilder, I believe where there is creativity, there is change, and the fewer attachments we endure with controlled structures, the more innovation we yield. "Woman," a separate initiative sponsored by CPBR, is channeling creativity through its undefined organizational structures, openness to new experiences, and enormous space for change.

Buddhist Influence on Peacebuilding

Religious influence has often been connected to social conflicts, while religious teachings provide us with a foundation (often overlooked by societies) that can be embraced as core in conflict transformation. The proof that religions can inspire violence and nonviolence in similar intensities is a developing idea that encourages a closer relationship between religions and peacebuilding. In this discussion, I will introduce the role of Buddhism and ways of channeling its religious resources to positively affect social change and conflict transformation.

Cause and Effect

In Buddhism, the existence of everything in the world is explained through cause and effect, and this phenomenon is called the Law of Cause and Effect. It determines all outcomes we come across in our environment. Cause and effect is made up of the following essential guidelines.

Noble Truths

In Buddhism, the four noble truths, integral to overcome suffering, are as follows:

1. Identifying suffering
2. Understanding the cause of suffering
3. Ending suffering by addressing causes
4. Following the way to end suffering

In my peacebuilding workshops, I introduce four steps to transforming violent conflict and extremism based on these four noble truths as follows:

1. Identifying conflict(s) and acknowledging that there is a conflict/violence
2. Identifying the nature and root causes and effects of conflict/violence
3. Identifying creative and alternative ways to address the root causes, engaging with the effects of violence/conflict, and adopting nonviolent approaches, mechanisms, and techniques
4. Implementing actions/solutions effectively and efficiently with contributions from all parties involved

We follow these steps as conflict transformation practitioners in a practical manner, interpreting religious thinking to engage and transform situations and people.

Violent Extremism Interpreted through Buddhism

Violent extremism is an "effect" existing within state, regional, and global power structures, born through a "cause" because of a "condition" and brought to life as a detrimental "effect." The Law of Cause and Effect shows that we need to address the "cause" and the "conditions" that led to the "effect" to eliminate the negative outcome or the "effect." Buddhists believe that the suffering in the world, such as poverty, injustice, and war (resulting in both structural and personal violence), is produced by ignorance (*Moha*), greed (*Loba*), and cruelty (*Dwesha*). In Buddhist practices, generosity, love, compassion, and selflessness promote and strengthen empathetic relationships among all beings. Buddhists believe that to relieve suffering one must attain enlightenment (nirvana) while wishing all beings to end suffering, including human, animal, and other living beings. Buddhist practices are in alignment with nonviolent strategies of peacebuilding that transform structural violence through mass mobilization.

David Loy, a scholar of Buddhist studies, points out the most important wisdom Buddhism teaches us is paying attention to the root causes of suffering. He further claims that these root causes have found their way into social institutions, and we should carefully examine their cause and effect on societies. Introducing Buddhist social theory, Loy expands on threefold suffering as institutionalized greed, institutionalized cruelty, and institutionalized ignorance, reinforcing and cultivating structural and personal violence. Individualized suffering and institutionalized suffering are interdependent, whereas the latter is the more powerful actor and can influence the former, not the other way around.

Countering violent extremism implies that individualized suffering is the root cause of institutionalized suffering. It is crucial to address the imperfections and ambiguities in this conviction that the violator lives outside society acting on his own self-interest. The reality is that the society has influenced or "caused" the "condition" to determine the "effect." Therefore, CVE strategies that do not focus on root causes cannot heal our societies in conflicts. This framing of the issue imposes its influence on the designs of CVE, which, for example, often proposes treatment of the individual isolated from his or her community.

The years 2008 and 2009 marked an important juncture in CPBR history. We were working with 120 religious leaders from four faith groups in three main regions of Sri Lanka. The country was going through the most brutal war in its thirty years of armed conflict, called the "final war." Initially, the CPBR team failed to bring together a group of Islamic religious leaders for a four-day conflict transformation workshop, and the Islamic leaders told us to leave their villages, go back to Colombo, and "influence the Sinhalese Buddhist politicians to stop the war" instead of engaging them in futile discussions. We spent two days in discussions to make them understand our purpose and what we represented before we could actually commence the workshops.

Naleemi, a prominent leader of a fundamentalist Islamic community, confessed his strong resistance and suspicions at the initial stages of our interactions. He said, "I came here to spy on you, but I am leaving totally transformed." Today, he is a messenger of peace, justice, and good governance.

Naleemi pioneered a community culture in his village that encourages young girls to pursue higher education. Since then, his village has produced many female professionals and political activists. They wear burkas and their ethnic, religious, and community identities proudly, representing a highly educated, socially conscious, and politically active group of women.

Naleemi became an inspiring religious speaker. His message of peacebuilding is composed of conflict transformation and Islamic religious concepts. He travels around the country delivering his message of peace at prayer meetings and public gatherings. Today, he is playing an important role in bringing Tamil and Islamic communities together, initiating dialogues with Sinhalese groups to bring justice through the compassion, empathy, and forgiveness embedded in their religious ideologies. During his revelations on his personal transformation, I have often seen his tears, moved by his own message. The trust in Naleemi's eyes when he looks at me gives me immense hope for our future as a multicultural nation and reinforces our strategies in peacebuilding. To him, we were humans, motivated by humanism as we connect through spiritual values beyond the truth embedded in our religious, political, intellectual, and intuitive dimensions.

CONCLUSION

Today, there is a trend toward increasing engagement between peacebuilding and CVE efforts to prevent communities from being exposed to extremist violence. CVE has evolved to combat violent extremism through policy, programs, and tools extensively within the last decade. A peacebuilder's broader mix of localized and sustainable tools and practices differs extensively from a CVE mandate. I recognize that peacebuilding and CVE may intersect in some respects, but the tactics of the two domains fundamentally differ, and a merger of the two is an imperfect solution to a complex problem. Among peacebuilders, our strength and purpose lies in how we introduce civil society–based propositions to the authoritative state structures, not in bringing directives from the state structure to the people. I share here some of the lessons I have learned about staying true to my purpose.

Protect Your Conscience

The most important tool we have against shortsighted peacebuilding strategies is our resolve to disqualify them with every opportunity presented to us. I have learned to protect my integrity and beliefs, focusing only on my vision in my initiatives, rather than being defined by funding criteria backed by debatable strategies. I have learned to find courage to speak up when I feel contradicted. Peacebuilding, as I see it, represents missionary work that needs personal, professional, and spiritual commitment. I find it healing to voice my concerns and take a stance before things settle too comfortably in my mind, against my better judgment. The peacebuilder in me believes that an oppressor, despite the degree of the effect on the oppressed—minimal or extensive—should not be granted mainstream approval and sophisticated tools to further subdue the oppressed.

Value Coexistence

Valuing coexistence, understanding root causes of conflicts, and engaging the parties in conflict in finding solutions is the key for peacebuilding. During my interactions with community groups in Sri Lanka, I understood that "people do not act solely on individual self-interest." It is an inadequate explanation for violent extremism that is deeply rooted in the failures of social responsibility and operational mechanisms. Diversity, in every form, is accepted and understood in our peacebuilding perspective, even if it takes the form of violent extremism. We believe that to eliminate violent extremism, first we must understand the causes of social conflicts, including the effect of oppressive social mechanisms.

Be Bold. Speak Up.

Every opportunity I get at a conference, workshop, or personal engagement, be it at a peacebuilders' retreat or at a destination in a foreign country, I speak of my concerns until the listener becomes aware of my position. I bring it up at all peacebuilding gatherings, be it a coffee break, social media, or conference, even when I see that I make people uncomfortable with my views. My advice to peacebuilding practitioners is simply "Speak up!" Don't sweep our problems under the rug, underestimate the damage CVE can do to our field, or be helpless bystanders to a real looming threat. Ask yourselves, "If we cannot protect ourselves, how can we help our many communities that we are accountable to in our roles?"

Take Action

We have to bring peacebuilding groups together to determine our roles within the new situation. Especially European peacebuilding communities have to take leadership in steering these discussions. Peacebuilders all over the world have to come out of hiding and strategize about what we can do to eliminate these initiatives. We have to rally out in the open without sulking in the background and taking handouts tagged with trendy names and noxious viruses. If we truly believe that we are against CVE initiatives and their harmful effects on societies, we have to come together with clear purpose. In every noted summit or conference, we have to appoint peacebuilders to carry this message. We have to take action against something that most of us don't believe in rather than assume the identity of innocent victims. If we don't act now and let CVE-infested peacebuilding in our field to the point that we lose our identity, we are as guilty as the designers of these strategies.

Policymakers should focus on delinking CVE and peacebuilding, even at this latter stage. Decision-making bodies should include civil activist participants who would play a crucial role in shaping strategy. In the discussions regarding peacebuilding policy, state actors should keep the state security and defense agendas separate in order to stay true to the peacebuilding mandate. We should request a recall of CVE strategies in peacebuilding, and those strategies should be placed solely under a defense agenda, where peacebuilders are not expected to tag along. Let peacebuilders be what they are, what they have always been, what they will continue to be—peacebuilders who give humanity "hope."

In our peacebuilding efforts, CPBR has remained true to its autonomy and unique identity, even when faced with the international pressures and trends in countering extremism being merged with peacebuilding. We have avoided working with the ambiguity of situations where we take on the directive of the policymakers and enforcers, who may be part of the social conflicts. Staying true to the do-no-harm methodology in peacebuilding, we have backed only the programs without unintended spiral effects that negatively affect communities.

Looking back, I have long had a distinctive image of myself as a peacebuilder and as part of an esteemed peacebuilding community that I took strength from when in doubt. I gained energy just by being around those peacebuilders. When at times I felt hopeless and struggled to carry on, I could reach out and gain focus and clarity from them easily. I used to look up to them and think that peaceful achievements would be possible for us one day, seeing their resolve and the progress they have made. They were my source of inspiration when it was hard to dream during harsh times. Now, I feel isolated. Now, even attending a conference feels like an ordeal filled with contradictions. Now, there's only one terminology, and everyone feels uncomfortable living under its shadow. We must walk toward being that wonderful community once again and choose whom we carry on our shoulders: CVE mandates or people who desperately need our championing?

NOTES

1. The Istanbul conference was convened by the Global Center on Cooperative Security, and the Astana conference was hosted by the government of Kazakhstan. Both June 2015 events were considered follow-ups to the (U.S.) White House Summit to Counter Violent Extremism of February 2015. For an informal summary of the proceedings, see Global Center on Cooperative Security, "Preventing and Countering Violent Extremism in South and Central Asia," U.S. State Department, https://www.state.gov/documents/organization/245705.pdf.

2. Leo Tolstoy, *War and Peace*, trans. Richard Pevear and Larissa Volokhonsky (New York: Vintage, 2008).

3. Karl Marx, *On Dialectical Materialism* (Firebird Publishers, 1977).

4. Though I sometimes feel alone in my efforts, there are other voices strongly criticizing the CVE paradigm. See, for example, Junaid M. Afeef and Alejandro J. Beutel, "CVE Critics Are Right, and CVE Is Still Necessary," *AltMuslim Ramadan 2016*, July 27, 2015, http://www.patheos.com/blogs/altmuslim/2015/07/cve-critics-are-right-and-cve-is-still-necessary, accessed May 5, 2017; Colm Campbell, "Beyond Radicalization: Towards an Integrated Anti-violence Rule of Law Strategy," in *Counter-terrorism: International Law and Practice*, ed. Ana Maria Salinas de Frías, Katya Samuel, and Nigel White (Oxford: Oxford University Press, 2012), 255–82; Naz Modirzadeh, "If It's Broke, Don't Make It Worse: A Critique of the UN Secretary General's Plan of Action to Prevent Violent Extremism," *Lawfare*, January 23, 2016, https://www.lawfareblog.com/if-its-broke-dont-make-it-worse-critique-un-secretary-generals-plan-action-prevent-violent-extremism, accessed May 5, 2017.

5. Global Peacebuilders Summit, September 4–9, 2016, Paretz and Berlin, Germany.

Part IV

Confronting Injustice and Trauma

Chapter Ten

Transforming Trauma

Wounded Healing in the Way of Jesus

Johonna Turner

Challenge: How do you deal with fear and traumatic experiences and help other people to do the same?

"When God chooses the plain, the ordinary, the weak, and the broken, God's power stands out more clearly."
—David Garland and Diana Garland, *Flawed Families of the Bible: How God's Grace Works through Imperfect Relationships*[1]

On a Saturday afternoon in February 2008, five young people, ages ten to seventeen, sat with me in the front room of a row house converted into an office space for youth organizers. Located on Martin Luther King Avenue Southeast, in Washington, DC., the office was just a few blocks away from the Anacostia Metro station, the Barry Farms public housing development, and the small bridge where a person can stand between the two and see the Washington Monument on the other side of the city. We were meeting every Saturday as part of the Visions to Peace Project, a short-term initiative I launched in 2007 to support youth-led organizing for peace. Supported by a Justice Fellowship from the Open Society Institute, I sought to engage youth in using the arts to promote creative and sustainable strategies for community safety that do not depend upon policing and punitive approaches.

Our first program, the "Flip the Script! Media Arts Workshop," provided a small team of Black youth with an opportunity to produce a documentary film that would highlight their voices and visions for peace and challenge the dominant narratives that too often criminalize African-American youth. Our

189

weekly popular education workshops focused on developing a deeper understanding of violence against youth as well as mapping how punitive responses are counterproductive to community peace. "What kinds of violence
affect your life and the lives of other youth you know?" I asked the youth
assembled in the room. "Gun violence! Domestic violence! Police harassment!" they called out one by one. Their final list ranged from shootings and
rape to incarceration and closing down public housing. How do young people
not only challenge these manifestations of violence but also heal from their
impacts on their lives?

This chapter examines my ongoing journey to transform fearful and traumatic experiences in my own life into sources of wisdom and possibility. It
also reflects my efforts to engage others, particularly Black youth in the
United States, in healing from trauma while working for peace and justice in
their neighborhoods. The Greek root word for trauma, *traumat-*, simply
means "wound." When events and circumstances in our lives overwhelm our
ability to cope, woundedness, or trauma, occurs in our minds, bodies, and
spirits. My Christian faith has deepened my capacity to let go of the fear and
shame caused by traumatic experiences in my life. Moreover, my faith has
transformed trauma in my life into a source of strength, insight, and compassion, which I can offer to others. In this way, I have come to see myself as a
wounded healer. The term "wounded healer," coined by psychotherapist Carl
Jung, refers to someone whose help to others is grounded in her own experiences of suffering and pain.[2] Traumatic experiences in the life of a wounded
healer release a unique ability to come alongside suffering others as a sister
or a brother who knows pain intimately, rather than as an objective or distanced outsider who lacks experiential knowledge. God has enabled me to
turn my experiences of pain into power and thus become a wounded healer.

As I explain in the next section of this chapter, "Foundations," the archetype of the "wounded healer" has been integral to how I understand the
identity and work of Jesus Christ, as well as how I perceive God's ability to
transform the most painful moments of my life. In the subsequent section,
"Challenges," I identify key obstacles that I have faced in my journey as a
"wounded healer"—namely, the lack of spaces to name and process trauma
collectively. Then, in "Responses," I tell the story of Let's Get Free!, the
arts-based healing program I founded as part of the Visions to Peace Project
to help young people come together to heal from trauma in their lives. Finally, I conclude by summarizing key aspects of our approach and highlighting
additional models for trauma healing informed by Christian spirituality.

FOUNDATIONS

"We do not have to convert the world before we console it."
—Kris Rocke and Joel Van Dyke, *Geography of Grace: Doing Theology from Below*[3]

In the Old Testament of the Holy Bible, there is a poem about a suffering servant who would be "pierced for our rebellion, crushed for our sins, beaten so we could be whole, and whipped so we could be healed" (Isaiah 53:5, New Living Translation). This poem is a prophecy of Jesus Christ, presenting him as the ultimate wounded healer. The poem's presumed author, the prophet Isaiah, proclaims that the wounds Jesus Christ willingly accepted to the point of death provide healing for all of humanity. As a wounded healer, Jesus Christ heals not only my brokenness but also the wounds in my life that result from the brokenness of others and the brokenness of our world. Brokenness refers to missing pieces: a lack of wholeness, completion, and health.

In both death and life, Jesus brought healing through his own experiences of suffering. Isaiah's poetic narrative of a wounded healer describes Jesus as one who "was looked down on and passed over, a man who suffered, who knew pain firsthand" (Isaiah 53:3, *The Message*).[4] He was considered utterly unattractive, rejected, and despised (Isaiah 53:2–3).[5] Jesus experienced life in human form as a member of a subjugated minority group—a Jewish person living under Roman occupation. Theologian Howard Thurman makes much of the historical facts that Jesus's economic, political, and social position put him in the same group as the masses of poor and disenfranchised people on earth.[6] Moreover, Jesus directed his life, ministry, and message to a disinherited people.[7] His ministry and message also put him at odds with the religious and political leaders within his own ethnic and religious community. As I read the Gospels, four different firsthand accounts of Jesus's life, I see Jesus, who was himself oppressed and persecuted, extending love and mercy to those most marginalized and hurting in his society—the women and children, people with chronic illnesses and disabilities, and those labeled as criminals, traitors, and cheaters. Throughout biblical accounts of his life, Jesus is described as seeing people with compassion—a term that means "to feel or suffer with." Could it be that Jesus's own intimate experience of suffering was connected to his willingness to experience and heal the pain of others?

Renowned writer and priest Henri Nouwen has written about how Christian leaders working for peace and justice might look to Christ's example to understand what it might mean for us to be wounded healers. "Thus like Jesus," writes Nouwen, "he who proclaims liberation is called not only to care for his own wounds and the wounds of others, but also to make his wounds into a major source of his healing power."[8] When I help others to heal from trauma through vulnerability and courage, I am participating in the work of peacebuilding and reconciliation to which Christ calls his followers. Trauma healing interrupts cycles of violence, facilitates inner peace, and lays the groundwork for reconciliation among people who have been hurt and those who have inflicted pain, often as a result of their own wounding. In these ways and others, my role as a peacebuilder is deeply connected to my identity as a Christian.

When I say I am a Christian, I am expressing my personal relationship with Jesus Christ, my commitment to follow his Way, and my participation in advancing the nonviolent, all-loving, radically merciful movement of Jesus Christ on earth. For me, advancing the Way of Jesus is more than sharing my faith with others; it is actively promoting shalom, a sense of wholeness, well-being, healthy relationships, and healing that is nourished by the grace of God. My faith in Christ began when I was a child under the guidance of my mother, a joyful and faithful woman of great humility and kindness, whom I witnessed rise early in the morning to pray and study her Bible. I also observed her courage in the face of many abuses and challenges. Though my mother modeled the graciousness of God in her everyday interactions, I nevertheless struggled with a transactional theology—often believing that God was most of all concerned with my behavior and that the Bible was much more of a morality tale than a love letter. Whereas my early understanding of salvation was individualistic and narrow, I now understand salvation as not only personal but also communal and as encompassing Christ's healing and justice.

I am a Black woman in the United States, the child of Black working-class parents from Mobile, Alabama, and Washington, DC, and the grandchild of southern women and men who laid bricks and picked cotton. When I was a child, my mother often told me stories about what her life was like growing up, illustrating for me her courage in the face of many oppressions. I imagine the many times she, as a Black girl child, had to urinate outside by the road during family road trips between DC and North Carolina—because "colored people" were not allowed to use public restrooms in the South. My maternal grandmother, too, told me stories of the indignities, violations, and losses that she and other family members suffered—such as the story of her great-aunt, a midwife, picked up by a white family to deliver a baby late one night and never brought back home. These intertwined legacies of slavery and segregation are part of my own story of trauma. The resilience and resistance of those who endured these and other assaults, rooted in the rich resources of their Christian faith, are part of my story of restoration.

Though many would not have suspected it, my childhood and early adulthood were rife with wounding, which God has been faithful in healing. As a child, I witnessed domestic violence in my household. I was also molested by a family member only a few years older than I was. During my first year of college, the name of a white supremacist group was scrawled on my dormitory door overnight, and the photo of my face, also on my door, was blacked out with a marker. While I was studying abroad during my second year of college, a student began stalking me. Later that academic year, after I returned to my home campus, one of my friends was killed by her boyfriend and found dead in her apartment. A few months later, a neighbor attempted to rape me the day after I moved into a new apartment building. Growing up as a Black woman in a racist and patriarchal society also means that I have been and continue to be subjected to ongoing structurally induced trauma. As I reexamine and revisit my experiences of deep wounding, I can see that Jesus has been present with me in my suffering. Laying these stories down side by side, I marvel at how God has kept me sane and made me incredibly resilient.

God has used many avenues in my life—both sacred and secular—to care for and comfort me and to prepare me to facilitate healing experiences for others. Arts and activism have been two major vehicles for my own recovery and restoration. During my teenage years, writing and performing poetry provided me with opportunities to break silence about issues such as sexual violence that were rarely discussed in public. Participating in a socially conscious poetry community as a teenager and young adult also afforded me the ability to give voice to my experiences of oppression and marginalization in society and to affirm my own culture and heritage. Through my involvement in the performing arts, I discovered an additional pathway for healing—participation in cultural and social activism. Along the way, I found that engagement in social change was a tremendous source of hope and healing. As I worked alongside others with similar stories, I came to understand that the harms I experienced in my life were rooted in overlapping and interconnected systems of oppression, including racism and patriarchy.

Recognizing and resisting multiple and interlocking systems of oppression as they manifest in everyday life is a hallmark of early Black feminist activism and has been recognized as a critical contributor to the mental and spiritual health of marginalized groups. In *Black Youth Rising: Activism and Radical Healing in Urban America*, sociologist Shawn Ginwright explains how developing a critical consciousness of oppression and working to transform societal conditions help Black youth to heal from the impacts of structural racism, internalized oppression, and other social toxins in their environment.[9] According to Ginwright, "Healing occurs when we reconcile painful experiences resulting from oppression through testimony and naming what seem to be personal misfortune as systemic oppression."[10] This was certainly relevant to my own healing journey. Identifying patterns of injustice and mistreatment against people who share my race, gender, socioeconomic status, and generation helped me to better understand traumagenic experiences in my life, as well as the role I could play in disrupting these patterns and interrupting cycles of violence. This awareness was instrumental to my pursuit of a vocation in justice and peacebuilding and particularly my call to restorative and transformative justice, philosophies of justice that emphasize collective healing.

CHALLENGES

"One doesn't need a psychologist to heal oneself. In many modern conceptions, healing is a collective challenge based on the recognition that my pain, your pain, the other person's pain are similar."
—Martha Cabrera, "Living and Surviving in a Multiply Wounded Country"[11]

While working in Nicaragua in the wake of a natural disaster, psychologist Martha Cabrera concluded that people were in dire need of spaces in which they could come together to talk about the pain in their lives. Cabrera recounts,

Working on the emotional recovery of the survivors of Hurricane Mitch, we found that while people wanted to talk about their immediate losses, they had an even greater need to talk about other losses that they had never voiced before. Many women in León and Chinandega would come up to us and say, for example, "Look, I'm really sad about losing my house, but I want to tell you about something else that was even harder . . ." And we began to listen to their stories. Many women told us things they had kept bottled up, such as: "You know what hurts me most? I suffer from insomnia. And you know why? Because I lie awake worried about my husband spending the night in my daughter's bed, touching her."[12]

Cabrera and her colleagues discovered that many women desired to name the devastation they experienced from domestic violence and sexual abuse in their homes. They also found that both men and women continued to suffer from traumas related to their nation's history of political violence. Nicaraguans were "multiply wounded," and the dearth of opportunities to process their pains led to new wounds. For example, many men who returned from the war expressed their pain by acting out violently toward their wives and children. Cycles of victimization and violence continue without adequate spaces for healing.[13]

While working alongside African-American teenagers and young adults in Washington, DC, I also heard the need for healing spaces. The stories of young people I met in schools, jails, community centers, and parks confirmed their urgent need, despite their deep resilience, to release the trauma in their lives that came from structural and interpersonal violence. Research has found that young people living in neighborhoods with high rates of violence face psychological impacts similar to those living in war zones.[14] Black youth experience structurally induced trauma as the result of the violence of racism manifested through stereotyping, criminalization (in which they are defined as criminals and targeted for arrest and incarceration), and decreased economic and social opportunities.[15] Like children and youth in communities throughout the United States and around the world, African-American youth are also impacted by gender-based violence, including domestic violence and sexual abuse. Forced displacement from their neighborhoods, police harassment and violence, and discriminatory suspension and expulsion from school are additional sources of trauma facing the young people I came to know within youth-centered social justice organizations. Reflecting on the factors that helped and hindered my ability to confront my own traumatic experiences has helped me to better understand how I might cultivate healing spaces for young people who are multiply wounded.

Most of the church communities to which I belonged as a young person did not make it easy for me to share my experiences of oppression and violence or to express my pain to God alongside and in the company of others. I regularly participated in expressions of celebration as part of Christian fellowship but rarely collective lament. According to Soong-Chan Rah, author of *Prophetic Lament: A Call for Justice in Troubled Times*, "Lament is not simply the presentation of a list of complaints, nor merely the expression of sadness over difficult circumstances. Lament in the Bible is a liturgical response to the reality of suffering and engages God in the context of pain and trouble. The hope of lament is that God would respond to human suffering that is wholeheartedly communicated through lament. Unfortunately, lament is often missing from the narrative of the American church"[16]

Liturgies of lament, a structured service or gathering in which people come together to mark the space of brokenness and loss together in the presence of God, can be utilized as a corporate healing response to a variety of hurts and wounds, including the death of a loved one, racism and other prejudice, environmental destruction, and addiction.[17] While I believe that this tradition would have been helpful for me in better understanding and releasing painful encounters, it was not a practice with which I was familiar until much later in my life. Similarly, some topics, such as gender-based violence, were simply not spoken about in my church experience.

When I joined an antiviolence organization for women of color in my city, I worked alongside other women within local and national campaigns to highlight and challenge multiple forms of violence against women, from police brutality to domestic violence, as well as their intersections and root causes. Our meetings as well as the events we organized, including marches and arts-based forums, provided a platform for me to process my everyday experiences of patriarchal violence, including the unwelcome advances I often experienced while walking down the streets of my city. These spaces, which combined storytelling with organizing, also helped me to express and heal from my experiences of sexual violence in college. A few years later, I participated in a support group offered by my local rape crisis center for adult female survivors of child sexual abuse. The support group enabled me to disclose that I had been molested to other members of the group, select friends and acquaintances, and, soon after, members of my own family. It also gave me the courage and ability to confront the person who molested me. Moreover, sharing my story with female friends and close acquaintances outside the group led many of them to share their own often-similar stories of abuse and victimization. Some of the components that were especially helpful in these experiences were the presence of community, the use of the arts, and an orientation toward activism and social change. However, the overwhelmingly secular nature of these spaces left out a significant part of my identity—my faith and spirituality.

There is a clear need for spaces in which people can address multiple forms of trauma in their lives and seek healing together. Moreover, there is a need for sacred spaces where young people alongside adults can bring our whole selves, share the multiplicity of our experiences, and cultivate hope for change. In the United States, African-American youth who face multiple forms of wounding are especially in need of such spaces to process their wounds. Growing up, I found too few of these spaces within Christian settings, particularly within the church. Without any direct encounter with the kinds of healing spaces I longed for, how might I, as a wounded healer, accompany young people in such a process? In Nicaragua, Cabrera and her team found that "accompanying people in processing their wounds . . . always involved acknowledging, expressing and reflecting."[18] What would it look like to create a space for African-American youth to acknowledge, express, and reflect upon their wounds together in the presence of God?

RESPONSES

"It is part of our task as revolutionary people, people who want deep-rooted radical change, to be as whole as it is possible for us to be."
—Aurora Levins-Morales, *Medicine Stories: History, Culture and the Politics of Integrity*[19]

In the introduction to this chapter, I described the Visions to Peace Project's "Flip the Script! Media Arts Workshop," which took place in February and March 2008. In June and July, we held a summer arts and organizing program that employed teenagers in the city's local youth employment program. Our summer organizers-in-training worked to identify and raise awareness of community-based strategies to create safety and peace and decrease support for punitive policies. They designed and led peace education workshops for other youth, interviewed seasoned organizers and other social change leaders on video, and organized neighborhood gatherings. In the process, they came to identify healing as one of the most crucial contributions to peace. At the end of that summer, the Visions to Peace Project transitioned from a project that I led as the full-time director with part-time volunteer staff to an entirely volunteer-led initiative with no external funding. Up to this point, the Visions to Peace Project had also operated as a secular organization. However, the project's youth leaders shared a similar religious background—Christianity—and I wanted to explicitly incorporate this dimension as we moved forward in our leadership-development and peacebuilding efforts.

In December 2008, youth and adults who remained committed to the work of the Visions to Peace Project met to reconnect with one another and figure out where we might focus next. It was at this juncture that our youth members articulated a desire for a structured program to help them heal from the pain in their own lives. We also began to discuss and envision the role that faith might play in the process. A few weeks later, I met Yevonnie Lowe, a licensed therapist, liturgical dancer, and poet, through a mutual friend. Yevonnie and I found that we had many things in common, including our faith as Christians, passion for the arts, experiences of trauma, and a call to serve as wounded healers, particularly among Black youth. I told her about the Visions to Peace Project, our youth leaders' call for a healing-centered space, and my vision of an arts-based trauma-healing program that would meet this need. Yevonnie immediately volunteered to help me design and lead the program. Over the next several months, she and I met to pray together over the vision and design the curriculum together. We shaped the curriculum to reflect our shared belief in the healing benefits of the arts, our commitment to theological praxis, and our recognition that many young people were "multiply wounded" from intersecting forms of violence as well as other sources of pain. We launched the program, Let's Get Free!, in April 2009.

Let's Get Free! consisted of eight weekly two-hour workshops in which youth engaged in journaling, discussion, and creative writing related to experiences of violence, breaking free from trauma, and releasing the power of healing. Cumulatively, the workshops we developed helped to cultivate a space for young people to seek healing from multiple forms of violence. We identified three themes to explore in the workshops and spent two weeks on each theme—moving from a focus on "personal healing" to "healing of families" and finally to "healing of communities." Across each theme, we employed arts and media to comment on interpersonal and systemic forms of harm, personal and collective trauma, and trauma healing. We selected popular songs and documentary video clips to share that were not only relevant but also likely to engage our youth participants, elicit discussion, and inspire their creativity and vulnerability. Youth also used the arts, particularly creative writing, as a means for their own expression. Let's Get Free! incorporated dance as an additional modality whereby youth learned dance movements to a fast-paced gospel song that spoke of God's healing power. The weekly workshops culminated in a performance for family and community members in which youth participants, as well as Yevonnie and I, shared some of the artistic pieces that we created over the course of the program.

In keeping with the Visions to Peace Project's emphasis on youth leadership development, Let's Get Free! was also designed to help youth begin to understand themselves as wounded healers within their families, schools, and neighborhoods. The program's theological foundation centered on the idea that God comforts our deepest hurts and equips us to comfort others. This idea, articulated in a New Testament letter written by the apostle Paul to an early church community, served as our biblical theme. "Praise be to the God and Father of our Lord Jesus Christ, the Father of compassion and the God of all comfort, who comforts us in all our troubles, so that we can comfort those in any trouble with the comfort we ourselves receive from God" (2 Corinthians 1:3–4, New International Version). Using these verses, we linked God's compassion and care for us to the release of our own pain, and the release of our pain to the destruction of barriers that keep others trapped within their traumas. We used this foundational scripture to emphasize that God has called us to be wounded healers. As we become free from pain in our own lives, we are well suited to help others to break free. Our experiences of trauma become transformed into powerful tools for healing. As the program's leaders, Yevonnie and I also sought to embody this theology by taking on the role of wounded healers—being transparent about our own wounds with young people, particularly those wounds that were already healed or in the process of healing. The theology was also put into practice by youth as they opened up to one another during the program and recited original poetry during the final performance that reflected upon their wounds and highlighted God's healing work in their lives. As we prayed together at each session's end, we recited a paraphrase of 2 Corinthians 1:3–4, "Praise God who comforts us so that we can comfort others!"

Each weekly workshop session followed a similar structure. First, we opened by playing a song that set the tone for the week's focus, inviting participants to listen to the notes and lyrics, reflect on the content quietly, or journal. Second, participants were encouraged to share reflections that came to them during the opening song or the previous week's session, but not to comment on what someone else had shared. Third, we provided a brief introduction to the focus of the day's session in the form of an additional arts or media piece and/or brief input by the facilitator. For example, for the second session on personal healing, we emphasized the idea that unhealed pain is often transferred to others and solicited specific examples from youth participants that demonstrated this idea. Fourth, we facilitated group discussion using questions we created for each session. This was followed by a short period for creative writing, reading our writing to one another, and then sharing what stood out for us from the pieces we heard. We ended each session with prayer and our closing ritual—collectively declaring our praise for a God who comforts us so that we can comfort others, while resting our arms upon one another's shoulders as in a large group embrace. In many ways, our closing ritual symbolized our ongoing process of reaching up to God while reaching out to community—a vertical and horizontal movement.

To begin our first session, we played the soulful song "Ready for Love" by India.Arie, centering the longing to give and receive love without limits within our quest for personal healing.[20] Continuing our focus on personal healing within the next session, we played the gospel song "Imagine Me" by Kirk Franklin, a song about struggles with abuse and low self-esteem and trust in God's unconditional love.[21] Our discussion explored the role of healing in interrupting cycles of violence as well as the labels often used to describe the various roles people occupy in situations of violence (victim, survivor, pedophile, rapist, murderer, batterer, perpetrator, abuser, etc.). With lyrics to the song "Misunderstood" by hip-hop artist Common in hand, we asked, What is the impact of these labels and what are alternatives?[22] We also talked about what we wanted to express through the poems and songs we would craft in each session.

During our "Healing of a Family" session, we began with another hip-hop song by Common, in which he lyrically unfolds the stories of three people reeling from deep hurts. The first verse tells the story of a young woman who was raped by her father as a child and finds some freedom from her pain by sharing her story with a close friend. Next, Yevonnie shared an original poem about child sexual abuse and then facilitated a group discussion focused on two questions:

What kinds of ways are entire families hurt or harmed?
What are the ways that families hurt us?

During the subsequent session on healing within family systems, we opened with "I'm Okay" by Christina Aguilera, a song about domestic violence and child abuse.[23] The brief introduction to this session consisted of remarks on the different approaches family members might take in relation to trauma and healing: "In some families, some members might not be ready to heal from hurts and violence within the family. Other families might not be ready to talk about the secrets within the family for various reasons or might not be able to deal with the hurt and pain. Still some families might talk about the pain in the family and it may or may not be helpful."

During the group discussion, participants talked about how their own families dealt with pain, how their families hindered and/or helped their healing, and what they wanted from their families emotionally. They also reflected on two additional questions:

> If you are ready to heal and your family is not ready, what can you do to begin or continue your process of healing?
> In what ways can you support others in your family?

During the time for creative expression, youth were encouraged to utilize any form of writing—for example, to write a poem, a story, a journal entry, a letter, or a script.

To begin our final two sessions focused on healing our communities, we returned to the hip-hop song "Misunderstood" by Common, this time playing the piece for participants. The song samples heavily from "Don't Let Me Be Misunderstood" by jazz vocalist Nina Simone. Yevonnie and I saw the song "Misunderstood" as not only about labels and stereotyping but also about how people end up in harmful situations because they lack options, often as the result of systemic oppression and structural violence. After a time for personal reflection and writing while the song played, we showed a clip from the feature-length documentary film *Chocolate City*, which was created in Washington, DC.[24] The film documents the forced displacement of four hundred families from a local public housing development. This issue was especially relevant to several youth participants who were facing potential displacement from their own homes within a public housing project. In the clip, a group of women share how being forced to move led to fragmentation in their lives and community and indirectly caused the death of a friend and neighbor. After viewing, youth shared their general thoughts, personal experiences, and reflections on how the clip related to violence against a community. Our guiding questions for this discussion included:

> What emotions and feelings did the women express as they talked about the destruction of their community?
> How did the destruction of their community affect the women emotionally and psychologically? Is this violence?
> What is safety? What threatens the safety of entire communities?

Participants classified gentrification, a process whereby a low-income neighborhood remains underresourced, then is later redeveloped into a neighborhood for higher-income people, as a form of violence against their neighborhoods. They also named some of the trauma that results. Some youth participants, who were also active in another youth organizing group, reported on their ongoing efforts to fight the redevelopment projects that were threatening the survival of their community.

The final two sessions of the program were dedicated to participants sharing, selecting, and practicing the pieces they would like to perform in front of their families, friends, and other guests. During the first of these sessions, one of the young men in our group, Harvey, was still struggling with what he wanted to release on paper and share in the final performance. [25] Instead of moving forward with our original plan, we played a video of a poem called "Knock, Knock" being performed on the TV show *Def Poetry Jam*. [26] The poet, Daniel Beaty, talks about visiting his father in prison after many years without his father in his life. By the poem's end, Harvey was sitting in one corner of the room—writing and writing and writing about the incarceration of his own father, which he had not talked about at all previously. I see this story as an example of the Holy Spirit's presence in leading our activities, even those that did not have an explicitly faith-based component, and orchestrating healing for each person within the group. We wrapped up the program on a Saturday night in which family, friends, and members of our networks showed up for a performance titled "Let's Get Free! Releasing the Pain of Violence and the Power of Healing." Collectively, our poems reflected the release of pain from many wounds, including the death of a cousin, the incarceration of a father, stereotyping and criminalization, and incest. By no means was it the end of the healing process, but it was an important beginning for many.

> *And it's God who gave me hope*
> *that things wouldn't always be this way inside of me*
> *But this history is still my history*
> *and because it's true I claim it publicly*
> *Yes, I was molested*
> *starting at the age of five.*
> *Yes, I heard the shouting and*
> *I still remember mom's black eye.*
> *Yes, I was assaulted by a neighbor*
> *who pinned me down and tried to rape me.*
> *Yes, I have often been afraid*
> *while walking down the street.*
> *And yet I heal*
> *and yet I love*
> *And yet I heal*
> *and yet I love*
> *And yet I heal*
> *and yet I love*
> *I know I'm not the only one.*
> *I know I'm not the only one.*
> *I know I'm not the only one.*
> *I know I'm not the only one.*

I wrote the first version of this poem during Let's Get Free! and performed it during our culminating event. I begin the poem by anchoring myself in my faith as a Christian and in my belief in a God who cares about me personally, partners with humanity for both personal and social transformation, and is the ultimate source of all healing. I continue by sharing stories, some of which I never had the courage to speak publicly about before. I move on with an affirmation of my ability to recover and to love. I end with the reason why I must tell my story—my freedom and healing are connected to the freedom and healing of others. In telling my story, I not only break free from strongholds of silence for myself. I also reassure others that they are not alone and that the strength, comfort, and hope that God has given me through my pain is also available to them.

CONCLUSION

"Healing takes place in community, in the telling and bearing of witness, in the naming of trauma, and in the grief and rage and defiance that follow."
—Aurora Levins-Morales, *Medicine Stories: History, Culture and the Politics of Integrity*[27]

Inspired by a theological vision of healing in community presented by the apostle Paul in his second letter to the Corinthian Church, Let's Get Free! was designed to help Black youth transform their own trauma by daring to name it, publicly express it, invite God to heal it, and through their example, help others to do the same. In other words, our goal—as a collective of youth and adults who envisioned the program together—was to emerge as wounded healers who would open up safe and sacred spaces for healing among our families and friends. Let's Get Free! was also birthed from a realization that healing from inner trauma is a critical pathway to peace and justice. We came to understand that dealing with our own pain together, in community, was necessary for ending cycles of violence in our lives, families, neighborhoods, and society at large.

Employing a range of resources—the popular and the sacred—we addressed individual and collective sources of trauma. Let's Get Free! engaged young people in drawing from spiritual resources through our participation in prayer for ourselves and one another, consistent affirmation of God's comfort, and our shared goal of being vessels of God's care and compassion in the lives of others. We recognized that our healing journeys were nourished by and nestled within God's unconditional love and grace. We also found it useful to draw from popular cultural resources, particularly music that young people enjoyed and found relevant, alongside creative writing as a means for personal expression. By employing cultural work to explore trauma in our lives and its role in the cycle of violence and acting in accordance with a theological vision of God's comfort manifested in us and through us, we tapped into our abilities as wounded healers and cocreated a community of healing. In doing so, we also moved toward a model of peacebuilding characterized by a "politics of integrity," or wholeness, an approach that integrates all of the dimensions of our lives, minds, bodies, and spirits and connects the multiple dimensions of reality, including power and pain.[28] Our commitment to resistance allowed us to identify and interrupt the ways in which systems of oppression limited our ability to speak out about the multiple causes of woundedness in our lives and to locate its roots in human brokenness as well as systemic injustice.

Since designing and directing Let's Get Free! in 2009, I have experienced and learned about additional approaches to trauma healing that integrate Christian spirituality and biblical frameworks. Key components of these models address some of the limitations of our program, although none of them were specifically developed for youth in U.S. urban communities. In 2010, I participated in a small group focused on trauma healing offered through my neighborhood church, which I had only recently joined. An elder at the church, who worked professionally as a social worker, led a sixteen-week small group gathering for women, using the *Healing Care Groups* curriculum created by theologian and educator Terry Wardle.[29] The curriculum melds psycho-education and biblical teaching to help participants better understand the impacts of early wounding in their lives, identify the false beliefs that they internalized as a result of those traumatic experiences, and replace the lies with truths from the Bible, especially the truth of God's unconditional love for them. I participated in the group, along with a few other women in their twenties and thirties who served in leadership roles in our church and/or within nearby Christian ministries.

Whereas the *Healing Care Groups* curriculum was not specifically created for clergy and other leaders, the American Bible Society's Trauma Healing Institute designs its programs for Christian leaders in countries around the world. The mission of the Trauma Healing Institute is to "equip local churches to care for people with deep emotional and spiritual injuries caused by war, domestic violence, natural disasters and other traumatic events."[30] Its core program, "Healing the Wounds of Trauma," integrates biblical and mental health principles to support leaders in first addressing their own trauma and then creating healing spaces for "people who have suffered horrific events like war, civil unrest, ethnic conflict, rape, and natural disasters."[31] The curriculum manual, *Healing the Wounds of Trauma: How the Church Can Help*, emphasizes the value of lament, facilitating the expression of deep pain to one another and to God. Its focus on leadership development ensures the continuation and advancement of trauma healing within the church and the ongoing formation and preparation of "wounded healers." The curriculum, utilized by leaders in Orthodox, Catholic, Protestant, and independent churches, has been made available in over 150 languages.[32]

In South Africa, the Ujamaa Center for Biblical and Theological Community Development and Research uses stories from the Bible to create safe and sacred spaces for marginalized people to find healing.[33] Through the center's

Tamar Campaign, socially engaged Bible scholars facilitate contextual Bible studies on the story of Tamar, the daughter of King David, who was raped by her half-brother Amnon. During the Bible study, participants collaboratively read and analyze the story (as told in 2 Samuel 13:1–22), discuss how the passage applies to their own contexts, and plan action steps based on what they have learned and discussed. At the end, facilitators always ask, "What will you now do in response to the Bible study?" and assist with the formulation of action plans. Some groups, for example, have started counseling programs for women in their congregations who have experienced sexual violence, whereas others have hosted workshops that teach men nonviolent ways of expressing their masculinity. This approach has been especially helpful for me in discerning faith-rooted approaches to peacebuilding that involve biblically informed strategies for trauma healing. I look to these models for information and inspiration as I continue to explore what it means for me to be a wounded healer in the Way of Jesus.

NOTES

1. David E. Garland and Diana R. Garland, *Flawed Families of the Bible: How God's Grace Works through Imperfect Relationships* (Grand Rapids, MI: BrazosPress, 2007), 16.

2. Galia Benziman, Ruth Kannai, and Ayesha Ahmad, "The Wounded Healer as Cultural Archetype," *CLCWeb: Comparative Literature and Culture* 14, no. 1 (2012), http://dx.doi.org/10.7771/1481-4374.1927.

3. Kris Rocke and Joel Van Dyke, *Geography of Grace: Doing Theology from Below* (Tacoma, WA: Street Psalms Press, 2012), 62.

4. Eugene H. Peterson, *The Message* (Carol Stream, IL: NavPress, 2002).

5. New Living Translation (Carol Stream, IL: Tyndale, 2015), BibleGateway.com.

6. Howard Thurman, *Jesus and the Disinherited* (Boston: Beacon Press, 1949).

7. Ibid.

8. Henri Nouwen, *The Wounded Healer* (New York: Doubleday, 1979), 82–83.

9. Shawn Ginwright, *Black Youth Rising: Activism and Radical Healing in Urban America* (New York: Teachers College Press, 2010).

10. Ibid., 9.

11. Martha Cabrera, "Living and Surviving in a Multiply Wounded Country," Medico International, https://www.medico.de/download/report26/ps_cabrera_en.pdf, accessed March 17, 2017.

12. Cabrera, "Living and Surviving in a Multiply Wounded Country," 1–2.

13. Carolyn Yoder, *The Little Book of Trauma Healing: When Violence Strikes and Community Security Is Threatened* (Intercourse, PA: Good Books, 2005).

14. Esther Jenkins and Carl Bell, "Community Violence and Children on Chicago's Southside," *Psychiatry* 56, no. 1 (1993): 46–54; Joy Osufsky, "The Impact of Violence on Children," *Future of Children* 9, no. 3 (Winter 1999): 33–49.

15. David Anderson Hooker and Amy Potter Czajkowski, *Transforming Historical Harms* (Harrisonburg, VA: Eastern Mennonite University, 2013).

16. Soong-Chan Rah, *Prophetic Lament: A Call for Justice in Troubled Times* (Downers Grove, IL: InterVarsity Press, 2015), 21.

17. Abigail Rian Evans, *Healing Liturgies for the Seasons of Life* (Louisville, KY: Westminster John Knox Press, 2003).

18. Cabrera, "Living and Surviving in a Multiply Wounded Country."

19. Aurora Levins-Morales, *Medicine Stories: History, Culture and the Politics of Integrity* (New York: South End Press, 1999), 20.

20. India.Arie, "Ready for Love," *Acoustic Soul* (New York: Motown/Universal Records, 2001).

21. Kirk Franklin, "Imagine Me," *Hero* (Inglewood, CA: Gospocentric Records, 2005).

22. Common, "Misunderstood," *Finding Forever* (New York: GOOD Music, 2007).

23. Christina Aguilera, "I'm Okay," *Stripped* (New York: RCA Records, 2002).

24. Ellie Walton and Sam Wild, dir., *Chocolate City* (DVD, Washington, DC: Wildlife Productions, 2007).

25. The name of this person has been changed for the sake of anonymity.

26. "Daniel Beaty—Knock Knock," video posted to YouTube by ServiceSpace, November 19, 2009, https://www.youtube.com/watch?v=8VLjZPqJqE0.

27. Levins-Morales, *Medicine Stories*, 16.

28. Levins-Morales, *Medicine Stories*.

29. Terry Wardle, "Healing Care Groups Participant's Guide" (Ashland, OH: Healing Care, 2002).

30. "About the Trauma Healing Institute," American Bible Society Trauma Healing Institute, http://thi.americanbible.org/uploads/page/THI-General_2014-02_EN.pdf, accessed March 19, 2017.

31. "Bible-Based Trauma Healing," American Bible Society Trauma Healing Institute, http://thi.americanbible.org/uploads/page/THI-General_2014-02_EN.pdf, accessed January 20, 2017.

32. "Healing the Wounds of Trauma: How the Church Can Help, Expanded Edition, 2016," American Bible Society Trauma Healing Institute, http://www.bibles.com/healing-the-wounds-of-trauma-how-the-church-can-help-2013-revised-edition.html, accessed March 19, 2017.

33. Ujamaa Centre for Biblical and Theological Community Development and Research, http://ujamaa.ukzn.ac.za/Homepage.aspx, accessed January 15, 2017.

Chapter Eleven

Peace from the Soul of the Nurturer

The Gender Question

Despina Namwembe

Challenge: How do you pursue and maintain gender balance
in faith-based peacebuilding?

Being a female Orthodox Christian, I am fully aware that my space at the "men's" table is always treated as secondary. As my religion challenges me with all the man-made theological restrictions, so does the strong cultural environment in which I operate. Although issues such as hierarchy and space in a religious setting, coupled with cultural dynamics, are at strong play, I still find my way out of the maze to offer peace work to a sometimes reluctant yet receptive community, notwithstanding my inner struggles.

It would be so easy for faith-based peacebuilding to flourish especially in Africa because Africa is regarded as a very religious continent that could easily promote its peace work through the diverse and ardent believers who exist at the different levels. Nonetheless, because this seems to be one-sided in the line of gender, cushioned by strong customs that put women second and men first, whatever their class level, the challenges facing women's full participation still exist.

Given these challenges, it is imperative that we study the dynamics at play in a particular society. If one is overly aggressive on such traditional matters, chances are high that failure of the entire program is bound to happen. However, one should know that having an individual-based working relationship with key male counterparts, whether religious or otherwise, is important. These can clear the air and give affirmation of the much-needed work. This has worked for me among the many strategies used. It is therefore important to leave the men in Africa to claim their traditional space while making them aware that they can achieve even much more if they work with the women. Ideally, the women who are targeted and supported to move up these societal ladders with the aim of breaking these stereotypes shouldn't be just women who show their faces, but women who can add value while at the same peace-negotiation table with men.

Religion in Africa is not simply enjoyed but rather ardently supported and practiced. This support and practice is statistically stronger among the female gender as opposed to the male. In many religious places, women are the majority, and they will always ensure that their children become as strong followers and believers as themselves. The formation of religious-based groups in these various institutions has helped women a lot in addressing gender-specific gaps that prevail within the many religious traditions. However, many still feel isolated in these groups as their voice is only heard by themselves and not necessarily by the male gender. With cultures that distance women from common participation with men, it is therefore imperative that work is invested in ensuring that women work together with men in a religious setting.

After a thorough investigation of the African cultural setup, the early Anglican and Catholic missionaries to Africa came with a clear strategy of strategically targeting men and ensuring that they were rewarded for their loyalty to ease their own entry points. The story of the Uganda Martyrs gives us a clear understanding of how Western religions were first embraced by men in the first catechetical (Christian religious) classes. The women's roles were confined to the kitchen, and they had no time to attend to these classes. For the case of Christianity, for example, the martyrs (twenty-three Anglican and twenty-two Catholic converts to Christianity) were executed between January 31, 1885, and January 27, 1887. They were executed at the orders of then king Mwanga, who felt that his powers were being surpassed as the martyrs started giving him less respect as compared to their God. All those killed were men. The missionaries therefore tailored religion to some of the men's favored cultural ways of living for easier following and adoption. Scriptures that favor men's supremacy were emphasized as compared to those that promote equal footing among both genders.

ORTHODOX CHURCH:
BRIEF HISTORY IN UGANDA

The Greek Orthodox Church is one of the Eastern churches. Eastern Orthodoxy and Roman Catholicism were originally branches of the same body—the One, Holy, Catholic and Apostolic Church—until AD 1054. This date marked an important moment as it was the period for the split between the Orthodox and Catholic churches, the first major division in Christianity and the beginning of the diverse Christian traditions that we have today. The divisions were spiritual, political, and cultural in nature, including spiritual interpretation pertaining to the Easter celebration and the Holy Spirit, according to Father Isabirye Anastasios, an Orthodox priest living in Kampala. Roman Catholicism and Orthodoxy celebrate Easter on different days according to different calendar systems, though both believe in the resurrection of Christ. The origin of the Holy Spirit was another major conflict. Roman Catholics believed the Holy Spirit proceeded from the Father and the Son, but the Eastern church felt both the Son and the Holy Spirit emanated from the Father. After this major separation in AD 1054, various Christian-linked traditions and churches arose and continue to do so to the current day. I personally think that some of these separations are informed by God to a certain degree, but the majority are manmade.

The Orthodox faith was introduced to Uganda in 1934 by Africans, particularly one called Sebbanja Makasa "Sparta" Reuben. Sparta was a soldier in the King's Rifles Army. This enhanced his communication with the outside world through access to literature. He opened a missionary school in the Degeya Luwero district and later an Orthodox church in the same area of Anoonya Degeya. He had converted to the Orthodox faith because, while reading, he stumbled on the word "Orthodox," which in Greek comes from two words, *ethos*, meaning "true," and *doxa*, meaning "teaching," hence "true teaching." Sparta and his friends Obadia Bassajakitalo, Theodoros Nankyama, and Ireneos Magimbi were at the helm of making the Orthodox Church a reality in Uganda. According to Fr. Isabirye, in 1919, Sparta and his friends sent letter to the different parts of the world asking about Orthodoxy until one U.S. citizen who was also of African ancestry, George Alexander McGuire, shared with them Orthodox literature on the noncanonical "African Orthodox Church." After reading and understanding this literature, Sparta and his colleagues did as the former missionaries had done, starting with the establishment of social institutions, hence the first Missionary Orthodoxy social institution in Degeya, which later expanded to many in different places in the country. This was the first Missionary Church to be introduced by an African.

Like many African traditions, the Orthodox Church maintains many traditions as they were practiced in the early years of the church. The Orthodox Church has no one singular head, as, for example, a pope as in the Catholic Church. The belief is that Jesus Christ is the head of the church. Nonetheless, the bishops or metropolitans congregate under a council called the Holy Synod, and there is a bishop who holds the leadership honorary title of "first among equals." There are no women on the synod; nor are there women on metropolitan councils in any local archbishopric, at least of the many I have interfaced with. In spite of this nonrepresentation, the women are given respect and are regarded as mothers to the church. The women are viewed in the image of Mary who gave birth to Jesus Christ. This therefore makes their roles and responsibilities to be viewed as inherently feminine in nature. Such roles include, among others, taking care of the church by cleaning it, ensuring that church vestments are in order, putting flowers in some areas of the church, and, in Africa especially, singing in the church choir, ushering, and organizing events. The Orthodox Church in Uganda remains small but is respected by many, including political leaders. For example, it was spared by the late notorious dictator Idi Amin in 1977 when he decided to ban all independent churches. Even today, with lesser statistical strength, it is recognized by the state as one of the important churches in the country.

FOUNDATIONS: FIRST STEPS IN A CHALLENGED LIFE

I was born into an Anglican family, making me Anglican by default as a child. Later, when I was a teenager, my brothers Aggrey and Isaac, who had become Orthodox through Father Isabirye, used to take me for prayers in the village Orthodox church. Moving to the city during my secondary education, I converted after doing some reading and undergoing basic theological education of listening to the words of wisdom from the late Metropolitan Theodoros Nankyama. To me the Orthodox faith not only had commonalities with my culture but preserved the ancient church doctrines and practice, which I found to be interesting. I loved the ancient stories of how martyrs like St. Barbara and St. Joan were revered in the church teachings, projecting their strength as women who went through a lot of suffering for their beliefs and exalting Mary the mother of Jesus. Additionally, there was a communal aspect about the believers and a lot of love, support, and warmth for one another in our faith cohort. Metropolitan Theodoros Nankyama was like a parent to all of us as young people. He never discriminated based on ethnic or social cultural differences; nor did he show hate for anyone. He never forced one to convert but was always there for anyone's well-being physically and spiritually. He allowed us as girls to read the epistles (written by the apostles Paul, John, Peter, James, and Jude as letters of instruction from the elders to the leaders and members of the Christian Church) out loud during the church service, something that was unheard of then.

The other thing that attracted me to this faith was the preservation of faith-based relics and Christian religious historical sites of worship that date from far back in the ages before Christ and immediately after the resurrection. This preservation of history is something that Africans treasure in their tradition so that information is preserved and passed on from generation to generation. The preservation of ancient relics of honor, like pieces of wood from the cross on which Jesus was crucified, the skulls of some of the saints, clothes from some of the martyrs, and the preservation of the tomb where

Jesus was buried, as found in the different holy sites in Greece and Jerusalem, meant a lot to me. These preservations made the understanding and deepening of my faith easier, more real, and more connected.

There are also many similarities between the Orthodox Church and the African way of life. From the beginning, I felt at home and continue to do so up to the current day. As we are a small faith community and always a minority in many places, everyone knows everybody else, which again promotes the communal and family aspect within the church. When you spend some time without going to church, many followers look for you, as their sister or brother, and feel very excited to see you. Our church is like a family, and I greatly value and appreciate that.

When we go for prayers, men and women are not supposed to sit together while in church. The women sit on the side of the icon of Mary, while the men sit on the side of the icon of Jesus Christ. These gestures symbolize the feminine and masculine identities depicted by Mary the mother of God and Jesus, respectively. In my simple understanding, I wanted to go to heaven through Jesus Christ, although I had, and continue to have, high respect for Mary the mother of God—which is the meaning of my name, Despina. I therefore remember sitting on the men's side as a lone female young person, which I continue to practice even today. In the early days, I remember being viewed with negativity, especially by the older folk. I, however, insisted on sitting there. I did not have a clear and strong valid explanation for the separation, and since the clergy never sent me away, I continued sitting there every time I attended church.

In my youth in 2001 with some older women, we organized the first female conference in our church on the role of women in the church. The conference, titled "The Role of Orthodox Women in the Church in the New Millennium," was held at the Orthodox Church headquarters in Kampala and supported by the World Council of Churches. We had speakers from as far away as Greece, Kenya, and Tanzania and also from other areas in Uganda. There were conflicting voices. Some discussants highlighted the importance of women's full participation in the church as not having any negative effect on the growth of the church spiritually, while others defended the appropriateness of excluding women, especially when it came to the priesthood, saying that it is one way of distancing temptation that may occur between men and women.

Additionally, the refusal of women to take Holy Communion during their menstrual cycle was and continues to be a challenge in the church. This is mainly based on the teachings in the Old Testament (Leviticus 15:19–24). This makes any woman feel inferior and her esteem greatly trimmed down. Taking Holy Communion in a Christian background makes one partake of the body and blood of Jesus Christ, which makes any believer experience a special and closer bond with Jesus. This act in the Christian faith symbolizes a central connection of the believers with Jesus, as it reminds them of his sacrificial living for their well-being. In his last days, he offered wine to his disciples, which he prayed for and called his blood; he then broke the bread and shared it with them, calling it his body. He was crucified a day later and died. These rituals therefore mean so much to any believer in the Christian faith, especially those who belong to the early churches. At the aforementioned conference on the role of Orthodox women, I took note of one speaker, Hellen Ganuri, a female theologian from Greece, explaining that it was wrong to say that women were unclean and not allowed to go for Holy Communion when menstruating, because no one could be unclean over something which is natural and one has no control over. I was so impressed with some of these discussions but still in search of a clear fulfillment in this area within my church.

Although these discussions were held, it was and continues to be clear that in our Orthodox Church, we have to let the priests not only lead us but also pray for us, even during events outside the church. This tradition doesn't prepare people enough to pray for themselves in situations of need and divine spiritual connection. It rather instills a spiritual dependence, which I find rather limiting.

I remember as a youth the late Metropolitan Theodoros Nankyama telling us to read the epistle as girls. This annoyed some of the priests, and at one point some bishops from Greece who had visited us couldn't hide their anger but openly refused to let us read the epistle. They couldn't believe that a female could even open her mouth in church apart from singing in the audience during the liturgy. Bishop Nankyama was stubborn on that and allowed us to not only read the epistle but also chant the forefathers' teachings. These teachings were standardized texts extracted by theologians from the early sermons and letters of the holy fathers to their faithful, which are universally read in the Greek Orthodox churches. Reading or chanting these texts was predominantly a male role in all the Orthodox churches in Africa, Greece, the Unites States, and so forth. Some priests would come and block us from chanting, and we as girls could only look on from the back. Even stepping beyond the church pews to be near the altar was seen as a negative. Bishop Nankyama, though, allowed us to sing from the side near the altar, and this gave us a bit of strength. In his absence we knew that we were expected to be a no-show for chanting. It took some good years for the priests and men to allow us to chant with ease even when the bishop wasn't around.

The church in Uganda started having Orthodox nuns in the late 1990s, thereby helping Ugandan women to access the altar for the first time. These were young girls and very loving of their church. I was so proud of this gesture and felt part of the church further. I continue to have a lot of respect for nuns the world over because their journey is characterized by living a sacrificial life. Although the nuns were and continue to be present, women are less active, especially in areas of leadership and at the discussion table where major issues pertaining to church life are discussed.

CHALLENGES AND RESPONSES: CAPABILITIES PUT TO THE TEST

It is usually hard for me as a faith-based peacebuilder to measure the impact caused in my works simply because of some of the attributes and time frames associated with measuring peace. As I struggle with this at the individual level, I can, however, say that the various actions I was involved in have brought a positive change in people's lives, and there are figures and descriptions of situations to that effect. Some of these contributions have been at the household, community, or even policy level. There were commendable positive life experiences that happened after using a mix of secular and faith traditions as catalysts for peaceful coexistence in the areas I worked in.

Rising to My Calling

I started doing women's work in the Orthodox Church Women's Union. As is typical of various women's groups, this was not devoid of drama. I was a youth then, and conflicts would arise from the small things between the older women to the big issues of governance. I was an onlooker then, but I always worked alongside the older women, and they gave me different responsibilities, most of which were small but called for commitment. As I grew older I assumed more executive powers, which would sometimes put me in situations of controversy even when it was for the good of all. Making decisions meant that I wouldn't be a favorite to all. The women started by having a strong team spirit and commitment; however, when financial resources came into play, some of that was lost.

I remember one day we organized a music competition in which we invited all-women choirs to make presentations based on such areas as their faith understanding, poetry, dance, and traditional background. We invited professional judges, and at one point, because time was running out, my friend Elizabeth and I, being on the women's leadership team, went to the judges and requested for time to be strictly adhered to, not knowing that the women had understood things differently. When the results were announced, the urban choirs that did not win went wild and accused us of being behind their loss. Chaos, fighting, and abuse among the women's groups themselves also ensued. We knew that this was not going to end well. After alerting the security in the area, we jumped into our cars and left. We, however, addressed it in the general assembly that followed, and as more and more women realized that we had nothing to gain by one choir winning over the other, the more they believed in us.

Every time I had a setback, I would sit down, reflect, pray, fast, and start doing something about addressing that setback. I started believing in myself as having the capacity to address those personal, institutional, and community challenges. I knew it wasn't going to be easy, but nonetheless I continued following my heart's desires. I just felt that I was getting suffocated by some of the internal church pressures. While most religious people may be good, we should know that there are some who decide to fail the very teachings they are supposed to uphold and preserve. The teachings about love, justice, and nondiscrimination are central in any faith. Similarly, we had individuals who simply wouldn't listen much to what you were offering as a woman simply because of ego. At one point one priest was open about my fellow woman, who was a medical doctor, saying that they couldn't support her proposals because she had to know her place as a woman and not to think that because she managed the Church Health Center that gave her the right to question their decisions. The female doctor later got a good job with the World Health Organization. However, there are incidences where women can be the problem for their fellow women, especially if you are moving up the leadership ladders quickly, and this was no different here. I knew that tradition was not on my side, and as a young person, I felt that my church was not helping that much either, especially after the death of Metropolitan Theodoros Nankyama in 1995. I wanted to explore, learn, and give at the same time. I also knew that all that called for personal commitment and strong dedication. I started on the journey by looking at my strengths and weaknesses. Some of these weaknesses led me to go back and add some academic papers, while others led me to continue with building strong networks both within and outside church circles. I started by working at one of the major national ecumenical institutions where I gained serious technical and institutional skills as well as national networks. I also became part of different national and regional women's and faith-based organizations. Later, I decided to join a global interfaith network organization as a member and attained global leadership around 2002, which expanded my connections even further.

During my early membership in the interfaith organization, especially in 2006, I was at first castigated in my church, and I heard the church leadership thinking that I had converted to another faith. To them "interfaith" meant being a lesser believer and a potential convert. I was relieved of some responsibilities, including representing the church on some institutional boards. Associating with some other faiths meant deviating from the faith's values and norms. I never interfaced with the religious heads who were more furious, reaching an extent of making a Sunday sermon out of it, but rather I engaged the priests one by one separately. It was good enough that some of them had started being part of the ecumenical and interreligious programs and hence had an open mind about interfaith engagements. Others, though, still sided with the faith leader, saying that in our religious doctrines, anything that is not blessed by the bishop is seen as a sin. In September 2009, I was employed officially as a female leader in this network organization, taking care of over six African countries. In my heart I knew that the interfaith organization I was working for actually had made me a stronger believer in my faith than before. Its intention was for me to deepen my roots in my own faith tradition while peacefully coexisting with those believers who were different from me, something that had nothing to do with conversion. I decided to ignore all this and stayed steadfast on what I wanted to do as a woman leader. I knew that although I loved and continue to love my faith that much, there would always be such inner and outer challenges or rejections and lesser trust but also situations of encouragement, love, and trust from those who are open-minded.

Land-Based Justice Program

The issue of land in the northern part of the country caused a serious rift between families. The Lord's Resistance Army rebel group and the government fought for almost twenty years, claiming the lives of almost 2 million people. When relative calm returned in 2005 through various peace agreements, another deadly war broke out between the returnees based on land ownership, boundaries, and laws governing such land. Twenty years is such a long time in a rural setting to know who used to be where and the exact demarcations of a person's land, let alone those who died, leaving behind widows and their children. The young men who grew up in camps and other war returnees used to spilling blood started roaming the villages on a killing spree in the guise of helping their widowed mothers reclaim their properties. The able-bodied men started using machetes to defend themselves but also to ensure that they were the ones in control of land and not the women. People were killed, houses burned, and property destroyed in various parts.

As an interfaith organization with our membership, we embarked on a community conflict-mediation program, which we based on the diverse faith teachings about property ownership and the prevailing land laws and policies as stipulated by government. I therefore involved policy personnel like the members of Parliament, district officials, and members of the security and the legal fraternity, in addition to the religious leaders, to ensure lasting solutions to the impasse. It is hard for a woman to be seen as a serious mediator in a rural setting, especially when even the language is foreign. Issues of conflict are always seen to be discussed at the table of men, and women who are given a chance to attend these events in many situations are taken on as spectators rather than active participants. Women were always the majority in our community dialogues, but their talking was less. They would always talk only among themselves as women until I made efforts to urge them to say something publicly. Even when they did so, the grumbling from the men, always feeling like the women had no place on issues of land, was evident. One man was bold enough and told me to be careful with what I was doing because "we" women had no role on issues of land. It was the men, according to him, who were responsible. "Giving women land would mean double acquisition from the father's house and then from her husband's place," he said. One woman stood up in anger, sharing how she is being sent away by the clan leaders from her husband's land because she produced only girls. There was an exchange of words between the men and the women on the other side. As it became intense, I whispered to the bishop and the police officer to calm the situation.

I very much knew that I was dealing with a remote grassroots community whose gender appreciation was pegged to a man being in control. Moving with a team of men and women and with security (mainly police officers) and then credible religious leaders in the area from the diverse religious and spiritual backgrounds was important. This was always the norm, especially on the first visit, when tempers were usually high. Sometimes it really didn't matter to me whether all the participants I moved with were men. My goal was to ensure that I was strategically protected, but I was also aware that these key personalities, especially the religious personalities, were more respected in these parts. On the subsequent visits, once the community had got accustomed to my presence, it was relatively easier for me to conduct grassroots meetings and engagements, but with a male companion who was more knowledgeable about the dynamics.

During the mediation process, we would sit in a circle to avoid promotion of hierarchy. Most women though would sit at the back, while the men were in the front rows. Sometimes the women would bundle up in one part of the circle too. We could use religious texts either from the Bible or the Koran to emphasize a point. Using these faith-based scriptures was always important, and it brought calm to the audience. There was always a wave of peace and understanding that they were fighting for something impermanent (land), something they can never take with them to the grave.

Using the local language was also important. In most of these places, especially in the northern part, I didn't speak the local language at all. I would speak English; then it would be translated by a volunteer during the mediation process. I saw that many were either not understanding me or were not very receptive. It looked like I was a foreigner trying to tell them what to do. It helped that the faith leaders, who were my very good friends, were from the area. Every time they would say something, the crowd would feel at home and happy. This made me strategize to learn a few words here and there from them. I would request them to tell me what a certain word meant, and I would say it during the mediation process. They crowd would then feel happy and even clap for me. I therefore became part of them and their problem. They started to feel less offended whenever I would request an interpreter, because even then I would drop in these local words here and there.

Engaging the Community on Religious Extremism

History shows that Uganda's politics was based on religion even during the early days. This political divide was based on mainly the Anglicans belonging to the Uganda People's Congress political party and the Catholics belonging to the Democratic Party, with the rest belonging to either of the two or one of the smaller parties. These were and continue to be the main faith traditions in the country, closely followed by Muslims. Religions and spiritual expressions have been in many ways fused with politics, and this has led to an enormous death toll. Every time a conflict breaks out in the country, religious groups end up taking sides based on sectarian interests at play. Those in the political realm know that when you use religion, not only do you recruit from the already existent huge numbers but also you get unquestioning followers. Many youths have either been abducted or even willingly given away by their parents to go and fight for a religious cause.

The overall goal of this project was mainly to unearth the drivers to violent extremism with a focus on the war on terror. During my engagements, I knew that meeting one faith group during the dialogue sessions would mean hearing negative propaganda about the faith that was not represented in the room. This therefore meant that unless I found it imperative to meet people of one faith, meeting people of many faiths as a collective of those in conflict was the best strategy. I therefore would hold focus group discussions with community members from the different religious backgrounds. I would target the areas that are so prone to religious conflict and just select both religious and lay people to be part of the discussion. Unlike in the land-based conflict mediations, religious matters come with a lot of sensitivity. One could hate the other for life for trying to tamper with a particular teaching. In Islam and Christianity in Uganda, women are portrayed as a weaker sex or a gender that is supposed to be submissive. A woman coming out to challenge the status quo alone would be seen in the negative.

Biologically I am currently a mother of three children, two girls and one boy. In Africa though, we end up being mothers to many, based on extended family support. During these consultations on the recruitment process of youth and children into extremist religious wars, I portrayed myself as a mother first and stressed that I was aware of the suffering of the mothers in these incidences. I would always refer to my children and how I would feel if my children were in a similar situation. This empathetic projection of my feelings made me also internally less judgmental of any individual or faith. I never portrayed a particular faith as the only one that caused mayhem because of the extremist ideology. Many faith groups in the country were culprits, only varying in numbers and the intensity of the situation. I gave examples of all the religious groups and how they had been involved, including the killings that had previously happened. For example, there were two breakaway priests: a prophet and an ex-Catholic priest who recruited many followers, and with the myths that surrounded the year 2000 as the beginning of a new millennium, it was easy for many, especially the rural folk, to believe and give in to any advice given by those they spiritually trusted. They told their followers to go and sell all their property, bring the money, and then set themselves on fire, thereby killing over one thousand people. Then came the restoration of the Ten Commandments by the Lord's Resistance Army rebel group, which was led by a former altar boy in the Catholic Church who mixed Catholic teachings with traditional spirituality for recruitment and whose almost twenty-year rebellion led to the death of almost 2 million people in northern Uganda. Lastly, the Al-Shabaab Islamist militant group (based in Somalia) initiated bomb killings in 2011, and the Shabaab-linked Allied Defense Forces recruited and brainwashed youth and children based supposedly on Islamic teachings, claiming many in the eastern and western parts of the country.

I could work with both men and women and religious leaders at the grassroots level in a diverse way at the same table and look at the issues not only with a human face but also with a nonblaming approach. Although women were always portrayed as weaker in these decisions, my approach was to project them as strong mothers whose love is unconditional. This approach contributed to the healing process of the conflict that had started between the Christians and Muslims in some villages in the eastern part of the country.

Gender Issues and the Environment

Protecting the environment has become a crosscutting issue in all the work that human beings do on earth. During an environmental training program for faith leaders and grassroots communities, I tried to address a conflict that had arisen because some men had refused to let their wives plant trees since the women were not designated as land owners. Some men became angry, saying that the women have no right because they can't plan for the land as they are more likely to leave anytime. "What if they plant trees in an area where I have my different long-term plans?" one challenged. "What if she starts selling the trees on my land and uses the money without my knowledge?" he continued.

My submission during the mediation was twofold: one was about having joint conversations in homes between men and women on the future plans they both harbor for land development, and the other was about how having a woman as a partner to fight environmental degradation was more useful and sustainable. I tried to show them that a mother has more use for trees in any rural setup. Although my upbringing and social life continue to be mainly urban based, I spent some good years growing up in the rural places, and I knew that a woman had more interest in preserving the environment and trees for that matter, probably more than a man. This was so because, in my view, she uses them for various purposes, including medicinal purposes for her children, firewood, and shade during cultivation. My submission touched many men who were fighting over the right for tree planting and land preservation. I further emphasized that women are less likely to destroy what can sustain their children, and having them as partners instead of adversaries brings in a lot of value addition. With the environmental officer and the religious leaders backing my line of thought, we resolved the issue. Actually we ended up giving about fifty seedlings to each woman and man present.

CONCLUSION: MEN BECOME MY IMPORTANT PARTNERS

One cannot easily win a battle working in isolation from the men in such patriarchal communities, especially in Africa. Whenever women are invited to take up leadership positions in the church, many refuse the responsibility. Others are involved less in the women's activities because of such events stretching into the evening or sometimes into the night. Since the women are considered as homemakers, including the cultural expectation to be back home before the men arrive, it was and continues to be hard to engage women in anything productive at a late evening time. Some men confront those of us women in leadership, saying we are promoting *omwenkanonkano* (literally meaning "equality," but in a negative way that indicates we are trying to control men or take away their power as heads of households).

Most of my current inclusion of men in the work that I do has been shared in various examples above. Since men are most of the religious leaders, heads of households, and leaders of various institutions and communities, there is no way one can work without them. The community further believes in them as the leaders, and partnering with them is important in hastening to resolve a challenge while reaching out to those in need of peace. I have become friends with clergy and laymen from the other faith traditions, and this has continued in the interfaith and secular networks. In the interfaith network family, I have found incredible men who have really mentored me, opened doors for me, and taken me as a real sister. Their support cannot be measured. On the other hand, I know that it is not easy for me to do peace work without men in the picture in my local setting, and this is not only because of the prevailing traditional stereotypes that continue to present themselves in the course of my work, but also for purposes of commitment and sustainability.

Practitioners also need to grow a strong network of friends beyond their initial community. Through grassroots, regional, and global networks, one can learn a lot. Working in isolation from the prevailing trends, achievements, and struggles only makes one a star in that particular locality, whose stardom can easily be lost as relevance fades because of monotony and lesser insight. These networks become important avenues for learning and practicing innovation. As the world continues to be that interconnected global village, many strategies and practices and much learning can be shared across the divide. It is important, though, to put into perspective the local dynamics so that whatever regional or global learning is achieved doesn't appear like an imposition on the local setting.

Female practitioners out there need to know that they will have to struggle to claim that space of practice and that it is not always easy, especially in areas where cultural traditions and faith backgrounds that restrict women are strong. It is therefore important to know that as the world where you live may be receptive, the world beyond could be less accepting of women's full participation. This therefore calls for being open to learning and persisting, but also being sometimes cautious and assertive without necessarily being aggressive.

Chapter Twelve

Reducing Violence through Better Theology

Qutub Jahan Kidwai

Challenge: How do you confront gender-based or sexual violence?

Woman's rights and gender-based violence are pressing issues among the Indian community in general and the Indian Muslim community in particular. In the last two decades, there has been a rise of radical elements, including myself, among Muslims—which ultimately meant to suppress their womenfolk in the name of Islam. Previously gender-based violence or any form of discrimination against women was understood as something cultural and customary, and it was attributed to poverty and illiteracy. But with the rise of violent religious extremist movements, the whole scenario has changed, and all of a sudden, many acts of violence and discrimination against the fairer sex are seen through the lens of distorted shariah law,[1] based on rulings from conservative Muslim seminaries and lawmakers.[2]

It began with more media coverage in the last two decades relaying news about religious extremist groups in Muslim countries punishing women publicly. Shariah religious leaders, *jirgas* (traditional courts that run on customary or tribal laws), and tribal norms all claimed to be working according to shariah rules. This dangerous claim has led to anti-Muslim prejudice among other religious communities. People now believe that Muslim women are not allowed to approach police or courts. Muslims are not seen as law-abiding citizens because they follow a parallel law system. Muslims are seen as inhumanely terrorizing people, including their womenfolk. Consequently, some media outlets and special interest groups now portray Islam as a point of discontent for global peace.

As a Muslim woman, I myself during my youth faced a dilemma regarding what Islam says about women. This ambiguity led me to study Islamic literature and jurisprudence, as well as the status of women in Islam. This chapter deals with my personal experience as a young Muslim woman and now as a feminist and peace activist during conflict and postconflict scenarios involving Hindu-Muslim tensions in India. I have tried to explain the dynamics of social and political turmoil during conflict that changed and affected many Muslim women in larger ways. The emergence of religiously based politics, the rise of traditionalists and religious extremist groups, the polarization of communities, and the politics of fear, which led to women becoming the most vulnerable group, are discussed. Thus, the purpose of my chapter is to share faith-based Islamic approaches to addressing gender-based violence and to highlight the humble achievements and the strong spirits of Muslim women who strive for rights and justice.

During my university days, I did an in-depth study of Dr. Asghar Ali Engineer's work on the Shah Bano issue (a controversy about marital maintenance in Muslim personal law[3] in India). Dr. Engineer was a renowned scholar of Islam, a philosopher, and a pioneer in promoting communal harmony in India. A progressive writer and a giant of knowledge, he penned forty-five books on Islam, Islamic feminism, and communalism.[4] I built on Dr. Engineer's work to prepare a seminar paper on the Shah Bano case and the rights of Muslim women, and it was very well received.

Later, in 2002, I came across a vacancy for a researcher's post at the Center for the Study of Society and Secularism, and I went for an interview. To my pleasant surprise, Dr. Engineer was right in front of me. He was the chairperson of the center! I was praying that I should be appointed for the post and should get a chance to work under him. I was blessed with a job offer. My first research was on the Uniform Civil Code and Muslim personal law in India from the perspective of Islamic rights. Being a Muslim and a woman, I found several issues incomprehensible, as far as Islam and the status of Muslim women were concerned. As for any layman in the community, what was inculcated during my upbringing was for me true and the only right information. Being from a family of political and religious leaders also brought with it a particular way of living, in which if you are a girl, the responsibility for family honor lies on your shoulders. However, Islam and its history as taught to me by Dr. Engineer were very different and a sheer revelation.

During my university days, we had engaged in gender studies and discussed at length the rights and plights of women in different communities. Somehow religion was always portrayed as the culprit in suppression of the fairer sex, because a religious commentator who has a strong prejudice against women will interpret the scripture accordingly. This antifemale interpretation had caused deep prejudice against holy scripture among rights-based activists and academicians. For example, activists often allege that wife beating, polygamous marriage, confinement of women, and inhumane female circumcision practices are promoted by the Quran. Any oppression of women in the name of customs, rituals, socioeconomic disparity, and violence leads to greater divides between religious leaders and intellectual and progressive civil societies. It's the need of the hour to highlight a better interpretation of Islam and also to reform Islamic law to safeguard Muslim women's safety and rights. The right understanding of theology is a must to counter these problems. It is the duty of all peacebuilders to generate a new image of the Muslim community through the right interpretation of Islam and to give proper status to Muslim women.

FOUNDATIONS AND CHALLENGES

Past relations between Hindus and Muslims in India were cordial and peaceful for centuries. This is a country built on syncretic traditions, including over 1 billion people, hundreds of languages, and eight major religions (Hinduism, Islam, Christianity, Sikhism, Buddhism, Jainism, Zoroastrianism, and Judaism) alongside numerous indigenous faiths. The recent Hindu-Muslim conflict is mainly the outcome of right-wing politics using distorted historical facts. A few political parties that were struggling to gain power and votes raised emotional religious issues to mobilize Hindus in India. However, common citizens perceived this as a threat to religion—whether Hinduism or Islam. In addition, the rise of conservative Muslim groups led to another parallel conflict, with Islam increasingly seen as a religion promoting killings and mass violence. Long-standing communal tension, which had existed since India and Pakistan were partitioned in 1947, later culminated in targeting the Muslim minority community in the name of antiterrorism. This is not a local phenomenon but has become global: any act of bombing or violence is seen through this one lens, and Indian Muslims are affected.

Effects of the Demolition of the Babri Mosque

As a young student, I experienced a lot of challenges after the major communal riots that followed the 1992 demolition of the Babri Mosque. Located in Ayodhya, it was one of the largest mosques in Uttar Pradesh state. According to the mosque's inscriptions, it was built in 1528–1529 on the orders of the Mughal emperor Babur (after whom it is named). However, according to Hindu sources, the Mughals had destroyed an earlier structure marking the birthplace of the god Rama in order to build the mosque. This claim was disputed by Muslims, and the political, historical, and socioreligious debate over the history of the site became known as the Ayodhya dispute. Starting in the nineteenth century, there were several conflicts and court disputes over the mosque. On December 6, 1992, the demolition of the Babri Masjid by militant Hindu nationalist groups triggered communal riots all over India, leading to around two thousand deaths.

After the demolition of the Babri Mosque, Muslim communities were ghettoized in many parts of Indian cities. Among Muslims, the emergence of conservative and fundamentalist groups led to greater suppression of women. I was in higher secondary school then. It's still so fresh in my mind to see some of my female classmates, who were previously free to come to school on their own, no longer allowed to attend by their families. I was the class representative and was supposed to look after the daily affairs of my class. These girls asked me not to inform their families that they were going for a study tour or other outing. Also, they were now accompanied by their brothers or other male relatives. My college principal, along with professors, counseled families and relatives but in vain. Minority community members who lost many in the violence were now feeling mistrustful and insecure.

Within a few weeks, some of the girls were stopped from pursuing their degrees and married off. It was shocking for most of us to know that girls were confined to their homes. In a month, the classroom strength was less than a half. Some of my Muslim classmates who still managed to attend school came wearing the *bindi*, a red circle sticker on the forehead usually worn by Hindu women, so that they would not be recognized as Muslim girls. They displayed the *bindi* on their foreheads to save themselves from being targeted.

My friends and I struggled to come to terms with why the girls were stopped from studying. My father was a social activist, and he was busy engaging youth to maintain peace and also helping police to secure localities. He followed the Gandhian philosophy and was disturbed to see the amount of violence between Hindu and Muslim communities. He would hold peace rallies and used microphones from mosques and temples to appeal for peace and brotherhood. But he never stopped me from going to school. I was wondering why he was not stopping me, when all my Muslim classmates' parents were concerned and had stopped their studies. I questioned him one night: "Don't you feel worried about me and my sisters?" My father smiled and replied, "I am very much concerned, and that's the reason I want you to go to school and set an example for other girls. Education is the best weapon for fighting ignorance. Also, education's wealth will never be snatched away from you, come what may."

I continued to attend classes amid curfews, and sometimes army personnel helped drop students off at the bus stands and railway stations. Every day my parents would advise me and ask me to be alert but remain brave and courageous. I tried to connect with my friends on the phone. In those days, there were no mobile phones or Internet, so we maintained communication through landline phones. We would cry listening to each other's voices.

Some of them lost their houses and also their near and dear ones. I was the most helpless soul at that time. Still, it was incomprehensible to me that communal violence was affecting the lives of Muslim girls. I prayed and consoled myself that at least my friends were safe.

The whole cycle of religious conservatism was taking shape both in the majority religion (Hinduism) and the largest minority religion (Islam). The minority community, which was highly affected, lived in ghettos and became more closed and insecure. When the school began its new term, we were hoping to see our friends return. Unfortunately, they were confined to their homes, and some were married off. Those who did turn up had begun to wear the *hijab* (head covering) and *burqa* (a black cloak from head to toe). Many of us were curious to know what made them change their appearance. The girls said it was their families who wanted them to wear the *hijab*, and also religious leaders in their sermons urged the community to observe strictness with their women to avoid a risk of sexual violence. I was shocked and unable to rationalize what was happening. The only trusted advice we received was from our professor and family elders. We continued to go to school, and the impact could be seen in my friends' lives. They were not allowed to go to school events, and they were asked by their family members to call from public phones to report their whereabouts. The fear and insecurity was the outcome of minority bashing and communal politics.[5] In my view, this mass shift of the community mind-set after the Babri Mosque violence was the beginning of an unjust system affecting the rights and lives of women.

Even in my own life, my relatives were pressuring my parents not to allow me to go for further studies. After clearing several entrance exams, I joined an Indian flying club to become a commercial pilot. I was the first Muslim girl to enroll in a flying club to become a commercial pilot, so this was widely covered by media. This led to my relatives' excommunicating my parents and my siblings. An unwritten fatwa issued against my parents stated that it is un-Islamic for a girl to be a pilot. The uniform I was wearing was against the tenets of Islam, according to their dictates. Also, this profession is male dominated, and women pilots rarely get respect, so it was not acceptable for a Muslim girl to learn to fly. I had to cope with the pressure of being a new trainee in the flying club and also, in the back of my mind, with my concern about my parents. There were strong misogynist dictates both in the name of Islam and family honor. My mother was the powerful voice behind me, who motivated me to go ahead and make history. My father was a Communist but a practicing Muslim and spent his life working for interfaith tolerance and peace. I continued my schoolwork and my flying course simultaneously. I scored at the top in all my school exams and worked hard to pass my aviation exams as well.

My university nominated me to represent India at the United Nations Youth Leaders Conference in Seoul, South Korea, in 1995. This was another big blow to the conservative flocks of my relatives and elders. For me, too, it was next to impossible to believe that my parents would agree to send me so far. I was only eighteen and was wondering how I could address youth leaders from all over the world. My father, along with my school principal and professor, encouraged and prepared me for the conference. I went and came back with two medals for projecting the role of youth in peacebuilding. The talk I delivered was from the core of my heart because I recalled those painful memories of communal violence in my city and country. My friends who were young and full of aspirations had had their lives ruined. Fear and insecurity will never allow a person to heal. Only a sense of justice and security will help peace prevail. On my return from Seoul, the then home minister offered his felicitations to me for this achievement. Until I graduated, I worked along with my professor to encourage girls to develop dynamic personalities and go for the professions of their choice—especially Muslim girls.

My Life Post-9/11

After 9/11, the whole scenario of conflict changed again. There was a complete shift in understanding the conflict, not just taking into account its political and economic dynamics. Religion, specifically Islam, was projected as a major harbinger of violence. The underlying drivers of this shift included an unjust global policy and bid for oil wealth, but it had an even more venomous effect at a local level. Indian Muslims were targeted. Then, the existing government was led by the same political party that had led the mob to demolish the Babri Mosque. Shortly after the September 11 terrorist attacks in the United States, India passed its own antiterrorism ordinance, the Prevention of Terrorism Act, following an attack on India's parliament building in December 2001. Among other potentially dangerous measures, the terrorism act allowed for 180-day detentions without charge, presumption of guilt, sketchy review procedures, summary trials, and trials in absentia. Misuse of this act along communal and minority lines was most glaring in states like Maharashtra and Gujarat.

In Gujarat, police invoked the terrorism act to arrest 123 Muslims allegedly involved in a vicious attack on a train full of Hindu passengers. The government declined, however, to use the act against Hindus involved in pogroms that had killed over two thousand Muslims. Shortly after the pogroms, Gujarat Chief Minister Narendra Modi justified the government's choice simply by stating that it was unnecessary to invoke the act against the Hindu rioters. The state government explained the violence as a "spontaneous reaction" to the train attack, despite evidence that the riots had been organized by right-wing Hindu groups. There are hundreds of innocent Muslims in jails, who haven't committed any crime. It has become common for the police to arrest Muslims without proof of guilt and to brand them as terrorists.

In the end I was forced to abandon my flying career by my parents. It's unexplainable what they must have gone through. I was depressed and looking for some normalcy in my life. Both my mother and father were sad, but they didn't lose hope. All they wanted was for me to be safe. My university invited me to join as a professor, and for a year I taught students. My teaching job was so monotonous that I was not finding peace. That is when I applied for a post at the Bombay-based Center for the Study of Society and Secularism.

RESPONSES: A LEARNING JOURNEY AND A NEW ROLE

Islamic Perspective on Gender Equality

I joined the center as a researcher, and my research focus compelled me to read about, discuss, and debate the Islamic perspective on gender equality. This idea still seemed incongruous to me. How can rights and religion be complementary to each other? Dr. Engineer would smile at my queries and teach me his concepts of religion, culture, and society. He said there are four aspects of religion. These are first the thought system, which should encourage reasoning, questioning, and change. The second aspect is the value system, which remains permanent and transcendent. The third is the institutional system, where one learns these values and behavior. Finally, the fourth aspect is the rituals, and this one is not likely to change.

Dr. Engineer also taught me that to understand the Quran, the verses can be divided into two categories: normative verses and contextual verses. Normative verses are not bound by place or time; they are generic and universal in their meaning. Contextual verses are best understood by taking into consideration place, time, community, and so forth. In both the Quran and the Hadith (the traditions of the Prophet Muhammad, PBUH), we need to understand the social context of the times. One cannot compare an advanced and developed society with a less developed one. Every society evolves, and consequently norms and behavior change. If the context in which a particular teaching was written is vastly different from our current social context, then we should question whether the teaching is normatively applicable. He also explained that shariah has a set of moral purposes (*maqased*), and the specific laws are devised in order to achieve these purposes. Thus, if the laws do not help to fulfill the purpose of shariah, then Muslims should change the laws, not the purpose of shariah.

During my ten years of training under my mentor, I discovered that the Quran intended to give full dignity to women and affirm gender equality.[6] Dr. Engineer discussed at length the rights of women in Islam, including rights in marriage, divorce, maintenance, property ownership, and so forth. To my astonishment, he even narrated several incidents in the history of Islam where women made tremendous contributions. But I still wondered, Do women really participate on the social, economic, and political fronts? I hesitatingly shared my perception that Islam wants women to be like the *umm-ul-momineen* (mothers of the *ummah*, wives of the Prophet, PBUH), living lives of total obedience to men and seclusion from male-dominated society. My query led to a discussion of a very crucial issue in the world of Islamic feminism, one that has an impact on the lives of all Muslim women.

In response, Dr. Engineer asked me to open the Quran and read out the verses on head coverings (*hijab*). Chapter 33, verses 53 and 59, say to tell your wives, daughters, and women believers to wear *jilbaab* so that they are not misunderstood or harassed, being mistaken for slave girls. This implied that wearing a head covering would be a mark of distinction for pious women. Chapter 24, verses 30 and 31, first command men to lower their gazes and safeguard their private parts, and then it commands the same for women. In the context of that time, tribal culture was transforming into urban culture, a nomadic culture was changing into a sedentary one, implying more exposure to people from outside the tribal family unit and thus more need for modesty.

The revealing outcome of our discussion was that all the verses in the Quran are duty based for men and, surprisingly, rights based for women. Islam began with rights-based discourse. There is no verse in the Quran that is duty based for women. However, in reality, the current practice is topsy-turvy, and the socially constructed gender role is legitimized by religious sanction. Head covering and seclusion have become duties defined by our patriarchal society, but they are not Quranic recommendations.

It is the need of the hour to frame a new shariah law incorporating only the Quranic verses that are meant to be normatively binding across contexts. At present, shariah contains *aadat*, or Arab cultural norms that were prominent in the context in which the Quran was written. Cultural customs and traditions should not be part of shariah, but they should be judged according to the values given in the Quran. Further, the Hadith is not a standard text unanimously endorsed by scholars. It is sometimes ambiguous, and it sometimes negates Quranic values. Thus, the normative verses in the Quran should be the only source for shariah.

The Holy Quran emphasizes reflection and observation before making a decision. A knowledgeable Muslim is one who is closer to Allah than anyone else and can use his or her faith and wisdom to discern the right interpretation. Reform in shariah is an inbuilt process, and it is very important to introduce reforms in conformity with Quranic principles and human rights values. This reform process needs to be safeguarded from customary laws and contradictory elements that negate the principles of Islamic jurisprudence. Such reforms would result in eradicating religious extremism and also in weakening the hold of politics over religion.

"Rights of Women in the Quran" and Saving Girls

The theological awakening that I experienced in learning from Dr. Engineer has given a new direction to my work as a scholar and activist. In the "Rights of Women in the Quran" workshop, we aimed to understand how the Quran reformed certain gender-biased practices of Arab tribes and how the Prophet personified the values of the Quran by treating women with utter respect. We also displayed posters in the community highlighting the roles of women achievers in Islamic history. For example, Khadija, the Prophet's first wife, was a businesswoman, and he accepted her freedom. His later wife Hafsa was the first custodian of the Quran.[7] The decision was taken after a long consultation about who would be the right person to secure the first copy of the Quran, and hence they all came to consensus that it was Hafsa. The response in the community was very positive. We found that now women express their happiness, as there are fewer restrictions and less domestic violence. Young girls are now allowed to continue their education. Women are now allowed to freely attend our meetings and workshops more frequently. Many have developed family-like relations with my team leaders.

Our Save the Girl Child campaign is an interfaith initiative in a western province of India called Rajasthan. The practice of killing newborn girl children is rampant in both Muslim and Hindu communities. So we invite religious heads called *moulanas* (Muslim leaders trained in madrasa schools) and pandits (Hindu scholars) to discourage the community from killing girls and to explain that such a practice is a sin. The *moulanas* and pandits, along with our members, share religious values and practices. There are programs held to honor parents who support girl children and help them get an education. Rallies with placards and flyers are held to celebrate life and save future generations. Posters are distributed in communities, schools, and colleges with messages from religious scriptures. Teachers are sensitized along with community members to inculcate these religious values and to denounce any form of violence. It's challenging work, though we are not able to get exact figures as to how many newborn deaths have taken place. The success we see is the increase in the number of participants in our work. Village heads, *moulanas*, and pandits all invite people to join this noble work. Secrecy is still maintained in places where this practice is rampant. Mothers who have allegedly killed their daughters are given counseling along with family members. The mothers share their trauma and their feelings of helplessness under pressure. Our campaign did make a difference when messages from the

Islamic Quran and Hindu Upanishad, denouncing such an act and calling it a grave sin, were displayed in the center and in villages.

Workshop on Women in Islam

One day I was sharing the idea of conducting a national-level training program for Muslim women activists, lawyers, journalists, and so forth. A grandson of Muhammad Ali Jinnah happened to be visiting, and he offered to sponsor this workshop. I was ecstatic and immediately worked on dates and started sending invitations all over India. There were forty-five women from all over India selected for this three-day workshop. In the workshop women were made aware of their Quranic and constitutional rights. We invited a senior mufti (Islamic legal expert) to address the women, and we covered subjects such as the history of Islamic law, the status of women during key historical periods, women's rights and freedom of expression in Islam, reforms in shariah law in other countries, and Muslim personal law in India.

While discussing Islamic feminism during the workshop, Dr. Engineer discussed the beginning of the Islamic feminism movement in the 1980s, challenging old concepts within the framework of Islam in Egypt, Morocco, Tunisia, and Algeria. Islamic feminists discovered that the Quran has proclaimed gender equality in every sense. The Quran has different levels. One is the practice in a particular historical context that is included in the text, and the other is the values that remain permanent. The Quran proclaims gender equality and through various verses supports this claim. For example, verse 71 of Chapter 9 says that both believing men and believing women are protectors of each other. Both men and women are given responsibilities to spread good words and contain wrong deeds. Both are required to enforce what is good and fight what is evil. This verse declares equality of sexes in all aspects of the society, whether social, cultural, political, or economic.

Some shocking revelations were shared by women workshop participants regarding certain divorce practices and mistreatment by Muslim leaders. One woman was orally divorced eight times by her husband, but even then he would never allow her to leave the house. This practice of instant oral divorce is quite rampant in India. Muftis often issue fatwas supporting verbal divorce, and nobody objects to a husband's behavior. In another testimony, a woman was forced to undergo *halala*, in which a verbally divorced woman must marry and divorce another man before she can remarry her first husband. The husband, who divorced her for a silly reason, later realized his mistake and wanted to take back his wife, but a *moulana* advised him that his wife must first undergo *halala*. The irony is that the husband committed a mistake, and the wife had to go through this ordeal of *halala*. The women also raised issues about gaining education and earning a living. There are many controversial fatwas saying that it is forbidden for a Muslim woman to work among people who are not her relatives or to earn money. Such fatwas are not legally binding on the community, but they do impact the lives of Muslim women. Also, the issue of the *hijab* and its enforcement in the name of community identity dwarfs the effort to help achieve women's empowerment. In every workshop, we heard about the pathetic practice of certain customs and misogynist behavior, which makes our work more challenging.

Evolution and Reform of Shariah Law

In 2009 I was appointed to an additional role as codirector of the Research Project on Codification of Muslim Personal Law, sponsored by the Indian Council of Social Science Research. This was an extensive research project highlighting the evolution of shariah law through both the emergence of Islamic jurisprudence and the study of reforms in shariah law in other Muslim countries. While drafting the blueprint for Muslim personal law, we interviewed different stakeholders, including two hundred muftis, *moulanas*, lawyers, and women's rights activists from all over India. I interviewed muftis, the heads of departments of religious studies from various Muslim universities, and madrasa leaders belonging to different sects, such as Sunni, Ithnaashari Shia, Deobandi, Barelvi, Ahle-Hadiths, Hanafi, and Shafi.

During the course of the interviews, my team and I encountered some strange behaviors. In one jurisprudence center of the Barelvi sect, I was supposed to interview the head mufti. He came in and sat facing the wall. I thought he would turn around, and then I would give him the questionnaire and pose questions. When I tried to begin, I was shocked and speechless to discover that he would not sit facing me and that I had to interview him without seeing him. That was a sheer humiliation for me. He believed that by seeing a woman, a religious person like himself could get provoked or invite wrong intentions. I said shame on him for using the name of Islam. Our Prophet never behaved this way toward women in his lifetime; nor did any of his companions. I stood up and told the mufti that I wished he would see women as full members of the Muslim community and as his mother, sister, and daughter. A faith that gets weakened by the sheer presence of women is not the true faith. I was truly upset and felt the agony of those women who are not able to speak or stand against such behavior.

Apart from this experience, the research also revealed the dualism of some religious leaders who try to use codification[8] of personal law to help Muslim women. We interviewed a mufti who was a judge in a shariah court in Lucknow and members of the Muslim Personal Law Board. There were notable contradictions, because the religious scholars agreed that the Quran doesn't support instant oral divorce or polygamous marriage, but they still allow it because it has been practiced for centuries. However, we held consultations in Delhi inviting lawmakers, scholars, and experts to gain their support. Though the rough draft of the law was ready, no one dares to do the legal drafting due to fear of backlash from powerful religious bodies. Half the population (i.e., women) in the Muslim community are deprived of their rights, and many lives are ruined due to the unjust practice of divorce. The problem is not considered as something alarming and serious among Muslim leaders. Activists and other campaigners are advised not to talk about codification as this will lead to communalization of the issue and encounter government resistance. Government doesn't want to engage as it is interested in votebank politics. It is a major challenge for us, though we live in the largest democracy in the world. India is signatory to the UN Convention on the Elimination of All Forms of Discrimination against Women, and our own constitution's principles stand against inequality; yet, ironically, in India women are suffering.[9]

Advocacy and Capacity Building for Muslim Women

When we conducted our first national-level women's training on "Rights of Women in the Quran," we got a tremendous response. However, the challenge for the women was how to understand these verses and related references. To search verses from the Holy Quran is a difficult task for any layman. So I decided to write a manual that contains selected verses from the Holy Quran that provide direct law on the right to education, right to earn, decision making, marriage contracts, the right to choose a marriage partner, maintenance, dowry, divorce, postdivorce maintenance, property and inheritance rights, and duties of the husband. All the verses are collected and compiled along with their meanings and commentaries in simplified language. This manual, "Rights of Women in the Quran," was printed and distributed for free to those who participated in our workshops.

We also supplemented the trainings with another initiative, called "Resolving Cases." Some cases come to women's organizations with the parties' consent for a panel to resolve them. Then we invite those couples and listen to their testimonies. A panel comprising myself, activists, and lawyers hear the details and give the decision according to the parameters in shariah law and make sure that justice is done as per the Quranic injunction and existing law in the country. Sometimes couples who have filed cases in court later agree to settle out of court after we help them find solutions. We help couples sign a declaration of agreement in which both husband and wife have permitted terms and conditions. Lawyers help in preparing documents and getting them notarized in court. Our team monitors a case for six months. The team and I work voluntarily on these cases.

A Step Forward

Before sharing this final story, I want my readers to know that I want to see my Muslim sisters as change makers, leaders, peacebuilders, and a voice that transcends all boundaries and limits. Let the women who went through the trauma of violence and death come out strong and become catalysts to heal other women. Islam in its history gives numerous examples of women who worked during war and served the wounded and provided help in every possible way. Empowerment needs to be reflected to send out a strong message.

In September 2014, a district in Northern Province of India experienced major communal rioting after a rumor that a Muslim boy had harassed a Hindu girl and the boy was killed by a Hindu family. Similarly, in a Hindu locality the rumor spread that a Muslim boy's family had killed a Hindu girl. The news spread like fire. Activists tried to verify the news by inquiring at the respective police stations. It was mere rumor, but things went out of control. A major killing and arson took place in Muzaffarnagar town and spread to adjacent villages. Some thirty thousand people got displaced and started living in relief camps. They left their houses and fields and were living in inhumane conditions as authorities failed to provide them with security and basic needs. Most who were targeted were Muslims, and they were owners of sugar cane farms. The riot was intended to displace the minority community and acquire their land. I, along with my women's group, went to Muzaffarnagar in December when the curfew was lifted. I was aware that the security situation was still tense, but I couldn't simply sit and watch. I wanted people to understand that it was not a religious fight but a politically motivated riot.

The women who accompanied me were the survivors of Gujarat's Godhra riot. The burning of a train in Godhra on February 27, 2002, which caused the deaths of fifty-eight Hindu pilgrims returning from Ayodhya, is believed to have triggered the violence. The riots resulted in the deaths of at least seven hundred Muslims and two hundred Hindus, with thousands of others injured. There were instances of rape, children being burned alive, and widespread looting and destruction of property. Many scholars and some commentators allege that the attacks had been planned and well orchestrated and that the attack on the train was a "staged trigger." Other observers see it as an instance of state terrorism.

I chose these women to accompany me so that they could share their own stories, interact with people in the relief camp, and help them with counseling to eradicate myths and fear. Healing was important for those who had lost their near and dear ones. These women could inspire them and with this hope, we visited one camp in Shamli Village. Conditions were pathetic and soul tearing. There were injured and wounded children and old people.

Women suffered as they lost their men and heads of family. In the camp, they were kept in open plastic tents and had no toilet facilities, no clean water or milk powder. Medicine and doctors were unavailable except in the initial few days. Private local groups and trusts helped provide food, blankets, and some medicines. My team did group counseling and explained that they should not hold religion or any particular religious community responsible for their plight. We asked them not to harbor hate or revenge.

The first day for me was very disturbing. I myself was not coming to terms with the treatment of innocent children and old people. Youth were angry and going through the trauma of not saving their dear ones. So on the second day, I thought of listing those children who would have been slated for class ten and twelve board exams, had the situation been normal. Our team consulted each family and listed thirty-two children. We also asked if there were teachers in camps. Fortunately, two teachers and a madrasa *moulana* came forward to help these children prepare for their exams. We managed to get a place near the camp where coaching class could be held. We sponsored the rent and meager remuneration for the teachers and *moulana*. We provided them with books, and our local coordinator made regular visits to know their needs and help children study without any fear. I was thankful to God when I heard all thirty-two children appeared for their boards, and none of them missed their exams. In addition to God, I also thanked and honored those two teachers and the *moulana* who came out as a ray of light in such a dark moment for these children. God dwells in such human beings who themselves were devastated but helped guide young ones on the right path. What an inspiration and selfless service they gave. These teachers too spread the message that no Hindus or Muslims can be the enemy of each other. We lived in harmony for centuries, so we should not now allow politicians to play tricks that create fear and divide us.

On my return, I made sure women who were victims of both communal violence and discriminative personal law received help to build their leadership skills. I also encouraged my team to engage more youth who are vulnerable in this era of social media, where they easily get radicalized. Youth are our hope and future, and if they are not brought into the mainstream, then survival of the nation will be bleak. Religion, which is misinterpreted, has become a major tool in luring youth and suppressing other communities. Therefore women and youth need to be empowered to help promote peace and justice. This way we can overcome the radical element in our society.

CONCLUSION

Reform is the best strategy to protect and empower the suppressed sections of society. Reforms in shariah law or theological understanding of social issues need to have more focus. Our objective is to equip women with a sound understanding of their status and rights in the Quran, giving a major thrust to empower them. We aim to equip them with the right knowledge so that they start questioning patriarchal and un-Islamic practices. Confidence building through asserting their place in the community as constructive members can lead to leadership. This confidence can only be gained by giving them the right understanding of Islamic rights. During communal violence in India, restrictions were laid on women, and the ratio of the Muslim girls getting an education fell drastically. They were confined and restricted, all in the name of protecting religious identity. But when these women are given true insight into their status, they will emerge as powerful players promoting peace and justice.

I would conclude that the myth of religion and faith playing a major role in undermining the rights of women all over the world completely disappeared after my experience of understanding the holy scripture and classical sources of Islam and simultaneously getting to learn about other faiths. The understanding of the Quran and its interpretation within the sociocultural and political context of its time gave a new thrust to my thinking. Values in any religion are universal and transcendent; they cannot be discriminating or unjust. Apart from understanding Islamic theology specifically with a gender perspective, I also learned that Islam is one of the promoters of peace and not jihad. A rational approach to understand any theology and scripture will help develop and evolve a balanced view. The scriptures condemn prevailing social malaise and provide new vision. Those who benefit from the new vision embrace the faith, and those who lose power in the new vision oppose the faith vehemently.

Today's dynamics of war and violence and the emergence of extremist groups show how religion over the course of time got converted into an establishment, and a power structure was developed around it. The fear of belonging to a minority community in India was deepened when there was planned violence against minorities. Prejudice and insecurity affected my rational thinking and led me to misunderstand my faith. However, after getting a chance to learn from a sane scholar who helped me understand the dynamics of all conflicts in the past and present, it is clear now how religion became part of the political establishment and lost its initial revolutionary thrust. The outcome was that religion came to be used more for distribution of favors than for spiritual enrichment.

It would thus be important to know that a journey that began with questioning sociocultural practice against the fairer sex ended with in-depth exposure to the divine message and theological understanding. The divine comes from God, and the theological buildup is human. This helped me build a premise of understanding religion in its true essence. Truth is a universal value in all religions. One has to face great problems in order to be truthful and face opposition from vested interests. The untold learning of the seen and the unseen in the Quranic message, I came to know from my teacher. It is vast and limitless. This transformed my soul and instilled a craving to learn more about the true essence of all religions. In my university days, I blamed religion for being unfair and oppressive to women. Today, I can say that the source of oppression is actually a source of liberation.

NOTES

1. Shariah laws are the rules Muslims are supposed to follow based on the Quran. Muslim countries vary in their implementation of such laws. There are debates on the interpretations and application of these laws too. These laws are divided into five categories: *adab* (behavior, morals, and manners), *ibadah* (ritual worship), *i'tiqadat* (beliefs), *mu'amalat* (transactions and contracts), and *'uqubat* (punishments).

2. In India, Muslim seminaries issue fatwas and rulings through centers of Islamic jurisprudence called *Darul Ifta*.

3. Muslim personal law often refers to a set of laws derived from the Quran that govern the personal affairs of the Muslim community in India. These laws relate to family affairs (divorce, marriage, inheritance, etc.). On nonpersonal affairs the Muslim community follows the civic laws that govern all other citizens of India.

4. See, among others, Asghar Ali Engineer, *Status of Women in Islam* (New Delhi: Ajanta Publications, 1987); Asghar Ali Engineer, *Rights of Women in Islam* (New Delhi: Sterling Publishers, 1992).

5. Asghar Ali Engineer, "Fundamentalism and Terrorism: Politics of Religion and Religion as Politics," *Tribune Online News*, January 5, 2003.

6. For other seminal feminist interpretations of Islam, see Amina Wadud, *Inside the Gender Jihad: Women's Reform in Islam* (London: Oneworld, 2006); Leila Ahmed, *Women and Gender in Islam: Historical Roots of a Modern Debate* (New Haven, CT: Yale University Press, 1992).

7. Nik Noriani, Nik Badlishah, and Yasmin Masidi, "Women as Judges," Sisters in Islam, 2002, http://www.sistersinislam.org.my/files/downloads/women_as_judges_final.pdf, accessed May 5, 2017.

8. Codification refers to converting shariah laws into specific legal codes to be used or applied by judges. For more information, see Tahir Mahmood, "Progressive Codification of Personal Law," Indian Law Institute, http://14.139.60.114:8080/jspui/bitstream/123456789/736/18/Progressive%20Codification%20of%20Muslim%20Personal%20Law.pdf, accessed May 5, 2017.

9. In August 2017, as this book was in press, the Indian Supreme Court did in fact ban the practice of instant oral divorce, declaring it unconstitutional, marking a significant victory for advocates for the rights of Muslim women.

Index

About the Contributors

Mohammed Abu-Nimer serves as director of the Peacebuilding and Development Institute at American University. He has conducted interreligious conflict-resolution training and interfaith dialogue workshops in conflict areas around the world, including Palestine, Israel, Egypt, Chad, Nigeria, the Philippines (Mindanao), and Sri Lanka. He is founder and president of the Salam Institute for Peace and Justice, and cofounder and coeditor of the *Journal of Peacebuilding and Development.* Professor Abu-Nimer also serves as senior advisor to the King Abdullah Bin Abdulaziz International Centre for Interreligious and Intercultural Dialogue.

Sushobha Barve is executive secretary and program director at the Centre for Dialog and Reconciliation near New Delhi, India. In 2004, she was named an Ashoka Fellow in recognition of her role as a leading social entrepreneur.

Nirosha De Silva has qualifications in business and human resources (HR) management, specializing in training and development. She has worked in the corporate sector and volunteered in peacebuilding, designing HR programs and training people in skill development, livelihood, and wellness. Nirosha has a passion for writing, including short stories, biographical literature, and over two hundred haiku, poems, and prose pieces. She lives in the Toronto area with her husband of twenty years and two teenage sons, having immigrated to Canada in 1998.

Peter Dixon, PhD, led the strategic peacebuilding work of Concordis International for eleven years, predominantly on Sudan and South Sudan but also on Kenya, Ivory Coast, Bahrain, Afghanistan, and Israel/Palestine. The focus was on inclusive, locally driven "Track 1.5" dialogue, aiming to help influencers of policy—including religious leaders—identify peaceful options. His PhD from the University of Cambridge is on cooperation in conflict intervention. His book *Peacemakers: Building Stability in a Complex World* (2009) aims to help Christians better understand pragmatic peacebuilding.

Michelle Garred, PhD, is senior advisor at CDA Collaborative Learning Projects and former associate director of peacebuilding at World Vision International. As a scholar-practitioner, she has worked to integrate peacebuilding into community development, humanitarian assistance, and faith-based service efforts in South and Southeast Asia, East Africa, the Americas, and the Balkans. Michelle is a pioneer in adapting conflict-sensitivity approaches for multifaith audiences. Her previous publications include *Making Sense of Turbulent Contexts: Local Perspectives on Large-Scale Conflict*.

Maria Ida (Deng) Giguiento is the training coordinator for the Peace and Reconciliation Program of Catholic Relief Services Philippines. In 2015, she was named a Peacemaker in Action by the Tanenbaum Center for Interreligious Understanding.

Azhar Hussain is a founder and president of Peace and Education Foundation in Pakistan, where he has been engaging religious leaders and supporting Islamic religious institutions in enhancing curriculum, promoting religious freedom, and building religiously motivated peacemakers. Hussain's project of religious engagement has trained more than thirteen thousand religious leaders and imams in Pakistan. Azhar's work exhibits a deeply held belief in the power of religion to heal, motivate, and empower people to bring about powerful social change within their societies.

Dishani Jayaweera is program designer, strategist, and cofounder at the Center for Peacebuilding and Reconciliation (CPBR) in Sri Lanka, where she has been working with clergy, women, and youth since 2002. She previously worked as an attorney and also holds a master's in conflict transformation. Dishani was named a Peacemaker in Action by Tanenbaum USA in 2012, and the CPBR team received a Niwano Peace Award in 2015 for its outstanding contribution to peacebuilding work in Sri Lanka.

Azza Karam, PhD, is a senior advisor on culture at the United Nations Population Fund (UNFPA). She represents UNFPA as coordinator of the United Nations Inter-Agency Task Force on Religion and Development; she is lead facilitator for the United Nations Strategic Learning Exchanges on Religion, Development and Humanitarian Issues. She coordinates engagement with UNFPA's Global Interfaith Network of over five hundred faith-based NGOs. She has published on political Islam, religion, and development. For a list of publications, see http://www.worldcat.org/identities/lccn-nr96011457.

Qutub Jahan Kidwai holds a master's degree in sociology from SNDT Women's University and a commercial pilot's license. She is regional coordinator of the west zone of India for the United Religions Initiative. For fifteen years, Qutub has been engaged in community-based peace and women's empowerment, as well as research on the Quran and the Hadith to support reforms safeguarding the rights of Muslim women. She is author of *Personal Law Reforms and Gender Empowerment*, among other titles.

Myla Leguro is a peacebuilding and development practitioner with twenty-seven years' experience in Mindanao, Philippines. She is well known in Mindanao civil society networks, having worked with Mindanao Peaceweavers and trained over sixty local organizations of different faiths. She holds a master's in international peace studies from the University of Notre Dame. In 2005, she was nominated with twenty-seven other Filipino women for the Nobel Peace Prize. Leguro currently directs a global initiative on advancing interreligious peacebuilding for Catholic Relief Services.

Rick Love is a peacemaker, ordained pastor, and certified mediator. Rick is a global citizen who has lived in Indonesia and England. He has traveled extensively, having consulted and lectured in over forty countries. Rick holds a PhD in intercultural studies from Fuller Theological Seminary and serves as president of Peace Catalyst International. He has authored four books, including *Grace and Truth: Toward Christlike Relationships with Muslims* (2013) and *Peace Catalysts: Resolving Conflict in Our Families, Organizations and Communities* (2014).

Despina Namwembe works with the United Religions Initiative as the regional coordinator in the Great Lakes countries of Africa and serves as director of Women and Girls–Africa on the global task force for Charter of Compassion's Women and Girls sector. She has special interest in peacebuilding work, gender issues, promoting the safety and future of the girl child, and promoting environmental work. Despina is also an author, contributing mostly to literature on women's empowerment.

Eboo Patel is a leading voice in the movement for interfaith cooperation and founder and president of Interfaith Youth Core (IFYC), a national nonprofit working to make interfaith cooperation a social norm. He is author of the books *Acts of Faith*, *Sacred Ground*, and *Interfaith Leadership*. A frequent guest speaker on college campuses and a regular contributor to the public conversation around religion in America, he served on President Barack Obama's Inaugural Faith Council.

Yael Petretti lived in Jerusalem between 1978 and 2010. Her training as a political scientist, her work as an Israeli tour guide, her involvement in Palestinian human rights issues, her Compassionate Listening skills, and her love for both Israelis and Palestinians have enabled her to help others understand what is happening there and why. She leads delegations to Israel and Palestine and conducts Compassionate Listening trainings in the United States. She is a volunteer Alternative to Violence facilitator in medium-high-security prisons.

Johonna Turner is assistant professor of restorative justice and peacebuilding at the Center for Justice and Peacebuilding at Eastern Mennonite University. For over fifteen years, she has worked with arts collectives, community-organizing coalitions, and other social movements to develop the leadership of young people of color, mobilize marginalized communities, and cultivate transformational approaches to safety and justice. Her education includes a PhD in American studies from the University of Maryland and a graduate certificate in urban youth ministry from Fuller Theological Seminary.